MARXISM AND SCIENCE

Gavin Kitching

MARXISM AND SCIENCE

Analysis of an Obsession

The Pennsylvania State University Press
University Park, Pennsylvania

Library of Congress Cataloging-in-Publication Data

Kitching, G. N.
   Marxism and science : analysis of an obsession / Gavin Kitching.
     p.   cm.
   Includes bibliographical references and index.
   ISBN 0-271-01026-6. — ISBN 0-271-01027-4 (paper)
   1. Communism and science. 2. Socialism. I. Title.
HX541.K54   1994
335.4'11—dc20   93-2304
                                                CIP

Published by The Pennsylvania State University Press,
Barbara Building, Suite C, University Park, PA 16802-1003

It is the policy of The Pennsylvania State University Press to use acid-free paper
for the first printing of all clothbound books. Publications on uncoated stock satisfy
the minimum requirements of American National Standard for Information Sciences—Permanence of Paper for Printed Library Materials, ANSI Z39.48–1984.

For S. J.

Language—I want to say—is a refinement,
"Im Anfang war die Tat."

Worte sind Taten.
　　　　　—Wittgenstein, *Culture and Value*

Contents

Part Four

Preface

Wittgenstein once revealed to his friend and student G. H. von Wright that he believed himself to be writing for "people who would think in a quite different way, breathe a different air of life, from that of present-day man. For people of a different culture, as it were." Such a statement would apply equally to this book, but there is perhaps a difference of spirit behind the words. Given Wittgenstein's rather curious personality, I suspect that these sentiments were originally expressed with grim satisfaction; in my case, they are reproduced in the spirit of depression and frustration that appears on their surface. These are not good times to be on the Left, and they have not been good times for the last twenty or so years. Those of us who wish to continue arguing for a socialist alternative to capitalism can do so only out of a sense of history's endless love affair with irony, and the conviction such a sense brings that those who capitulate to the mood of *any* historical moment are likely to end up with a retrospective pie in the face.

But if such reflections give us the courage to swim against the contemporary tide, they must not lead us to do so by simply repeating the old certainties, the old recipes. For times *have* changed, and in that changing they have demonstrated beyond reasonable doubt that the old notions of socialism—the notions that have held sway on the Left from somewhere in the middle of the nineteenth century until now—cannot any longer be sustained. This book argues that case, echoing what a number of others have said and adding a few points of its own. But it also argues that a suitably reformed conception of socialism—a market socialism—though it may lack the utopian qualities that inspired the imaginations of so many fine men and women over the last hundred or more years, still offers the prospect of a much better form of human society than that currently to be found in Major's Britain or Clinton's America or Yeltsin's Russia, and a form that is feasible and achievable, as well as desirable. It follows therefore that a socialism which takes seriously the lessons of the twentieth century, and is amended and developed in the light of those lessons, continues to be something well worth fighting for.

This book, however, is not really meant as a serious weapon in that fight, nor even as an outline plan of campaign. It is, in fact, no more than a small prolegomenon to the fight for a feasible and desirable market socialism. In its assault on Marxism's claim to be a science, it aims not primarily to undermine socialism's opponents but to ready its friends for the fight—that is, to help socialists get rid of some unwieldy intellectual kit, an out-of-date hangover from long-gone campaigns, which they have no need to carry now and which simply weighs them down. Or, to play with another metaphor, this book simply tries to empty a ridiculous Victorian portmanteau and to replace its cumbersome contents by some suitable modern clothing—simple, attractive, durable, and easy to wear.

That is the political purpose of the book. Its history and genesis are rather different, however. Historically, this book and its predecessor, *Karl Marx and the Philosophy of Praxis*, were originally conceived as one project, with the provisional title "Marxism: a political and philosophical reconstruction." I deeply regret that for reasons beyond my control it has not been possible to publish them as such, for the two books are closely symbiotic. Issues ignored or treated superficially in one are normally dealt with in some detail in the other, so that a critical reader is likely to think the better of each book for having read both. However, the changing economics and politics of the publishing industry are beyond my control, so I must content myself with expressing my frustration in this preface.

As for its genesis, this book seems, in retrospect, to have originated in an experience that for a long time I could not explain. This was, simply, that while I can still read Marx himself with pleasure and profit, I find most modern Marxist writing (with a few outstanding exceptions) neither pleasurable nor profitable to read. I long thought that this reflected badly on me. I believed that it was a sign of growing ennui, of that ever-present sense of déjà vu that seems an inevitable concomitant of age and experience, even perhaps a symptom of my growing moral and political demoralization.

Wittgenstein, however, has taught me differently and has also given me the courage to come to a conclusion that is in essence extremely simple but in implication extremely complex. To take the simple part first, I have decided that much modern Marxist writing fails to compel attention because its spirit is dead. It has simply lost that revolutionary fervor and belief that informs every word of Marx and that gives his writing such passion and power, even today.

The complexity arises in saying how, precisely, one knows this is the case. In other words, the real difficulty lies in getting one's intellect to explain what one's intuition already knows. And as such an effort this book is only a very partial success. In it I identify one characteristic of modern Marxist writing that makes so much of it a chore to read, its lack of a subject; or, more precisely, its deliberate linguistic repression of subjectivity in the name of "objectivity" and "science." But if there is no subject present, then one does not know who is speaking or why (in the deepest personal sense of "why") they are speaking, and so they are unlikely to command attention, let alone persuade or convince. This repression of subjectivity also has other symptoms—the underuse of transitive forms of verbs and the overuse of intransitive forms (and particularly passive intransitive forms), for example. This does *not* mean, however, as the addendum to chapter 5 makes clear, that I am now a devotee of so-called poststructuralist or postmodernist thought, much of which seems to me equally purposeless. It simply means that good Marxist writing must have a reflexive dimension based in an awareness of the dialectical relationship between the observer and his or her observations.

But this is only part of the story. For the rest of it, having no explanations, I can only enumerate symptoms. These will be familiar to anyone who has struggled with modern Marxist social science (and indeed with a good deal of non-Marxist social science)—the mangling of syntax, the plodding Latinate wordiness, the piling of scholastic distinction upon scholastic distinction. All these things bespeak the death of a political spirit even as the formal assertions and the perpetuation of a certain vocabulary seem to mark its continuance. The problem is that while I can *assert* these things and intuit that they are correct, I do not feel that I at present have the analytical acuity of a Wittgenstein to *explain* all these connections, to make them transparent, and perhaps I never shall. But if others wish to take up the task, as part of Marxism's intellectual and political renewal, I shall be delighted.

I feel certain of only one thing, and that obscurely. It all has something to do with a loss of sense of *importance* in what one is doing, with a feeling that the *only* practical consequences of such writing will be professional—curriculum vitae lengthening, departmental promotion, and the rest. It is hard to write at all, let alone to write well, without some sense of the significance of the task. And in some wonderful but mysterious way, a loss of a sense of significance gets "automatically" expressed prosaically as a kind of dilatory wordiness and (in academic prose) as scholasticism (which is just a form of wordy, dilatory thinking). So much, as I say, I can assert, but not prove—at least not yet.

Finally, I have some acknowledgments to make that are also an aspect of this book's history. *Marxism and Science* was begun in the United States in the late 1980s while I was a Fulbright scholar at the State University of New York. I thank Frank Hearn, Dev Kennedy, and Henry Steck (all of SUNY–Cortland) for keeping me sane while I tried to get the project off the ground. I was not able to continue the book when I returned from America to the (then) Polytechnic of North London, because I was working in a higher education institution undergoing Thatcherite butchery, but Winston James, Eileen O'Keefe, Jennie Somerville, and Jenny Mellor all rendered me much the same psychological service until I could board a plane to Australia.

Once I was in Sydney and at the University of New South Wales School of Political Science it was possible to begin serious work again. I owe a particular debt of thanks to two people for aiding me in different but equally vital ways. Professor Conal Condren encouraged me to get the manuscript out of a folder and consider it as a possible book again; Pat Hall-Ingrey has helped me in myriad practical ways, including putting up with my disastrous impact on word processors and printers. I also express my profound thanks to Sandy Thatcher for also helping me to believe in the book once more, and for simply being a witty and sympathetic publisher.

But of course I owe the most of all to my family, Pamela, Ewan, and Samjack, who came with me to the southern hemisphere and shared all the consequences—good and bad—of that decision. As always, this book has cost them much in deductions from my time and attention. *Marxism and Science* is dedicated to my younger son, Samjack. May he grow up in a better world, and may he make some contribution, however small, to rendering it so.

PART ONE

Introduction

This book is in part about that tradition in Marxism, beginning with Karl Marx himself, which has wanted to claim that Marxism is a science—not a "soft" social or human science, but a "hard" science, wholly on a par with other natural sciences.

In Part One of this book I argue quite briefly, but I hope convincingly, that this claim cannot be sustained, that Marxism fails to meet even the minimum requirements of a natural science and has always failed to do so. Parts Two and Three, however, contain its core and deal with the issues that were the major stimulus to its writing. The second part takes up the vital question of the motives that have led many Marxists to claim that Marxism is a hard science, and in it I identify two types of such motives, psychological and political. This is a more-or-less useful analytical distinction, but I suggest that in the history of Marxism there has been a continuous interaction of politics and psychology in the repeated attempts to validate it as a science. Finally, in Parts Three and Four I turn from critique to constructing an alternative, and I consider how Marxism may be thought of if not as a science. I explore the idea that it is a point of view, and I analyze both the literal and metaphorical uses of this concept to bring out its epistemological, practical, and political implications.

It will become clear as the reader proceeds that this book, like the short textbook on Marx that preceded it, relies heavily on the later philosophy of Ludwig Wittgenstein for important parts of its specific analysis and for the complete epistemology and view of language that underlies it. Wittgenstein was almost unique among modern philosophers in his refusal (at least in his later work) to separate or rigidly distinguish philosophy and psychology. On the contrary, it is not too much to say that for the later Wittgenstein philosophical problems were a curious species of psychological problem.[1] In his view, many if not all philosophical problems derive from the psychological inability of those doing philosophy to understand, or even perceive, the implications of their "ordinary" uses of language. To quote one of his most famous aphorisms on this subject: "A main source of our failure to understand is that we do not command a clear view of the use of our words—Our grammar is lacking in this sort of perspicuity."[2]

A great deal of this book concerns the way in which Marx and Marxists, in their attempts to think deeply about human society and thought, have also abused the language on which they have drawn, and in ways remarkably similar to those philosophers whose uses of language form the main target of Wittgenstein's *Philosophical Investigations*. I argue that this similarity is by no means accidental, revealing as it does the close relationship and common heritage of certain scientistic traditions of Marxism and other scientistic traditions of Western thought—notably logical empiricism and positivism— against which Wittgenstein's later philosophy is pitted.[3] But my analysis also goes beyond Wittgenstein. I see Marxist abuses of language not merely as the product of a certain psychologically induced blindness to various subtleties in the use of language—I see that psychological blindness itself as a product of a certain political situation in which Marxists have continually found themselves since the first days of "the founders."

To put it most simply, the semipermanent addiction of Marxists to an objectivist view of both language and the world (and to the so-called correspondence theory of truth that is nearly always its epistemological concomitant) derives, in my view, from a deeply felt need for an absolute set of

---

1. K. T. Fann, "Wittgenstein and Bourgeois Philosophy," *Radical Philosophy*, no. 8 (Summer 1974: 26–27. See also the Preface to Hanna Fenichel Pitkin, *Wittgenstein and Justice* (Berkeley and Los Angeles: University of California Press, 1973), especially xi–xii; also Stanley Cavell, *Must We Mean What We Say?* (Cambridge: Cambridge University Press, 1969), 72, and Brian McGuiness, "Freud and Wittgenstein," in his *Wittgenstein and His Times* (Oxford: Basil Blackwell, 1982). For Wittgenstein's own views on Freud and on psychoanalysis in general, see his *Lectures and Conversations on Aesthetics, Psychology, and Religious Belief*, ed. Cyril Barrett (Oxford: Basil Blackwell, 1967).

2. *Philosophical Investigations* (Oxford: Basil Blackwell, 1953), remark 122.

3. Although many contemporary Marxist philosophers attack empiricism—and logical positivism in particular—as the quintessential modern empiricist tradition, at least some of the Vienna Circle thinkers saw themselves as inheritors and developers of the scientific Marxist tradition, and a number took up very radical political positions. On this, see Otto Neurath, *Empiricism and Sociology*, trans. Paul Foukes and Marie Neurath, ed. Marie Neurath and Robert S. Cohen (Dordrecht; D. Reidel, 1973), especially the manifesto of the Vienna Circle (*Wissenschaftliche Weltauffassung: Der Wiener Kreis*), published as chapter 9.

revolutionary truths to compensate for an ever-threatening sense of impotence in the face of the massive, omnipresent actuality of capitalism.[4] Capitalism *was* and *is*. Communism is at worst a mere intellectual postulate and at best a nascent actuality hopefully being constructed (in the former USSR, China, Cuba, Nicaragua, or wherever else hope may passingly be pinned).

In such a situation, the need to be able to think and feel both the passing of capitalism and the construction of communism as more than postulates, more than hopes—as, in fact, scientifically guaranteed necessities—has been persistent and pervasive. It is also a psychological and political need that is almost impossible to fulfill if any reflexive or subjective element is allowed into Marxist epistemology or Marxist conceptions of language. Hence the continuing shunning of such elements in the name of a hostility to "idealism" (and this despite their importance in Marx's own early philosophical writings).

In short, one aim of this book is to contribute to a deepening of the Marxist understanding of ideology by treating Marxism itself—or at least one important and probably dominant strand in it—as an ideology, and by providing, through the use of Wittgensteinian techniques, a detailed account of how it works linguistically as an ideology. I also hope that this account may provide a model for further advances in the theory of ideology. For techniques of language analysis derived from Wittgenstein do, I think, provide the beginnings of a method through which epistemology, psychology, and politics may be linked and their immensely subtle connections traced, even though it was no part of Wittgenstein's own project, in first developing and using these techniques, to provide a method of analyzing ideology.

Since scientific realism is currently the most fashionable version of epistemological objectivism in Marxism, it is the focus of critique in the first part of the book. Here it is suggested that whatever may be the merits of realism as an epistemology of natural science, it has fundamental and damaging weaknesses as an epistemology of social science, and most especially as an epistemology of Marxism. To state a complex case briefly, realism breaks down as an epistemology of Marxism because the account that it provides of natural-scientific unobservables (like molecules, atoms, and subatomic particles) cannot be extended to cover Marxist social-scientific unobservables (like labor values or modes of production) as is done in Marxist ver-

---

4. On "objectivism," see chapter 2 of David Rubinstein, *Marx and Wittgenstein: Social Praxis and Social Explanation* (London: Routledge and Kegan Paul, 1981), 27–62, and Richard J. Bernstein, *Beyond Objectivism and Relativism: Science, Hermeneutics, and Praxis* (Philadelphia: University of Pennsylvania Press, 1983).

sions of realism. This is because natural-scientific unobservables are known and their existence confirmed through forms of experimentation and manipulation that cannot be reproduced by Marxists or by social scientists in general.

I then go on to argue that because the experimental means by which natural scientists know their unobservables are not available to Marxists, the latter (unlike the former) are driven to a dogmatism about the existence of these entities, which, like all dogmatisms, relies in the end on nothing more than repeated assertion. These assertions may, however, be more or less thinly disguised as some form of deduction from a set of abstract premises.

However, as I have already said, the principal aim of this book is not to destroy or demolish. For I do not wish simply to reject realist and other objectivist accounts of Marxism as science. I wish, rather, to present another picture of Marxism, a conception of it as a "point of view." As this very term suggests, my alternative conception of Marxism requires attention not only to the objective observations, whether theoretical or empirical, made by Marxists, but to the values and purposes of those subjects, those people—Marxists—who actively make such observations. Without wishing to be pretentious, I aim to present in most of the pages that follow what may be called a post-Einsteinian conception of Marxism. It stresses that Marxists, too, are not and cannot be absolutely privileged observers, standing in some Archimedean spot in absolute time and space from which some uniquely privileged, uniquely true account of the social world can be given. This does not mean, however, that there is no sense in the claim that Marxism provides an objective or even objectively best account of capitalist society. It just means that any coherent post-Einsteinian reading of objectivity must have reference to the purposes of the observer, to what he or she wishes to see, before any coherent account can be given of the objectively best perspective or position from which to see it.

An exercise of this sort undertaken at the end of the twentieth century may seem a complete anachronism. Neo-Thatcherite conservatism is still firmly in power in Britain. Russia and eastern Europe appear to be moving to a much closer involvement with the world capitalist system externally and to much more market-oriented social systems internally, while in the United States of America free-market economics is still in the ideological and political ascendant despite President Clinton's recent electoral victory. It is well over a decade now since Marxism was influential (or even fashionable) among students and intellectuals in the West, and there seems no immediate or even medium-term prospect of that situation changing. Marxism is, and is likely to remain, a distinctly minority taste in thought and politics; indeed, in the particular institutionalized form of Marxism-Leninism (i.e., of centrally planned dictatorial states under one-party Communist rule) it seems likely, after the extraordinary events of 1989, that Marxism will very soon disappear from the geopolitical map of the world.

However, despite all this, I hope and believe that this book is in no way anachronistic. For this will not be yet another of that long sequence of books in the Marxist tradition that show their idealism even as they propound their materialism. This book does not argue that Marxism is a rapidly dwindling intellectual and political force in the world because it claims, falsely, to be a science. For this is simply implausible, amounting to little more than the old intellectual's trick of redefining what one cannot change into something that one can change in order to compensate a gnawing and desperate sense of impotence. Rather, this book argues that the decline of Marxism may well be irreversible for good material reasons. But if there is to be any chance—any chance—of Marxists reversing that decline, then they must at least rid themselves of an ideological burden that they simply have no need to bear and that has deeply damaging effects on their political practice.

An introduction is no place to argue at length for what is to be demonstrated in the main body of a text, but I can simply state what I take to be the principal political advantage to Marxists of adopting the position for which it argues. In short, seeing Marxism as a point of view rather than as a science has the advantage (I shall try to show why it is an advantage) of making it the kind of thing of which other people have to be rationally persuaded or convinced, of making it in fact a position to which people have to be moved. By contrast, thinking of Marxism as a science makes it the kind of thing that only has to be applied in a manner that makes processes of persuading or convincing at best a marginal concern and at worst an irrelevance. It is hardly surprising, therefore, if orthodox Marxists have often proved themselves appalling persuaders and convincers, babes in arms in comparison with their ideological opponents and indeed often indulging in forms of politics more designed to alienate than to convince.

Of course, within the orthodox tradition there have supposedly been good theoretical justifications for this indifference or even hostility to the demands of rational conviction and persuasion. Two in particular have stood out. These are:

(1) that the working class or popular masses will, in the right conjuncture (usually a crisis of some sort) come to perceive their real, material interests as requiring the revolutionary overthrow of capitalism without any need of outside persuading or convincing.

Or conversely:

(2) that the passivity of conservatism of the working class and popular masses in advanced capitalist societies is secured by an ideological "over-determination" against which rational persuading or convincing are equally of no avail, since it is a necessary effect of the very functioning of such societies. In other words, the vast majority of people who live under capitalism are neither Marxists nor socialists because the very roles that they play in the system somehow ensure that they cannot be.

I consider both these views to be profoundly false, but two important points can be made about them both. First, they are, as may be obvious, logically interchangeable. That is, in a moment of supposed or presumed crisis in the system one can switch, without logical contradiction, from deep political gloom predicated on position (2) to anticipatory euphoria predicated on position (1). Conversely, if the crisis does not quite live up to expectations one can—equally without contradiction—switch back to the gloomy determinism implied by position (2). Second, both positions, diametric opposites though they may appear to be, have the effect of neatly excusing Marxists from seriously addressing themselves to issues of persuading and convincing sensible and intelligent people that it might be a good idea to be a Marxist or a socialist. But this may be the principal psychological and emotional appeal of both positions. For, especially in the case of small and impotent political groups with few or no resources to range against the vast propaganda machine (as it is seen) of the capitalist mass media, theories of essential revolutionary interests and theories of ideological overdetermination both have the enormous merit of not requiring such groups to do what in any case they cannot do. Impotence displaced to theoretical profundity certainly feels much better.

This book argues that now, in the late twentieth century, Marxists and socialists have very good reasons to be both gloomy and depressed and that, in reality, neither Marxist theory nor Marxist science can or should provide any hiding place from that gloom and depression. Indeed, if Marxism is to remain even remotely capable of changing the world, it must provide a means of facing harsh political realities and not escaping from them, for facing such realities is prerequisite to changing them. Thus I will argue that the supposed science of Marxism gives us no remotely scientific reason to believe that the world capitalist system will collapse into revolutionary transformation in however long a term one may wish to conceive this process. (Although capitalism will no doubt continue to experience periodic economic crises of various kinds). More important, however ("more important" because this view has a much greater credence among contemporary Marxists than the one above), I will also argue that Marxism gives us no remotely valid grounds for believing that the Marxist conception of capitalism—as an exploitative and historically transitory mode of production that can and should be transformed into a higher form of economy and society called "socialism" or "communism"—is one whit more scientific than the view of that ordinary citizen of a Western nation who believes it to be a tolerably acceptable system that has done much for herself and her family and that is, at the very least, better than any of the other alternatives around.

Indeed, the third part of this book will argue that the latter view, far from being a quintessential piece of capitalist ideology to be exposed by the science that underlies the Marxist view of capitalism, is a perfectly reasonable and rational view to hold, at least as reasonable and rational as its Marxist alternative. And if this is the case, then it suggests that the Marxist attitude to such views should be very different from the contempt that has traditionally been rationalized and justified by such notions as "ideology" and "false consciousness." In fact, it suggests that the most that Marxists can and should do when faced with such views is to argue that there may still be some advantages to reasonable people in taking up the Marxist position, the Marxist point of view on capitalist society, insofar as that position is not in contradiction with this "commonsense" view of capitalism and insofar as it allows certain things to be seen that cannot be seen from the commonsense point of view.

But this is to put things far too negatively. For the third part of this book also argues that grasping and accepting a conception of Marxism as a point of view opens up some exciting possibilities for Marxists and Marxism, possibilities for a more open and welcoming intellectual and political practice, possibilities for writing and speaking more eloquently and more persuasively, and—in conjunction with progressive changes in actually existing socialist societies—possibilities for a new kind of radical politics that can be optimistic because effective, rather than despairing because totally ineffective. In fact, the third part of this book has much to say about "possibility" (and "potentiality"). For it argues that these notions are, and ought to be, at the heart of Marxism. Indeed, it argues that these "quasi-performative" concepts are revelatory, not only of the essence of Marxism itself as a form of praxis, but of the human condition as a whole. But that is to anticipate analyses and conclusions that lie many pages ahead. For the moment it is only important for readers to know that, if they bear with the often harsh tone of criticism pervading the first two parts of what follows, they may find themselves led, in the third part, to conclusions and to a perspective (another central word in this book) from which the prospects for Marxism and for socialism may look somewhat better than the readers might have imagined and that may inspire a continued commitment to that radical political activity (another key phrase) without which Marxism is nothing.

1

Natural Science as a Practice

It has become a commonplace of the contemporary literature in the philosophy of science that any attempt to produce a single criterion by which science may be distinguished from nonscience is futile. It is futile at least in the sense that the history of those practices and disciplines that we now call scientific will quickly reveal one—and usually far more than one—example of sciences and scientists not abiding by whatever criterion is chosen. Indeed, it is now seriously doubted whether those practices that get called sciences and those people who get called scientists have anything *at all* in common when one examines them closely, save the names themselves.

Thus, some natural sciences are heavily mathematical (like physics) and others (like geology and meteorology) are not. Some rely almost exclusively on results obtained from highly controlled and closed experiments (subatomic physics, biogenetics, most forms of organic and inorganic chemistry) and others (again like geology or meteorology or like astrophysics) do not, or at least not nearly to the same degree. Some sciences and scientists still claim to be able to make exact predictions based upon alleged universal laws of nature, whereas many others now see such laws as simply statements of probability based on observations of statistical frequency. Indeed when, under the influence of Thomas Kuhn, philosophers of science turned their attention to the detailed history of science (including quite contemporary history), and away from what might be termed an *a priori* epistemology of natural science, the vast jumble of things that emerged as accepted (i.e., accepted by some group of scientists at some point in time) theories, methods, and practices of natural science seemed so diverse as to enable some philosophers of science, like Paul Feyerabend, to argue that that history showed there to be no such thing as "a" or "the" scientific method.[1] There was just a vast mishmash of ideas, hunches, practices, and speculations chosen on the basis that they might or did "get results." The only methodological rule of natural science that Feyerabend thought could be derived from its history was "anything goes," which is of course no rule at all.[2]

In this situation it may seem rash, to say the least, to argue that Marxism does not meet even the minimum requirements of scientificity; on the above interpretation of the contemporary literature of the philosophy of natural science, no such requirements can be identified. However, I do not think that an out-and-out Feyerabendist anarchism is justified by a balanced reading of that literature. For, at least to me, the vast bulk of it does seem to concur in identifying two regularly present hallmarks or criteria of natural science as a practice. These are *experimentation* and *application* of experimental findings or results. This is to say, in all the literature that I have consulted (save Feyerabend's own writings) natural science as a practice is distinguished by the presence of one or both of these criteria. To be more precise, *all* natural sciences involve some form of controlled experimentation, and most involve the application of experimental results to the solution of one or more "practical" problems in the world.[3]

It is true, however, that not all the writers who make mention of these two practices use them as the defining criteria of natural science either singularly or jointly. Some writers do so; some do not. Furthermore, some writers pick these two criteria along with others; some pick them in subordination to others. Very often, especially in the most recent literature, the search for invariant criteria of science having been given up, these two practices just appear in a list with many others (such as model building,

---

1. Paul Feyerabend, *Against Method* (London: Verso, 1975). A good overview of the debate appears in the Introduction to Ian Hacking, *Representing and Intervening: Introductory Topics in the Philosophy of Natural Science* (Cambridge: Cambridge University Press, 1983), 1–17.

2. Feyerabend, *Against Method*, 23–28.

3. See Hacking, *Representing and Intervening*, chapters 9, 10, and 11; Larry Lauden, *Progress and Its Problems* (Berkeley and Los Angeles: University of California Press, 1977), 1–8 and 121–51; and I. Lakatos, "Falsification and the Methodology of Scientific Research Programmes," in *Criticism and the Growth of Knowledge*, ed. I. Lakatos and A. Musgrave (Cambridge: Cambridge University Press, 1970), 91–196. It is noticeable, however, how little of the literature on the philosophy of natural science concerns itself *in detail* with the history of scientific experimentation and application. In general this is left to historians of science, such as Gerald Holton (see below, note 7). It may be that this omission is itself a cause of weakness in the literature and feeds into its strongly "theoreticist" bent. Certainly both Hacking and Holton believe this to be the case.

theorizing, calculating, measuring, predicting, etc.) as the kinds of things some scientists get up to sometimes.[4]

However, unlike theorizing or model building (but like calculating, measuring, and predicting), experimentation and application possess the characteristic of being defeasible practices; they may, and often do, go wrong. The anticipated results of an experiment are not in fact obtained; the intended application does not work. This, I will argue, is an enormously important attribute of these practices; indeed, it is the characteristic that is central to the identification of natural science as science. From the point of view of defining the specificity of natural science as a practice, it is in fact more important that experiments often fail and applications sometimes do than that experiments sometimes succeed and applications usually do.

The reason is that experimentation in natural science and application of scientific findings are both examples of what philosophers (including philosophers of science) call nondiscursive practices. That is, they are human activities that involve something more than thought (cerebration). I mean by "thought" both introspectively known mental phenomena and (more important) all symbolic systems of the kind created and used by human beings—written and spoken language, mathematics, symbolic logic, and so on. Experimentation and application, of course, always involve the use of language and may often involve the use of mathematics and statistics, but they also both involve a considerable surplus nondiscursive element as well. This element includes a myriad of specific activities: the design, production, and deployment of a physical experimental apparatus; the isolation or synthesis with that apparatus of some new physical, chemical, or biological phenomenon; the sinking of shafts into the ground; the building of telescopes; the orbiting of satellites around the earth; the taking of blood and tissue samples from animals and humans; the physical, chemical, and biological analysis of these samples in a vast number of ways; the collecting of fossil samples; the classification of such samples; the creation and application of conditions of extreme cold or heat; and so on and so forth.

Clearly this list could be extended at will for one more page or for ten more pages, depending upon the levels of detail or aggregation used in describing all the various activities that may be involved in different forms of scientific experimentation and application. But they are all, in one way or another, nondiscursive forms of *intervention* in the world that are carried out—along with a mass of discursive practices—with the aim of realizing a

4. See, for example, Hacking, *Representing and Intervening*, 137.

myriad of different, scientifically defined purposes by a certain class of human beings whom we have come to call "natural scientists." And sometimes those purposes are realized and sometimes they are not.

My choice of experimentation and application as the twin defining characteristics of natural science should not, however, be taken as the adoption of a "verificationist" or "falsificationist" epistemology of science. For leaving aside the classical Humean objections to verificationism, we have known since Kuhn that a falsifying experimental result, or a whole sequence of them, does not necessarily lead to the overthrow of a scientific theory or hypothesis, since there are plenty of other strategies available to scientists for dealing with such outcomes.[5] They can, among other approaches, question the experimental design or conditions, assign the results to the category of a minor anomaly, or amend or qualify the theory or hypothesis to allow for the results.

The point, therefore, of insisting on the centrality of experimentation and application to natural science is not to reinstate naïve verificationism or falsificationism. It is, rather, to insist that it is of the essence of the scientific enterprise that the theories or hypotheses that scientists are using or developing should *work*, and that the process of experimentation and application *define* for a scientific community what "work" means in this context. Thus, if after a thorough check and recheck of the experimental design and conditions a natural scientist cannot account for some experimental results that continually run against her or his expectations, then such results are always a setback for that scientist. Indeed, it is a matter of formal procedure in all natural science that a researcher will not publish her or his results until she or he has experimental data in line with theoretical or hypothetical expectations. Indeed, having such data is what having results *means* in any natural-scientific community.

And what has been said above about experimentation applies *a fortiori* to application. For if unexpected or anomalous experimental results are always a setback, applications that do not work (vaccines or other drugs that have unforeseen side effects, machines that prove unreliable, space shuttles that explode) are always a disaster. These kinds of episodes do not merely call into question the validity of the whole natural-scientific enterprise, they nearly always involve a considerable amount of suffering, and they also—at least in the West—involve the companies engaged in de-

5. Thomas Kuhn, *The Structure of Scientific Revolutions* (Chicago: University of Chicago Press, 1970), especially chapter 7, 77–91.

veloping such applications in considerable legal and commercial losses. Thus it is not surprising that in modern, highly institutionalized and commercialized applied science such spectacular end-product failures are very rare. (That they are so rare is of course what makes them such a scandal when they do occur.) And the reason such misfires are so rare is that natural-scientific inventions or developments are not applied in commercially marketed products until both the developments and the products in which they are embodied have been thoroughly tested and retested.

In fact, in modern natural science experimentation and application are hardly discrete processes. For up to the moment when a product is marketed commercially (and in many cases afterward) it is subjected to a *continuous* process of experimentation, which may begin with the original innovative experiments of the research laboratory and continue right through the testing of a product in the workshops of a commercial firm. The pure natural scientists may regard what the commercial group or groups are doing as the mere application of their findings, but the latter groups may, with equal validity, regard what they are doing as pioneering experimental work designed to make the end product effective and fault free.[6]

The central point is this: in putting their theories, hypotheses, and predictions to nondiscursive experimental tests (and, where appropriate or possible, to the ultimate test of application), natural scientists are "giving nature a chance to answer back" as it were—to surprise them by not producing the results that they want or expect, or perhaps simply to be mischievous by both producing the results they wanted or expected and some additional results, some surplus element, unlooked for and (as yet) unexplained.

To repeat once more, this does not amount to naïve "falsificationism." When such results do occur, though they are always treated as setbacks, setbacks can be dealt with in a variety of ways, from altering the experimental design, to amending or complicating the theory or hypothesis, to simply treating the results as minor anomalies. But while all these responses, and others, are available to natural scientists faced with unexpected or anomalous experimental results, one response is not available to them—to erase or amend the results by an act of will or imagination. Indeed, not only can experimental findings not be erased or amended by imagining them to be different, they cannot be obtained by mere willing or imagining, either.

This is, of course, because of the central characteristic of scientific experi-

---

6. See, for example, D.S.L. Cardwell, *The Organisation of Science in England* (London: Heinemann, 1980), chapter 8.

mentation mentioned earlier—that it always involves both extradiscursive and discursive activities. Thus I can imagine what may happen to the molecules of a gas under extreme heat (especially if I am an informed theorist of gases), but I cannot put a gas under extreme heat just by imagining it. Or again, I may imagine (if I happen to be a subatomic physicist) that a quark has an electrical charge of ⅓e, but I will need a cooled niobium ball to prove it.[7]

It follows that pure thought experiments are *not* experiments in the sense in which I am using the term. Nor are they, I am arguing, scientific experiments in the sense in which that term and practice is understood by natural scientists. Natural scientists do, of course, conduct thought experiments. They conjecture, hypothesize, and theorize, and doing so is an important part of natural-scientific work at particular conjunctures, perhaps even at some of the most creative of them. But natural scientists do not *just* conjecture; they confirm or refute conjectures through experimentation. They do not just hypothesize; they validate or falsify such hypotheses by experiment. They do not just theorize; they test, develop, and (occasionally) overthrow such theories by experiment. And to repeat: what I mean by "experiment" here, and what they mean, is something more than a thought experiment, with that "something more" being a myriad of nondiscursive practices or practical interventions in the world.

It also follows from the view outlined here that mathematics is not a natural science, since all experimentation in mathematics is entirely discursive—that is, it occurs within the system of symbols that is mathematics. Mathematics is, however, a tool of nearly all natural sciences, and the principal tool of some of them (e.g., subatomic physics). But to say that mathematics is not a natural science is not to condemn it as some kind of illegitimate activity (anymore than to say that Marxism is not a natural science is to condemn it). It is simply to say that "natural science" is the name that we give, now, to certain forms of practical intervention in the world, forms in which controlled experimentation is a definitive central

---

7. I refer to the experiments by which Robert Millikan, an American physicist, claimed to have measured the charge of an electron and to have shown that all such charges were multiples of a unique magnitude. These experiments were important in establishing widespread belief among physicists in the reality of electrons. The experiments and their philosophical implications are described and discussed in Gerald Holton, *The Scientific Imagination: Case Studies* (Cambridge: Cambridge University Press, 1978), chapter 2. They are widely referred to in modern philosophy-of-science literature; see, for example, Hacking, *Representing and Intervening*, 22–23, and Bas C. van Fraasen, *The Scientific Image* (Oxford: Clarendon, 1980), 74–77.

practice. Mathematics is not a form of practical intervention in the world, and therefore it is not a science. It is, however, a highly creative and rigorous intellectual activity whose results can be applied, very successfully, in such interventions. Some of its results, however, have no practical implications whatsoever—or at any rate none that can be currently foreseen[8]—and this is just as we should expect.

Marxism, by contrast, is a form of practical intervention in the world, but it is a form of intervention—one of many—that is not defined or definable by controlled experimentation. It is therefore equally not a natural science, though none the worse for that. This is to anticipate, however. For before coming to a fuller discussion of why Marxism is not any kind of natural science, we must deal with a number of objections that may be made to the view of science outlined above.

A first objection may simply be that not all natural sciences do depend upon experiments in the way in which I have suggested; one could perhaps point to geology or meteorology or astrophysics as examples. However, this objection confuses what may be termed "closed system" experimentation with experimentation as such. It is true that astrophysicists cannot produce closed or controlled environments in the manner in which nuclear physicists or biochemists do, but telescopes of all types are pieces of experimental apparatus that enable observations not available to the unaided human senses (and are in that respect like electron microscopes, for example). Second, both meteorologists and geologists *do* conduct experiments in simulated environments designed to model or reproduce processes in nature that may be difficult to perceive (because, for instance, they take a very long time in nature, as in geology, or because they are complicated by other crosscutting factors, as in meteorology).

A second and much more important objection to my thesis is that a focus on experimentation and application as the twin criteria of natural science amounts to a version of philosophical pragmatism or instrumentalism. Am I not simply arguing that the natural sciences are true because they work in some more or less practical way? And if so, is this argument not open to the usual objection—namely, that the sciences are not true because they work, but that, on the contrary, they work because they are true? That is, they are made up of true theories and hypotheses about the natural world that may be confirmed by experimentation but do not depend upon it for their truth.

8. For a similar view, see Morris Kline, *Mathematics in Western Culture* (London: Allen and Unwin, 1954), Introduction, 9–11.

However, although it may seem somewhat like it at first sight, my thesis does not amount to a variety of pragmatism. For I am not arguing that scientific theories or hypotheses are true because they work. I am arguing, rather, that putting scientific theories to the test of experimentation and application is a part—in the case of natural science a central part—of the process by which they are found to be true. There are, of course, other parts of the process: the formulation of theories and hypotheses, the intellectual testing of such theories for consistency with some relevant body of data or with some cognizant body of theory, the cross-checking of experimental results with those of other researchers in the same field, the checking of measures and calculations, and the like. All these, too, may be part of the process, may play a role, in the finding of some theory or hypothesis to be true. But what has been argued above is that experimentation and application are the truth-finding processes that set the natural sciences apart from other intellectual practices in which it is equally important to sort out true from false ideas.

If one wanted to say that the pragmatic effectivity of scientific ideas—as demonstrated in experimentation and application—is of central importance in the natural-scientific enterprise,[9] I would have no objection to this interpretation of my thesis, provided that it is not supposed that what I am offering here is a "pragmatic theory of truth" or some such. For as will become even clearer as this book proceeds, I think it crucial both for science and for Marxism that they avoid the hopeless snares and delusions that are the so-called philosophical "theories of truth," whether these be correspondence theories or coherence theories. This is because *all* such theories rest, in my view, on subtly but profoundly flawed premises. Most notably, they are all grounded on what John Dewey called the "spectator theory of knowledge."[10] That is, they all rest on the notion that knowing is a *cognitive* rather than a *practical* activity, and on the closely related notion that it is a one-time state of affairs rather than a continuous process. However, all this will be spelled out in much greater detail in later sections of this book when I examine some recent epistemological debates within Marxism. For the moment, I only want to insist that the great strength of the natural sciences

9. This is now a quite widespread position among both those who take a realist view of natural scientific entities and forces and those who take an antirealist view. See, for example, Hacking, *Representing and Intervening*, chapter 4, and most especially van Fraasen, *The Scientific Image*, chapter 5.

10. Hacking, *Representing and Intervening*, 62. See also Richard J. Bernstein, *John Dewey* (New York: Washington Square Press, 1966), 57–74.

is that, in practice, they avoid the snares of philosophical epistemology. Natural scientists pursue highly specific truths (rather than a singular "Truth"), and they pursue them through a whole variety of practices and procedures of which experimentation and application are central and, in my view, definitive. However, as this book proceeds I shall argue that, as practices that are at once discursive and nondiscursive, both experimentation and application in natural science do have broader philosophical implications—in particular, that they have powerful implications, of a mostly devastating sort, for the claim that Marxism is some kind of natural science.

Third, and finally (in this list of possible objections to my thesis), some recent philosophers of science have argued that there are particular areas of modern natural science (especially the area of subatomic physics) in which experiments are conducted that are in principle indefeasible. The argument here is that experiments in this area involve the creation of such highly artificial and controlled environments that in effect they produce the very phenomena of whose existence they are supposed to be the test. That is, it is clear that these phenomena (various types of subatomic particles) do not exist except under these experimental conditions. Clearly, if true, this points to a serious flaw in the thesis outlined in this chapter. For it is essential to my thesis that both experimentation and application should be defeasible— not in the sense that every, or even most, experiments should fail, but that at least some do and all can, and that some experiments should also surprise (i.e., provide some additional or unexpected findings) even if they succeed.

However, a close examination of the literature on this admittedly opaque and rapidly changing field seems to me not, on balance, to support this interpretation. For there is a serious ambiguity in the verb "produce" in the preceding paragraph. It seems that what experiments in particle accelerators do is to abstract or isolate physical phenomena that do not occur in nature (i.e., without the intervention of the physicist). The experiments do not, as it were, simply create the entities required to match those imagined or postulated in some preexisting theory.[11] And so, while it may be true that subatomic physicists "produce" the phenomena that they are investigating, these phenomena are still not purely discursive, because the experiments in which they are created are not purely discursive. Thus, such

---

11. This is well discussed in Moritz Schlick, *Philosophy of Nature* (New York: Philosophical Library, 1949), 94–119 (an appendix, "The Concept of the Atom"). See also Holton, *The Scientific Imagination*, chapters 1 and 2, and Hacking, *Representing and Intervening*, chapter 9.

experiments do not invalidate the theory of the specificity of natural science that I have put forward in this chapter. It also seems, incidentally, that experiments in subatomic physics *are* defeasible, at least in the sense that they have continually led to surprising or surplus results, results that have usually been interpreted as the discovery of new particles.

2

Marxism and the Philosophy of Science

The thrust of chapter 1 was to argue that natural sciences are human practices distinguished by the centrality of the extradiscursive activities called "experimentation" and "application" by which scientific theories and hypotheses are tested and utilized. In this chapter I shall argue that Marxism is not a science because its theories and hypotheses are not experimentally testable in the above sense and because none of its theories or hypotheses can be applied.

Both the assertions in the preceding sentence will have to be justified by detailed argument. Before I do this, however, I wish to make it clear what precisely is being said, and what is *not* being said or implied, in the sentence which denies that Marxism is a science. In denying that Marxism is a science I am *not*:

(1) stating or implying that all Marxist theories or hypotheses are false or worthless. On the contrary, I believe that a number of propositions about the world that derive from Marxism are true, and importantly true. They are not, however, scientifically true, which just means that they cannot be established as true by the methods that I have argued are definitive of natural science. However, natural-scientific truths are not the only truths in the world, and one should most certainly not conflate "true" with "scientific," let alone "Truth" with "Science." Human beings establish that propositions are true in a great many ways, and they believe that propositions are true for a great many—often very good—reasons. Natural-scientific truths are such because they are established by particular procedures. Some propositions in Marxism are

not established by scientific procedures, or by any rational procedures, because they are false. Others, however, are true, and their truth can be established by rational procedures, though not by the procedures definitive of natural science.

Equally, I am *not:*

(2) denying that Marxism may be classed among the social or human sciences, conceived as a body of practices that must employ qualitatively different procedures from the natural sciences. Marxism may certainly be thought of as a *Geisteswissenschaft* if one so wishes. Indeed, those traditions of Marxist thought (notably the "Frankfurt School" or "Critical Theory" tradition) that would wish to class it as such have always insisted that the annexing of Marxism to the natural sciences was and is a fundamental mistake, albeit one initially perpetrated by Marx and Engels themselves.[1] Hence this book is not addressed to those Hegelian and "humanist" Marxists who would wish to defend this broader, German conception of science and have Marxism classed as a science *(Wissenschaft)* in this sense. For this tradition does not believe that there are, for example, "laws" of the development of human society that are part of, or a parallel to, "laws of nature"; nor (therefore) does it believe that Marxists are, or can be, in command of such laws or that humanity can be free only by being obedient to the historical necessities that they reveal. It is because the harder versions or streams of Marxism have made claims of this scope and certainty that they have given rise to a certain psychology and to a certain form of politics, both of which have had profound effects in the real world. Indeed, it is these breathtaking claims that have long made Marxism such a worthy and impassioned target to both attack and defend, and this book is just one of many that since Marxism's beginnings have taken a side in the debate about such claims. Humanist Marxism of the Frankfurt School variety may, in a certain sense, be more intellectually sophisticated than "scientistic" Marxism, but its claim that Marxism is some kind of *Geisteswissenschaft* is also much easier to defend because much less follows from it than from the claim that Marxism is, or can be, some sort of full-blown *Naturwissenschaft.*

Since, therefore, it is the psychological and above all the political effects

---

1. See, for example, Leszek Kolakowski, *Main Currents of Marxism* (Oxford: Oxford University Press, 1981), vol. 3, *The Breakdown*, chapters 7, 8, and 10.

of Marxism in the real world that is the central concern of this book, this alternative vision of Marxism ("Marxism as Critique" as Gouldner calls it) finds almost no place in its pages, even though it has deeply influenced other parts of my work.[2] I will, however, have something—something rather critical—to say about the political project of the Frankfurt School when, in chapter 6, I try to reformulate the Marxist point of view as a rational one in the contemporary world.

In stating that Marxism is not a science, I *am*, however:

(1) arguing that all attempts, from Marx and Engels onward, to present Marxism or "historical materialism" as a science on a par with other natural sciences cannot be sustained and ought to be abandoned. This is true both of the attempts of the founders themselves and of more recent efforts, notably those made by Louis Althusser and his followers and those deriving from an application to Marxism of Roy Bhaskar's *Realist Theory of Science*.

I *am* also:

(2) arguing that Marxism and Marxists would actually be in a stronger intellectual and political position if they abandoned the attempt to present Marxism as a *Naturwissenschaft*. By "stronger position" I mean simply that they would have a slightly greater chance of realizing their revolutionary purposes if they frankly admitted that Marxism is not any kind of hard science than if they continued to maintain this position. I will present an argument for this view in the third part of this book.

I *am* also:

(3) arguing that Marxists do not need either a "theory of science," or, indeed, any of the "theories of truth" offered by philosophy in order to identify or defend those propositions in Marxism that are true. As will become clear as my argument develops, I now hold, along with the later Wittgenstein, the view that what propositions like "X is true" or "X is a rational belief" mean is an essentially contextual matter, and that little or nothing of any interest can be said about such propositions outside of the context in which X is specified.

It is of course the case that when we claim that "X is true" or "X is rational" we very often claim to have verified this in some way, or to have falsified counterclaims that "X is not true" or "X is irrational." But the

2. Alvin Gouldner, *The Two Marxisms* (London: Macmillan, 1980), chapter 2, 32–63.

variety and combination of procedures that may count as verification or falsification in different contexts is so great that any attempt to unify or generalize them in philosophical "theories of truth" will always result in oversimplification, usually by omission. In other words, the terms "true" and "false," "rational" and "irrational" are used to refer to a family of human practices that resemble each other in various ways; this variety, however, cannot be grasped by the application of any single, abstract criterion (e.g., "correspondence to reality," "logical coherence," "verification by sense data"), even if, as seems doubtful, any of these criteria can be given a clear meaning. In the most general way it can be said that what makes this family of practices a family is that they are all concerned with the allaying of doubt, either about observations and propositions ("true/false") or about judgments ("rational"/"irrational"). The ultimate test, therefore, of any set of procedures for demonstrating that "X is true" is that in that context (the "X" context) they do allay the doubt that "X is true"; likewise, the ultimate test of any set of procedures for demonstrating that "X is rational" is that in that context (the "X" context) they do allay the doubt that "X is rational." This also means of course, as Wittgenstein stresses, that words like "true" and "false," "rational" and "irrational" only come into play in the everyday language game when a (specific) doubt has arisen.[3]

This, in turn, raises the possibility that what is wrong with all philosophical theories of truth is that they try to specify the criteria for our believing that *any* proposition is true in an abstract context in which no *specific* doubt either has arisen or can arise. In other words, philosophical theories of truth are attempted answers to the question, How can we know that *anything* is true? I, along with Wittgenstein, would want to say that this is a question which does not require an answer, because it is one that nobody, except deeply deluded philosophers, ever asks.[4] It is certainly not a question that any practicing scientist ever asks. Rather, natural scientists, like all other human beings, ask, How can I know that X is true, since I have now come to doubt X? (X here is a specific proposition or set of propositions.)

It is important to say all this because the central argument of this book

3. See Ludwig Wittgenstein, *On Certainty* (Oxford: Basil Blackwell, 1979), especially remarks 78–237, and the important commentary and elucidation in Thomas Morawetz, *Wittgenstein and Knowledge: The Importance of "On Certainty"* (Brighton: Harvester, 1980). See also Stanley Cavell, *The Claim of Reason: Wittgenstein, Skepticism, Morality, and Tragedy* (Oxford: Oxford University Press, 1979), chapters 6 and 8.

4. *On Certainty*, especially remarks 115–27. "If you tried to doubt everything, you would not get as far as doubting anything. The game of doubting itself presupposes certainty." (remark 115).

will be that Marxism was a rational point of view that embodied certain important truths, but that this point of view has been made increasingly irrational by historical change and thus needs to be fundamentally altered if it is to remain a rational point of view. In other words, I write in a context in which fundamental doubts have arisen both about whether Marxism as a whole is any longer a rational point of view and about the truth of specific theoretical and empirical propositions to which Marxists have traditionally been committed, and I write to address those specific doubts.

I also argue, however, that Marxism is a point of view that has been, and can be, constructed and defended in accordance with the highest standards of scholarly objectivity. I believe, though, that all these arguments can only be validated within the detailed context of what follows, and that demonstrating their validity does not require—and would not be aided in the slightest—by my defining in an abstract or contextless way what I mean by "truths," "rational point of view," or "scholarly objectivity." Rather, what I mean by these terms will be shown in what follows, and my argument will be validated (or not) in that showing.

Marxism and Scientific Realism

Before constructing any argument that Marxism is not any kind of natural science, it is first necessary to examine how, on what basis, it has been argued to be such. I think there is no doubt of what is, and always has been, the predominant "orthodox" Marxist position on this issue. It is that Marxism is a science insofar as, like a number of other natural sciences, it is able to delve beneath the mere appearance of phenomena to reveal the underlying realities that explain those phenomena. A number of quotations from Marx himself are usually adduced in support of this orthodox view:

> All science would be superfluous if the outward appearance and the essence of things directly coincided. (*Capital* 3:797)

> It is the work of science to reduce the visible, merely external movement into the true intrinsic movement. (*Capital* 3:307)

> That in their appearance things often represent themselves in inverted form is pretty well known in every science except Political Economy. (*Capital* 1:573)

The final form of economic relations, as these are visible on the surface, in their real existence, and also in the ideas which with the bearers and agents of these relations seek to gain an understanding of them is very different from—indeed the very reverse and the opposite of—their inner, essential but concealed core-form and the concept corresponding to it. (*Capital* 3:311)

In [the] completely estranged form of profit, and in the same measure as the form of profit hides its inner core, capital more and more acquires a tangible form, is transformed more and more from a relationship into a thing, but a thing which embodies, which has absorbed, the social relationship . . . in this form of *capital* and *profit* it appears as a ready-made precondition on the surface. It is the form of its actuality or rather its actual form of existence. And it is the form in which it lives in the consciousness of . . . the capitalists, in which it is reflected in their ideas. (*Theories of Surplus Value* 3:483)

William Suchting has shown how nearly all the crucial terms that appear in these quotations —"appearance" (*Erscheinung*), "essence" (*Wesen*), "representation" (*Darstellung*), and "semblance" or "illusion" (*Schein*)—were taken by Marx from Hegel's *Science of Logic*, which he read just before he began writing *Capital*.[5] And it is important here that in his *Logic* Hegel himself appears to have been influenced by the natural science of his day in exemplifying the relationships between these categories. Thus, for example, in the first subdivision of that part of the *Logic* dealing with the doctrine of essence (entitled "Matter and Form") Hegel treats the molecular structure of matter—the molecular forms themselves and their laws of behavior expressed in mathematical forms—as essential forms of an appearance (*Erscheinung*). This appearance is matter itself, which Hegel treats as a mere "semblance" or "illusion" (*Schein*) insofar as it is not grasped as the appearance of these forms, but which is also "actual" (*wirklich*) insofar as matter just *is* the "necessary appearance" of these forms.[6]

In trying to further clarify what Hegel is saying here, Suchting himself takes the example of "Eddington's famous 'two tables'":

5. W. A. Suchting, *Marxism and Philosophy: Three Studies* (New York: New York University Press, 1986), 37–39.

6. Hegel's *Science of Logic*, trans. A. V. Miller, Foreword by Professor J. N. Findlay (London: Allen and Unwin, 1969); see especially book 2, section 1, chapter 3, 447–50 and 458–61.

Eddington takes the table as represented by physical science (a fairly stable structure of molecules whose individual sizes are very small in comparison with their distance apart) as the "real" table, and the commonsense table (a structure that densely fills a certain portion of space etc.) as mere illusion. But there is in fact nothing illusory about the commonsense table in the sense that this is just how the scientific table is "projected" at the level of ordinary sized objects. This is the fully determined "appearance" of the scientific table. Finally, to understand the commonsense table as being *nothing but* the scientific-table-in-such-and-such-relations is to conceive it under the category of actuality.[7]

In short, it is very important to realize just how deeply natural science has been involved in the Marxist conception of science from its very beginnings. For it is not just that Marx himself was clearly writing with certain natural-science examples in mind when he discussed appearance and essence or illusion and actuality. It is not just that modern Marxist scholars such as Suchting continue that tradition by using examples like Eddington's "two tables." It is that Hegel himself, from whom Marx got this vocabulary, developed it, in large part, by generalizing, philosophically and epistemologically, from what he understood about the natural sciences of the early nineteenth century.

And, as we can see, the most transfixing area of natural science for Hegel and for Marxists, from the early nineteenth century to the present day, has been what we might broadly term "the molecular and submolecular world" (including the atomic and subatomic world), revealed by organic and inorganic chemistry (including biochemistry) and by physics. The reason, of course, is that this is the paradigm case of the scientific explanation of sensibly perceptible phenomena—the phenomena of the ordinary world, if one likes—by non-sensibly perceptible entities, ones that in fact are only knowable or perceptible by the specialized methods and techniques of natural science. To put it crudely (and to a degree inaccurately, but forcefully)— Marxists from Marx onward have taken the defining characteristic of natural science to be that it explains what can be naïvely seen by what cannot

---

7. Suchting, *Marxism and Philosophy*, 39; for further details on Sir Arthur Eddington, astronomer and super-scientific realist, see A. D. Kline, Introduction to the section "Theory and Observation," in *Introductory Readings in the Philosophy of Science*, ed. E. D. Klemke, R. Hollinger, and A. D. Kline (Buffalo: Prometheus Books, for Iowa State University, 1969), especially 145.

be seen, or rather by what can only be seen by the application of scientific methods. Thus, in the Preface to the first German edition of *Capital*, we find Marx saying:

> The value-form, whose fully developed shape is the money-form, is very elementary and simple. Nevertheless, the human mind has for more than 2000 years sought in vain to get to the bottom of it, whilst on the other hand, to the successful analysis of much more composite and complex forms, there has been at least an approximation. Why? Because the body, as an organic whole, is more easy of study than are the cells of that body. In the analysis of economic forms, more-over, neither microscopes nor chemical reagents are of use. The force of abstraction must replace both. (*Capital* 1:7–8)

If, therefore, there is something seriously misleading about this analogy or comparison, if the kind of unobservable entities and relations discovered through Marxist science are significantly different from those discovered by the sciences of the molecular and submolecular world, if the "force of abstraction" is not an adequate replacement for microscopes or chemical reagents (or particle accelerators for that matter), then the claim that Marxism is a natural science will be severely, even fatally, weakened. I will argue that this is the case, that there are significant differences here, ones that are vividly illuminated by an examination of the role of experiment and applica-tion in natural science. But this is to anticipate. At the moment, I simply wish to establish that the sciences of the molecular and submolecular world are hegemonic in the Marxist image of science. For this implies that in order to discuss the central problems of Marxism as science we will have to ana-lyze in some depth the Marxist equivalents of atoms and molecules in the social world—namely, labor values and modes of production—to see whether they are in fact proper equivalents.

As a prelude to that analysis, however, it should be noted that, although the molecular and submolecular world provides the dominant paradigm of science for Marxists, it is not the only such paradigm. Thus Ben Brewster has argued that when, in the third volume of *Capital*, Marx juxtaposed the "true intrinsic movement" of the capitalist mode of production to the "vis-ible, merely external movement," the comparison he is invoking is that of Ptolemaic astronomy versus Copernican/Keplerian astronomy. So that while the Ptolemain sees the "merely apparent" or "merely external" move-ment of the sun setting beneath the rim of the earth, the Copernican or

Keplerian sees the "true intrinsic movement" of the earth rising above the line of visibility of the sun.[8]

Again, and certainly more familiarly, we know that Marx was in some ways deeply influenced by Charles Darwin's *Origin of Species* (of 1859), whether or not it is true that he wished to dedicate the second volume of *Capital* to Darwin.[9] Certainly in the Prefaces to both the first and second editions of volume 1 of *Capital* Marx makes loose reference to some similarities between his theory and the theory of evolution, a comparison that Engels was to develop and to treat much more seriously in the years after Marx's death. I have argued elsewhere that for Marx himself the analogy between his work and Darwin's probably did not extend much beyond the notion that human history, like the history of species, proceeds in a broadly evolutionary way, although the mechanisms of that evolution had nothing to do with those (like natural selection) posited by Darwin for plants and animals.[10] Certainly it is clear from their correspondence on the matter that neither Marx nor Engels was a social Darwinist, although Marx did manifest a distinct liking for biological analogies and metaphors in describing social and historical processes.

I therefore conclude that both astronomy and evolutionary biology are distinctly secondary motifs in the Marxist picture of science and that that picture has been dominated, both in Marx's time and since, by the sciences of the molecular and submolecular world. Therefore, we must now examine the use made of this picture of science both by Marx himself in *Capital* and by most orthodox Marxists after him.

Marx's *Capital:* Social Atoms and Social Molecules

Capital is the foundation of the Marxist science of the economy. It is scientific in applying Marx's scientific method; and in accordance with this method it is able to analyse the economy in abstraction

8. Ben Brewster, "Fetishism in Capital and Reading Capital," *Economy and Society* 5, no. 3 (August 1976): 347.

9. For diametrically conflicting views, see David McLellan, *Karl Marx: His Life and Thought* (London: Macmillan, 1973), 424, and Leslie R. Page, *Karl Marx and the Critical Examination of His Works* (London: Freedom Association, 1987), 117–21.

10. Gavin Kitching, *Karl Marx and the Philosophy of Praxis* (London: Routledge, 1988), 61–63. For an opposite view, see Page, *Karl Marx*, 122–32.

from politics and from the other aspects of society. The broad outlines of Marx's scientific method are well known: science must reveal
the hidden forces behind the appearance of phenomena, but this in
one form or another is the criterion of all methodologies and it is
necessary to consider Marx's specific method more carefully. . . .

Starting from existing notions science progresses by forming
highly abstract (simple) concepts and, through a process of reasoning, producing ever more complex, less abstract (but nevertheless
abstract) concepts until the concrete is reproduced in thought. For
Marx, therefore, science implies a hierarchical relationship between
concepts and, what is more, this pyramid is related to the hierarchical
relationships of determination which link phenomena in reality.[11]

Laurence Harris then goes on to cite "values" and "prices of production"
and "surplus value" and "profits" as instances of the way in which the
"hierarchy of concepts" in *Capital* is also a "hierarchy of determination"
in reality. That is, on Harris's account, values determine prices of production in reality and surplus value determines profits in reality, as well as
values and prices of production and surplus value and profits being linked
hierarchically (as more or less abstract concepts) in Marx's scientific model
of the capitalist mode of production. These two paragraphs are from one
review article by one contemporary Marxist economist, but they clearly
and succinctly state an orthodoxy that would be accepted by many contemporary Marxists who attest to the scientific status of Marxism.[12] The following is my summary of this orthodoxy.

In the first volume of *Capital* Marx presents an abstract model
of the capitalist mode of production. It is severely abstract in
that it abstracts both from particularities of time and place
(although it uses, illustratively, some data on nineteenth-
century British capitalism) and from many social and political
features that are found in any actual capitalist society. The
model of capitalism set out in volume 1 is thus very abstractly

---

11. Laurence Harris, "The Science of the Economy," *Economy and Society* 7, no. 3 (August
1978): 284–85.

12. For an influential work that attempts to develop the realist conception of Marxism into
a "methodology" for Marxist (and other) social scientists, see Andrew Sayer, *Method in Social
Science: A Realist Approach* (London: Hutchinson, 1984). See also R. Keat and J. Urry, *Social
Theory as Science* (London: Routledge and Kegan Paul, 1975), especially chapters 2, 5, and 8.

economic and postulates a situation in which all commodities exchange at their values (or in proportion to the amount of socially necessary abstract labor directly and indirectly embodied in them). This happens because in the "volume 1" model the relative money prices of commodities directly reflect these values. This being the case, then human labor power, sold by the working class to the capitalist class, also exchanges at its value, it being, in this respect, a commodity like all other commodities. In addition, machines and raw materials of production, the monopoly property of the capitalist class, also exchange at their labor values. All this being the case, it can be shown that the capitalist class as a whole can only obtain a profit from production by exploiting the labor power of the working class, since it is a unique property of human labor power that it is the only commodity capable of producing a mass of commodities greater in value than itself. In essence, this exploitation is accomplished by the capitalist class using its monopoly control over the means of production to force the working class to work for a period of time in excess of that necessary to replace the value of means of production and to produce the value of its own labor power. This unpaid or "excess" labor time Marx calls "surplus value" and he claims it to be the sole source of profits in the capitalist system.

In volumes 2 and 3 of *Capital* Marx makes his model of the capitalist mode of production gradually more "complex" or "concrete," introducing such factors as the circulation of money and commodities, the expansion of the system through increases of capital investment, and, in volume 3, competition among capitals. Among the complexities introduced by competition is that commodities no longer exchange at their values but at their "prices of production," prices that will be above or below values, depending upon the organic composition of capital in the sector involved. However, Marx demonstrates in volume 3 that the effect of varying prices of production is simply to share out the mass of surplus value among different capitals as different sectoral rates of profit. This does not alter the fact that the total mass of profit available to be shared out is determined by the mass of surplus value expropriated from the working class. Moreover, Marx demonstrates in volume 3 (on the basis of his analysis of production in the first volume) that as capitalism develops technologically there is a necessary tendency for the overall rate of profit to fall, a tendency brought about by the gradual expulsion of the only source of surplus value and profits (living labor power) from the production process through ever-increasing mechanization. This law of the tendency of the rate of profit to fall can be offset for a while by a number of counteracting tendencies in the system (also analyzed in volume 3), but it is not annulled by them, and it manifests itself in periodic crises of the system.

It will therefore be seen that, according to this orthodox account, a realm of entities is postulated in volume 1 of *Capital*. These entities (which Marx terms "labour values," varied quantities of labor time embodied in commodities), are, it is universally agreed by both Marxist and non-Marxist economists, empirically imperceptible and unmeasurable in any actual capitalist economy,[13] but changes in their magnitude are nonetheless deemed (at least by orthodox Marxist economists) to have empirically measurable *effects* on empirically measurable phenomena in the real world.

Thus, for example, if there is a long-term decline in the amount of socially necessary abstract labor (SNAL) embodied in a commodity or group of commodities (i.e., in the value of that commodity or group of commodities), then, according to Marx, there will be a long-term decline in the empirically measurable *price* of that commodity or group of commodities. This fall will not necessarily be in the nominal money price of the commodities in question but in their price expressed as a proportion of average money earnings when inflation is discounted.[14]

Or again, if, according to Marx, the value in SNAL of "constant capital" (i.e., the amount of SNAL directly and indirectly embodied in plant, equipment, and raw materials) rises faster than the amount of SNAL embodied in wage goods ("variable capital") and in surplus or profit goods ("surplus value"), then over time the empirically measurable average monetary rate

13. See, for example, Joan Robinson, *An Essay on Marxian Economics* (London: Macmillan, 1942), chapter 3. See also Diane Elson, ed., *Value: The Representation of Labour in Capitalism* (London: CSE Books, 1979), and A. Sen, "On the Labour Theory of Value: Some Methodological Issues," *Cambridge Journal of Economics* 2, no. 2 (1978): 175–90.

14. See my *Karl Marx*, 83.

of profit in the capitalist system will fall, a fall that in turn will bring about a number of other empirically measurable phenomena (especially economic crises of various types).[15]

All this being the case, we see how and why Marx was heavily influenced by areas of natural science in which invisible or unobservable entities were deemed to have sensibly visible or perceptible effects or to take sensibly visible or perceptible forms. We can also see why twentieth-century Marxists have been deeply influenced both by further scientific developments of the molecular and submolecular world (most notably subatomic physics) and by the debates in the philosophy of natural science to which such developments have led.

For, wedded as they are to this conception of science, it is clear that neither Marx himself nor contemporary Marxists can be at all sympathetic to empiricist philosophies of science. For these latter claim that the only real phenomena in the world are those that are sensibly perceptible by human beings and that all other entities are simply imaginary postulates, perhaps helpful to human beings in providing explanations of sensibly perceptible phenomena but in no way as real as these phenomena themselves. On the contrary, it is clear that given the form of scientific explanation in *Capital* orthodox Marxists *must* be philosophical realists of some sort. That is, they have to hold that there are real entities in the world that are not sensibly or naïvely perceptible by human beings but that nonetheless really exist and either have sensibly perceptible *effects* (for example, those of electromagnetic fields of force on iron filings) or take sensibly perceptible *forms* (as when atoms combine into molecules and molecules combine to form the vast multitude of sensibly perceptible things in the world).

Ian Hacking has usefully distinguished two types of realism in the modern philosophy of natural science, "entity realism" and "theoretical realism." He notes that it is possible for philosophers of science to be one or the other or both without contradiction, but that it is not necessary to be both and some realist philosophers of science are not. Broadly speaking, those philosophers of natural science who are entity realists hold that the physical entities identified by experiments in the molecular and submolecular world (e.g., molecules, atoms, electrons, positrons, quarks) are real,

---

15. See, for example, Meghnad Desai, *Marxian Economic Theory* (London: Grey-Mills, 1974), chapter 18; G. Hodgson, "The Theory of the Falling Rate of Profit," *New Left Review*, no. 84 (1974); and Joseph Gillman, *The Falling Rate of Profit: Marx's Law and Its Significance to Twentieth-Century Capitalism* (London: Dobson, 1957). The "law" itself is set out in *Capital*, vol. 3, part 3.

while those who are theoretical realists hold that a number of entities identified in scientific theories, rather than in scientific experiments, are real. These theoretical entities would include "energy," "force," "momentum," "acceleration," "electricity," "electromagnetism," and the like (i.e., broadly speaking, all those entities in natural-scientific theories whose existence can only be known of through their *effects*). Entity realists are usually theoretical realists as well (but do not have to be), and theoretical realists are usually entity realists as well (but do not have to be).[16]

To see what is involved in these disputes about realism in natural science, it is perhaps best to begin with what an out-and-out antirealist philosopher of science, such as Bas van Fraasen, would say about a theoretical entity like electricity or an experimental entity like a quark. In the first case he would simply apply something like Russell's "theory of descriptions" to such theoretical entities as electricity. In other words he would want the term "electricity" replaced by sense-data descriptions of a vast number of events (light bulbs illuminating, ring coils heating up, computers functioning), followed by a proposition such as "X (electricity) is postulated by human beings as the common cause of these events." Electricity would thereby be relegated firmly to the status of a mental or cognitive phenomenon, which for out-and-out empiricists like van Fraasen is an allocation to an unreal or at least less-real status. In the case of quarks, he would similarly take any description of an experiment in which they appear and say something like "A quark is that entity postulated to explain why a magnetometer measures the passage from a positive to a negative electrical charge on a supercooled niobium ball at $+\frac{1}{3}e$."[17]

It will be seen, then, that out-and-out antirealism about natural science requires some kind of instrumentalist doctrine about things that cannot be perceived by the senses.[18] That is, it requires some doctrine to the effect that such things are simply convenient fictions or postulates produced by scientists to help explain sense-perceptible phenomena in their experiments. Insofar as these explanations seem plausible, and, more particularly, insofar

---

16. See Hacking, *Representing and Intervening*, chapter 1.

17. See van Fraasen, *The Scientific Image*, especially chapter 3. For a fascinating review of the realist/antirealist debate in contemporary philosophy of science, see Paul M. Churchland and Clifford A. Hooker, eds., *Images of Science: Essays on Realism and Empiricism* (Chicago: University of Chicago Press, 1985), especially Van Fraasen's "Reply" to a series of realist criticisms of *The Scientific Image*, 245–305.

18. For "instrumentalism," see, for example, E. Nagel, *The Structure of Science* (New York: Harcourt, Brace and World, 1961), chapters 5 and 6, and S. Toulmin, *The Philosophy of Science* (New York: Harper Bros., 1953), chapter 4.

as natural scientists can produce sensibly perceptible phenomena through the alleged manipulation of these entities, then we must believe that such fictions or postulates are "empirically adequate" and practically efficacious. But, according to van Fraasen, we do not have to believe in the real existence of the entities (whether theoretical or physical) that they postulate, or that natural scientists claim to have experimentally discovered or isolated.[19]

I turn now to what a philosophically informed and interested natural scientist might make of this attack on the reality of the entities in which she or he deals. It is probable that the average natural scientist would in fact be a philosophical realist about the unobservable forces and entities in her or his theories, or at any rate about those old and well-established forces and entities in her or his field (like energy, electromagnetism, molecules, atoms, etc.). This is because there is a tendency in all the natural sciences, well documented by Hacking, for such entities to graduate over time from the status of mere postulates or conjectures to that of real things, mainly through their being identified or isolated by experiments.[20] But note that though most natural scientists would probably be philosophical realists about nonnaïvely perceptible forces and entities, *they do not have to be.* Given the centrality of experimentation and application in their professional practice, it is possible for natural scientists to be epistemologically agnostic or cynical about the reality of the forces and entities in which they deal. In other words, it is open to natural scientists to say, for example:

> I will accept, if you like, that neutrons are just convenient explanatory fictions, and not necessarily real. But nonetheless I can build, and have built, a machine that will produce a naïvely perceptible ray, and when this ray is trained on a number of other naïvely perceptible things it will have certain naïvely perceptible effects, effects which I can and will demonstrate for you now.

It is equally open to natural scientists to say, for example:

19. Van Fraasen, *The Scientific Image,* chapter 4.
20. Hacking, *Representing and Intervening,* 30. See also D. W. Theobald, *An Introduction to the Philosophy of Science* (London: Methuen, 1968), chapter 7 ("Science and Physical Reality"), where this precise point (about the indifference of the practicing scientist to realist or instrumentalist descriptions of what she or he is doing) is made, only to be dismissed as *philosophically* unimportant or irrelevant. It seems to me, however, (as it did to Wittgenstein), that two descriptions of a practice, the choice between which has *no* implications for the actual conduct of that practice, are probably both forms of "idling language." Mary Hesse also seems

> I will accept, if you like, that the DNA molecule is just an explanatory fiction and does not really exist. But nonetheless I will undertake certain experimental procedures, which I will describe and explain, making reference to this entity; these procedures will result in the production of two-headed pale green mice. Moreover, I will produce such mice at will through these procedures and in unlimited numbers.

In short, it is open to the natural scientist to be a principled realist or a cynical instrumentalist about naïvely unobservable scientific forces and entities because her or his practice as a natural scientist does not depend *simply* on theories or concepts in theories. In other words, the centrality of experiment and application in natural science implies that scientists do not merely describe or explain naïvely unobservable phenomena; they intervene in nature to *manipulate* such phenomena. Moreover, nearly all these manipulations can be made to take forms that will have naïvely perceptible effects or consequences. These effects or consequences can then be claimed to be due to, and only to, the manipulation of the postulated unobservable entities. Generally speaking, the more successful these manipulations are (i.e., the more frequently and reliably they can be undertaken) the greater will be the belief, among both scientists and nonscientists, in the reality of the entities that are supposedly being manipulated in order to produce the naïvely perceptible effects.

It is of course true that there are some natural sciences that operate, not in closed or artificial experimental environments, but in "open systems" where the capacity for the manipulation of phenomena is usually much less. I am thinking here of such sciences as geology, meteorology, or astrophysics; although experiments are carried out, the principal application of the science is in the prediction of natural phenomena rather than the manipulation of them. In Roy Bhaskar's *Realist Theory of Science* these kinds of open-system natural sciences are implicitly compared with social science as a way of defending the possible scientificity of the latter. However, I do not believe that this comparison is a valid one, and I certainly do not believe that it can be used to defend the scientificity of Marxism.

The reason is that such open-system experiments are not concerned with

---

to be struggling with the same problem in her highly muted defense of scientific realism (*The Structure of Scientific Inference* [London: Macmillan, 1974], 283–302). Having outlined a highly qualified form of realism, she is forced to admit that her "network theory" of science may also be seen as a form of instrumentalism (300)!

observing or isolating the unobservable entities and forces of the molecular and submolecular world. On the contrary, they all take the existence of these biological/chemical/physical entities and forces as already established by other sciences. In one case they are concerned with the behavior of some much larger phenomena that these entities and forces produce on the planet Earth (geology, meteorology). In the other they are concerned with some universe-scale phenomena that they produce beyond the planet Earth (astrophysics). In either case, therefore, these open-system sciences and forms of experiment do not concern the reality of the kind of unobservable entities that have provided the dominant paradigm for the Marxist conception of science and of Marxism's own scientificity. It is on the validity of this analogy between the molecular and submolecular world and the unobservable entities of Marxism that Marxism's claim to be a science primarily depends, and these forms of open-system experimentation do not affect this issue at all.

However, I will say somewhat more about this when I come to consider Bhaskar's work in detail, and in particular the claim that his realist theory of science can help validate the scientificity of Marxism. For the moment, I wish to concentrate on bringing out what I take to be the crucial difference between Marxism and the natural sciences of the molecular and submolecular world—crucial, that is, to assessing the claim that Marxism is any kind of hard science.

We can most simply and easily approach this difference by noting that, unlike the natural scientist confronted with questions about the reality of his or her unobservable entities and forces, the Marxist is compelled to be a dogmatic realist about values or modes of production *because the Marxist has no experiments or applications to which she or he can point to sustain a cynical epistemological agnosticism or instrumentalism.* The Marxist cannot offer any propositions equivalent to "neutrons may not be real but I can produce a ray" or "DNA molecules may not be real but I can produce two-headed green mice," and we can see this clearly if we consider what propositions the Marxist might adduce of this type.

Possible candidates might be "Values may not be real but I can predict that the industrial rate of profit will fall," or "Values may not be real but I can predict that there will be a major economic crisis in five years' time," or "Modes of production may not be real but I can predict that the next Marxist revolution will be in Thailand." But these examples just have to be adduced for the major problem with them to be obvious. For even should all these predictions come true, it will not be possible for the Marxist to demonstrate that his or her explanations of these events (in terms of values or modes of production) are either the only possible ones or even the best available ones. The reason of course is that the Marxist cannot experimentally manipulate the unobservable entities she or he is postulating in order to produce the predicted event at will. A Marxist who could experimentally reduce the value rate of profit to see if this would actually reduce the monetary rate of profit, or a Marxist who could actually articulate two modes of production in varying proportions to see which proportion was the most objectively revolutionary, would be a Marxist who, like the natural scientist, could ultimately shrug off the realism/antirealism debate. But of course we know that Marxists cannot do this. Thus radical antirealism, whether of an empiricist or pragmatist kind, is threatening to the Marxist in a way in which it is simply not to the natural scientist inured by his or her nondiscursive "manipulatory" practices.

Antirealism menaces the orthodox Marxist precisely because, since he or she cannot manipulate unobservable entities through nondiscursive experiments and applications, he or she is always open, even in the best case, to objections of the form "Well, yes, the rate of profit did fall, but for reasons which have nothing to do with values, the rising organic composition of capital, and so on"; or "Well, yes, a crisis did occur, but for reasons that have nothing to do with a rising value mass of C"; or "Well, yes, there was a revolution in Thailand, but for reasons that have nothing to do with modes of production." Confronted with such objections, it is impossible (I mean logically impossible) for the Marxist to demonstrate that his or her explanations of these phenomena are superior to whatever non-Marxist explanations are being proffered. For the only conclusive way to do this is to produce or reproduce the phenomena by manipulating the Marxist theoretical entities, and then to show that they cannot be produced or reproduced by manipulating the non-Marxist theoretical entities—neither of which experimental wonders the Marxist can perform.

However, some Marxists would deny the radical distinction set out above by asserting that Marxists can and do conduct experiments—thought experiments—of which (they could say) *Capital* is a classical case. On this well-known account, the process of abstraction undertaken by Marx in constructing the theory and argument of *Capital* is some sort of equivalent to natural-scientific experimentation in that the entities produced by that process of abstraction are indeed real abstractions. That is, they are entities that are either real in themselves or that have real effects. My reply to this case (which is, broadly, the classical Althusserian case for a Marxist science) is simply to assert that thought experiments are not experiments, or at any rate not scientific experiments, precisely because as thought experiments they have no nondiscursive or extradiscursive elements to make them defeasible.

Perhaps the best way to clarify what I mean here is to consider a well-known section of Wittgenstein's *Philosophical Investigations* in which he is discussing the possibility of a "private language," one constructed by, and only comprehensible to, one person. Wittgenstein concludes that such a language is an impossibility, a conclusion that has been much debated and disputed. But here we need not consider the validity of his conclusion, but simply note the form of argument by which he reaches it. In the most famous passage dealing with the issue, he says:

> Let us imagine the following case. I want to keep a diary about the recurrence of a certain sensation. To this end I associate it with the sign "S" and write this sign in a calendar for every day on which I have the sensation. I will remark first of all that a definition of the sign cannot be formulated—But still I can give myself a kind of ostensive definition—How? Can I point to the sensation? Not in the ordinary sense. But I speak, or write the sign down, and at the same time I concentrate my attention on the sensation—But what is this ceremony for? for that is all that it seems to be! A definition surely serves to establish the meaning of a sign—Well, that is done precisely by the concentrating of my attention; for in this way I impress on myself the connexion between the sign and sensation.— But "I impress it on myself" can only mean: this process brings it about that I remember the connexion *right* in the future. But in the present case I have no criterion of correctness. One would like to say: whatever is going to seem right to me is right. And that only means that here we can't talk about "right."[21]

By analogy, let us say that I believe that the entities created by abstraction in the first volume of *Capital* are real. "Values," "constant capital," "variable capital," "surplus value," and "the law of the tendency of the rate of profit to fall" are all "real abstractions" produced by a "scientific" (rather than "ideological") process of abstraction. I am then asked how I know this. I can reply either by simply repeating the assertions above (which was

21. Wittgenstein, *Philosophical Investigations*, remark 253.

Louis Althusser's strategy at his worst), or I can say that they are real because they have "real effects." I am asked what these effects are, and I reply, "The long-term tendency for prices to fall as a proportion of average earnings is an effect of rising relative surplus value." Or I say, "The secular tendency for the rate of profit to fall, the tendency for capital to centralize and concentrate, and the regular occurrence of capitalist economic crises are all effects of C rising relative to $V + S$." To these replies my skeptical inquirer points out that all such effects can be explained in other ways, ways that do not involve postulating any of the entities of which they are supposed to be the effects. At this point I must either take issue with each of these alternative explanations (and take issue in ways that do *not* involve assuming or postulating the very entities—values and the like—that are in question) or I am driven back to dogmatic assertions about scientific abstractions producing the concrete in thought and so on. In other words, my problem here (and Marx's) is that

> "I have no criterion of reality. One would like to say: what-
> ever is going to seem real to me is real. And that only means
> that here we can't talk about 'real.'"

It is important to say what is meant by a "criterion of reality." What Marx lacks here is not someone to check up on, or even agree with, the process of abstraction he has undertaken in *Capital*—plenty of Marxists have done so. Nor does he lack for plausible explanations constructed with the entities he has abstracted. (In all these respects he is, of course, much better off than the philosophical solipsist against whom Wittgenstein's argument was originally directed.) What he lacks, and what the natural scientist has got, is something nondiscursive he can *do* with these entities so as to have nondiscursive effects. For the position that I am arguing here does not endorse van Fraasen's empiricist view that only phenomena known through the senses are real and that any other use of the term is an abuse.[22] Nor does

22. There is no doubt that the principal problem of van Fraasen's otherwise brilliant anti-realist argument is the position he is forced to take on observation, particularly on "unobservables" in science. Van Fraasen has to find a basis for arguing that observing the printed word with the aid of spectacles, for example, is somehow *qualitatively* different from observing large molecules through a high-power optical microscope. For it is essential to his thesis that one "sees" type in some totally unproblematic and "naïve" way in which one does not "see" molecules. But it seems very hard to deny that one is dealing here with matters of degree and that no form of human observation is totally naïve in the manner in which van Fraasen needs it to be. See van Fraasen, *The Scientific Image*, 13–19; see also Klemke, Hollinger, and Kline,

my position involve an endorsement of the more naïve scientific realism in which molecules or atoms, or neutrons or positrons, are held to be "as real as" (the familiar exemplars) "this jacket, that skirt, that television set," and so on. The position for which I am arguing is rather that the word "real" is probably too loaded with empiricist connotations (connotations continually reinforced by just these comparisons—"this jacket," etc.) to be anything but confusing in talking about natural science.

Hence the important point about the unobservable entities identified and manipulated by natural scientists is not whether we should agree to call them real or not, but that we should be clear about what such scientists do—can do—nondiscursively, with them. And it is less important to say about naïvely unobservable social things that one cannot manipulate as natural scientists do (such things as values, modes of production, etc.) that they are not real, than it is to say that they are *not scientific*, not scientific things, not things of science, whatever else they may be. So my position is not to say, with the empiricists, "That which cannot be sensibly perceived is not real," but to say "That which is naïvely unobservable and which one cannot manipulate nondiscursively is not scientific, whatever else it may be." And I would add, "And calling such things real does not, in itself, make them one whit more scientific."

Finally, we may note one recent formulation of a realist theory of science that has proved particularly attractive to Marxists. This is Roy Bhaskar's work, which has the great merit, for Marxists, of making a clear distinction between forms of scientific explanation that are appropriate and possible in "open systems" and those that require "closed" (or experimentally produced and controlled) systems.

Bhaskar argues that far too much philosophy of science, especially empiricist and Popperian theories, has drawn spuriously universal criteria of

---

Introductory Readings, part 2, 152–83, and Hacking, *Representing and Intervening*, chapter 2. This issue also forms a major part of the debate in Churchland and Hooker, *Images of Science*; see especially the essays by Churchland, Musgrave, Hacking, and Wilson, and the replies to these by van Fraasen, notably 255–58, 297–99, and 302–5. On p. 256 in particular, van Fraasen makes what seems to me a rather unconvincing defense against the charge that his theory of science may be circular "because I define empirical adequacy in terms of observability and point to science as the source of information about what is observable" (250 n. 7). The point here is that van Fraasen treats as "empirically inadequate" any theory which contains a statement that "X is unobservable" if "in fact" X is observable. This hardly seems very helpful, in that realism is a theory about the status of those entities and forces that are naïvely *unobservable* but "scientifically" observable. It is not a theory about entities and forces that are deemed scientifically unobservable but then turn out to be "naïvely" observable (significantly, van Fraasen gives no example of such a case).

science from the analysis simply of closed-system science. This is particularly true of Humean theories of causality, which require a constant conjunction of events only producible in closed systems, and Popperian falsificationism, which requires a capacity for prediction that is equally only possible (Bhaskar argues) in closed systems.[23]

Bhaskar's realist theory of science postulates instead of all this that science aims to identify the real "generative mechanism" of nature, mechanisms that are nothing less than the "causal powers of things."[24] However, the causal powers of such natural things will normally produce predictable effects (in the sense of some kind of perceptible event) only in closed systems. In open systems, by contrast, the causal powers of one thing may be nullified by the causal powers of another, or several different causal powers may crosscut in complex ways. In open systems, therefore, causal powers will manifest themselves, if at all, only as "tendencies," and these tendencies may not be "actualized" in any perceptible event or set of events. Moreover, these events, even if they occur, may not be perceived or perceivable by human beings.

The appeal of Bhaskar's theory of open-system tendencies as "powers which may be exercised without being fulfilled or actualised (as well as being fulfilled or actualised unperceived by men)"[25] is that it appears to fit certain aspects of "Marxism as science" perfectly and to deal with some of its most difficult problems. For example, the law of the tendency of the rate of profit to fall can be conceived as a perfect case of an open-system tendency that may not be actualized because a number of countervailing tendencies (enumerated by Marx in the third volume of *Capital*) continually cut across it and nullify its influence for long periods. Hence of course it may not be perceptible in any actual event or pattern of events (i.e., in any actual tendency for the measurable price rate of profit to fall). On Bhaskar's account this would not negate the existence of a real generative mechanism at work in capitalist society (say, the accumulation of C faster than V + S), which generative mechanism might in turn be seen as one causal power of a real thing or things—labor values.[26]

However, in my view appearances are highly deceptive here. Bhaskar's open-system realism cannot be brought to the rescue of Marxism in the way that some have supposed. The reason is that, as a theory of natural

23. Roy Bhaskar, *A Realist Theory of Science* (Sussex: Harvester, 1978), 14.
24. Ibid.
25. Ibid., 21.
26. A. Sayer, *Method in Social Science*, especially chapters 3 and 4.

science, Bhaskar's realism is as dependent on nondiscursive forms of experimentation as is the antirealist account I have provided in this chapter. For if one asks of Bhaskar how the generative mechanisms, the causal powers of things in nature, can be known to exist if they do not necessarily manifest themselves even as actualized tendencies in Nature's open system, he refers one immediately and explicitly to closed-system experimentation!

In other words, Bhaskar's objection to what he terms "epistemic realist" (i.e., empiricist) and "transcendental idealist" (i.e., theoreticist) accounts of closed-system science is to the descriptions they give of what goes on in closed-system experiments. Broadly speaking, the empiricists talk about such experiments demonstrating constant conjunctions of events (seen as sense-date phenomena) from which "causal laws" are inferred. The theoreticists see such experiments as simple embodiments of cognitive theories whose results are only given meaning by being theoretically categorized in some way. Against these two adversaries Bhaskar wants to advance a realist theory in which closed-system experiments, or at least some of them, reveal the actual causal powers inhering in real natural things, which things may themselves be revealed by such experiments.[27]

We do not have to consider here whether Bhaskar's descriptions of the various closed-system experiments that he uses as examples are more or less convincing than the descriptions that he is attempting to rebut. All that is important for us to note is that—given his descriptions of what closed-system experiments do—Bhaskar can then provide his indulgent account of the acute limitations that may confront natural-scientific explanations in open systems. For he can be confident that these limitations do not threaten the reality of his "intransitive" things of nature, with their "causal powers" and "generative mechanisms," this reality having already been confirmed by experimentation in closed, or controlled, systems.

But of course this does not help the case of the Marxist scientist one bit, precisely because, as I have already argued, closed-system experimentation is not available to him or her at all. Moreover, it is clear that Bhaskar would not classify purely discursive thought experiments (in which systems are closed purely by a process of intellectual abstraction or simplification) as experiments of the type that his theory requires.

In short, whatever may be the merits of Bhaskar's work as a theory of natural science (and for our purposes we can remain agnostic about that), the very structure of its argument disqualifies it as a defense of Marxist

27. Bhaskar, *A Realist Theory of Science*, chapter 1, 28–62, and chapter 2.

social science precisely because its realism depends totally on closed-system experimentation. I can only think that this has not been noticed by social scientists, and especially by Marxists, because (a) Bhaskar is one of the relatively few recent philosophers of natural science to devote some close attention to social science[28] and (b) because of the apparently congenial—to social scientists—things he has to say about explanation in open systems. However, neither of these aspects of his theory alter its basic logical structure, a structure deeply inappropriate for the defense of a Marxist science.

Conclusions: Nondiscursive Practices and the Limits of Epistemology

I shall now summarize the argument of this chapter, an argument that sums to the contention that Marxism is not a hard natural science. I argued in chapter 1 that nearly all modern philosophy of science stresses the centrality of nondiscursive experimentation and application in natural science. I have argued in this chapter that since these forms of experimentation and application are not available to Marxists, and since thought experiments of intellectual abstraction and simplification are not adequate substitutes for nondiscursive forms of experiment (because the absence of a nondiscursive element makes reality claims for any social unobservables indefeasible), then the central realist argument for equating Marxism with natural science does not hold.

The foregoing is the form of my argument that Marxism is not a natural science. If this were all there was to it, however, it would simply be a species of analytical truth. For I would have defined natural science in a certain way, a way that excludes Marxism (and indeed most social science), and then have deduced from this definition that Marxism was not a science. But this in itself is hardly very convincing, since clearly by changing the definition of natural science one would radically change the conclusion.

It is important therefore to understand that the analytical form of the argument above obscures, to a degree, its central point and merit. That point is, essentially, that *the centrality of certain nondiscursive practices in natural science makes natural science as a practice immune to purely "epistemological" critique.* In other words, there is a very good and deep

28. Ibid., 123–25 and 195–97.

philosophical reason why, at a pinch, the natural scientist can afford to be, and can actually be, an amused agnostic or cynic in the realist-antirealist debate. The reason is that both realism and antirealism, like nearly all philosophical epistemologies, presuppose what John Dewey called the "spectator theory of knowledge." That is, they both presuppose that the problematic knowledge relation is that between a given and passive subject and a given and passive object, with the central epistemological question being how the subject can have or obtain true knowledge of the object. In these kinds of conception knowledge is always cognitive (so that, for example, it incorporates "knowing" how to blow glass but not the actual *act* of blowing glass). It is also always conceived as some kind of inherently mysterious "mapping" relationship, so that knowledge is somehow a map or copy or representation of what is known. In fact, nearly all epistemologies are what Wittgenstein called "picture" theories. In some way or other knowledge is conceived as a "picture" (correct or incorrect) of the known.[29]

It is one of the ironies of intellectual history that Karl Marx himself, in his earlier philosophical writings, was one of the relatively few nineteenth-century thinkers in the West to perceive that there was something fundamentally wrong with this epistemological picture of knowledge (as "picturing"). In his early writings Marx offered the suggestion that the way to escape epistemology was to conceive knowledge as a *practice* and therefore as a *process in time*, rather than as a synchronic (or "one off") picturing. He also stressed that human beings as a species are essentially active or acting creatures who use thought as a part of a myriad of nondiscursive practices. Hence the whole epistemological tradition stemming from Descartes, which wants first of all to solve the problems of knowledge so that human beings can then act in the world on the basis of true knowledge, fails to see (for Marx) the essential point about knowledge—that it is both formed and tested as a part of nondiscursive practice. Hence, one might say that the only problem of knowledge lies precisely in the conviction that there *is* such a problem to be solved apart from practice![30]

However, it is just as important to say that the escape from the epistemological picture by way of such notions as "practice" and "knowledge as process" and "as part of practice" is only partially effective. It is only

29. Wittgenstein, *On Certainty*, remarks 1–21, 89–105, 115–23, and 193–232. See also Richard Rorty, *Philosophy and the Mirror of Nature* (Oxford: Basil Blackwell, 1980), chapter 4, and R. J. Bernstein, *Beyond Objectivism and Relativism*, part 1.

30. On the "Cartesian anxiety" in philosophy, see R. J. Bernstein, *Beyond Objectivism and Relativism*; see also Cavell, *The Claim of Reason*, chapters 6–8.

partially effective because if left in this discursive form it can simply be appropriated as another epistemological picture, or as a development or "dynamization" of the previously static picture. Therefore, the true and complete escape from the epistemological picture is not via the concepts of "practice" or "process" or "nondiscursivity." Rather, one truly escapes epistemology by actually pipetting "this" element into "this" compound, by powering up "this" particle accelerator and firing "this" beam of electrons at "these" atoms, by blowing "this" glass vase, by growing "these" cells in "that" liquid, and so forth. And note that although "what" is being done nondiscursively cannot be described without language, it can be *done* without language. (There is that much to Dr. Johnson's refutation of skepticism!) And equally, although the effects of these experiments cannot be described without language, they can be experienced (though perhaps they cannot be understood) without language.[31] It is precisely these nonlinguistic elements of such practices that make them nondiscursive, and it is the way in which these practices escape epistemology that makes the natural scientist's cynicism or agnosticism both possible and more philosophically profound than she or he may know. "They may not be, but hold this sheet of metal in front of that laser beam" is not merely the cynical, it is the philosophically profound reply to, for example, "Electrons aren't real."

In short, (and as Gaston Bachelard, among others stressed), it is through extradiscursive forms of experimentation and application that natural science escapes and transcends epistemology, that it knows in ways that defeat all of philosophy's supposed epistemological rules for knowing.[32] It does so precisely through a dialectic between theory and practice, a dialectic that just *is* experimentation and application. And, ironically, while the young Karl Marx saw that it was through practice that knowledge escapes epistemology, he went on, in later life, to develop a conception of Marxism as science that cannot escape epistemological questioning—and indeed has been plagued by such questioning throughout its history—precisely because it cannot make use of the forms of extradiscursive practice that can inure its explanatory social unobservables against epistemological skepticism.

It is because it cannot remain indifferent to epistemological questioning of its crucial explanatory unobservables (something we see demonstrated again recently in agonized debates over "realism") that I argue that Marxism

---

31. See van Fraasen, *The Scientific Image*, 15.
32. Gaston Bachelard, *La formation de l'esprit scientifique* (Paris: Librarie Philosophique, Vrin, 1960), chapter 3.

is not a natural science.[33] So my position is founded on more than a definition. It rests on the contention that the types of nondiscursive practices on
which natural scientists can rely and Marxists cannot (experimentation and
application) mean that natural scientists can *do* things—both practically and
philosophically—with their unobservables that Marxists cannot, that in fact
such unobservables play a totally different *role* in the practice of natural
scientists than they do in the discourse of Marxist realism. The difference is
precisely that in Marxist realism Marxist unobservables are purely discursive
entities, while in the natural sciences of the molecular and submolecular
world they play both a discursive and nondiscursive role. To repeat, it is
this inurement to epistemological questioning that is the essential strength
of the natural sciences, of *Naturwissenschaften*, as practices, and it is the
absence of that strength that is definitive of Marxism as something other
than a hard science.

33. The literature on Marx as realist and nonrealist is considerable, but for two directly
contrasting accounts see Richard J. Bernstein, *Praxis and Action* (London: Duckworth, 1972),
chapter 1, and Andrew Sayer, "Abstraction: A Realist Interpretation," *Radical Philosophy* 28
(1981): 6–15. See also Alvin Gouldner, *The Two Marxisms*, especially chapters 2 and 3.
Gouldner's whole account is constructed around an ideal typical distinction between what he
calls "scientific Marxism" and "critical Marxism" and his analysis continually abuts on the
issues that currently divide realist Marxists from antirealists, although he never uses this terminology. (In any case, this terminology is just the latest conceptual packaging for arguments
that are as old as Marxism itself, originating, as Gouldner rightly insists, in unresolved tensions,
even contradictions, in Marx's own thought.)

PART TWO

3

The Psychology and Politics of Marxism as Science

Having argued in chapters 1 and 2 that Marxism is not any kind of hard science, I turn here to a somewhat different and, in my view, rather more interesting question: Why have Marxists wanted or needed to believe that Marxism is such a science? That is to say, I am concerned in this chapter with the psychological and political advantages that accrue to Marxists if they believe it is true that Marxism is a science.

I should make it clear, however, that I am not confusing or conflating the question of the intellectual reasons that Marxists might have for believing Marxism to be a natural science with the question of the psychological and political advantages that may follow from holding such a belief or from persuading other people who are not Marxists to hold it. I take it that the intellectual reasons that Marx himself, and many other Marxists, have had for believing that Marxism is (or is like) a hard natural science are of the type reviewed, and rejected, in chapter 2. However, having discarded such arguments and given my own reasons for doing so, I can now turn to the psychological and political aspects of the issue. It may be, of course, that in some particular case a Marxist, including Marx himself, might have believed or might believe that Marxism is a natural science for a combination of the reasons reviewed in the last chapter and the psychological and political factors examined in this chapter. But even if that was or is so in any particular case, it is an irrelevance from the point of view of the analysis in this book. For analytically I am treating the psychology and politics of Marxism as science as a totally separate question from the intellectual merits of Marxism as science. I do so both to avoid psychological or political reductionism and to avoid reproducing the kind of crude psychological assaults on Marxism (as some kind of totalitarian "psychosis," for example) that were made by *Encounter* ideologues many years ago.[1]

In this chapter, therefore, I proceed throughout on the assumption that all or most Marxists have believed that Marxism is a hard science for the kind of reasons that I have reviewed and rejected. However, what other psychological and political advantages have flowed from such a belief? In asking and answering this question, it should be noted that the distinction between psychological and political advantages is to a degree artificial. Considerable political advantages could accrue to Marxists in any situation in which a large number of people other than Marxists came to believe, for psychological reasons, that Marxism was a science. However, I think that the distinction is a generally useful one, insofar as Marxists have usually been a very small minority of the population in most societies. The psychological advantages that may have been bestowed on them by the belief that Marxism is a science have very rarely translated into large-scale political advantage in the way that a mass belief in Marxist science might do. However, even a minority belief that Marxism is a science can translate into institutional political advantages (in universities or other institutions of higher education, for example, or in political parties), if not into mass political advantages.

The Psychological Advantages of Marxism as Science

For Marx and Engels Themselves

It seems fairly clear that the principal psychological (and political) advantage to Marx and Engels of their conception of Marxism as science was the radical disjuncture this made between Marxism (or "scientific socialism") and the various forms of what they termed "utopian socialism." These latter had antedated Marxism in the socialist movements of Britain, France, and Germany, and they competed with Marxism for the allegiance of the most politically aware sections of the European working class throughout the lives of both Marx and Engels. The battle between scientific socialism and utopian socialism (especially anarchism) was a marked feature of the politics of the First International, but it continued in somewhat varied forms in the

1. See, for example, Lewis S. Feuer, "Karl Marx and the Promethean Complex," *Encounter* 21, no. 6 (December 1968), and "Lenin's Fantasy," *Encounter* 25, no. 6 (December 1970).

Second International as well.[2] In those conflicts the main use made of the notion of scientific socialism was to juxtapose Marxism to any and all socialist creeds that saw socialism as some kind of ethical or political prescription, as some kind of ideal state of affairs to be aimed at, either by the working class, or the dispossessed, or humanity in general.

To all such notions Marx and Engels counterposed socialism and communism as, in the oft-quoted phrase, "the real movement which abolishes the present state of things."[3] That is, they saw socialism, not as a set of prescriptions or blueprints of an ideal society provided for the working class by "outside" intellectuals or other dreamers, but as a set of values and institutions created by the working class itself in the course of its struggle against capitalism. The enormous enthusiasm and excitement with which Marx greeted the democratic forms of government developed by the working people of Paris during the Paris Commune of 1871 was due to his perceiving the Commune as a perfect example of that "real movement" which would abolish the present state of things.[4]

The author of an excellent recent book on the relationship between Marxism and utopianism has argued that the insistent and highly rhetorical attempts of Marx and Engels to distance scientific from utopian socialism has served to disguise from Marxists the extent to which the founding fathers were indebted to the utopian socialists (especially, perhaps, Robert Owen and Henri de Saint-Simon) both for their analyses and critiques of capitalism and for their ideas about socialism, however fragmentary and reluctantly expressed these latter may have been.[5] I am sure that this is correct. But I am equally sure that the psychological effect of this polemical distancing was to disguise or suppress the awareness of this indebtedness in Marx and Engels themselves. And this was especially so as they got older, became embroiled in First International factional fighting, and then attained the status of founders and developers of a particular ideological and political strain of socialism (called "Marxism") with its own institutional interests to defend.

The other issue most frequently raised in regard to scientific socialism is

2. See Kolakowski, *Main Currents of Marxism*, vol. 1, *The Founders*, chapter 11, and McLellan, *Karl Marx*, chapter 7; see also Vincent Geoghegan, *Utopianism and Marxism* (London: Methuen, 1987), chapter 2.

3. Karl Marx and Friedrich Engels, *The German Ideology* (part 1, with selections from parts 2 and 3,), ed. C. J. Arthur (London: Lawrence and Wishart, 1970), 56–57.

4. Karl Marx, "The Civil War in France," in Karl Marx and Friedrich Engels, *Selected Works* (hereafter *MESW*) (London: Lawrence and Wishart, 1970), 248–307.

5. Geoghegan, *Utopianism and Marxism*, chapter 2.

the psychological support this notion may have provided to Marx's teleology. This is the question of whether scientific socialism enabled Marx to carry over the teleological strain in Hegel's philosophy of history into Marxism. For there seems only a small step, psychologically, between the proposition that socialism *must* be a natural outgrowth of the self-activity of the working class and the proposition that socialism *will* be the outcome of that activity because socialism is somehow inscribed in the essence and destiny of the working class in the way in which self-realization and total self-consciousness is inscribed in the essence and destiny of Hegel's "Absolute Idea." Certainly, those people who believe that Marx did carry over a "materialist" version of Hegelian teleology into Marxism often seem on strongest ground when they point to Marx's apparently implacable faith that the institutions and forms of politics thrown up by the working class in the course of its struggle against capitalism just would be socialist and communist forms and just would issue in a communist revolution against capitalism. What could have sustained such a belief, ask Paul Hirst and others, except some teleological conception that communism was somehow the manifest destiny of the working class inscribed in its essence, its identity, as a class?[6]

I think the evidence that Marx himself (as against, say, the early Lukács) held such a teleological conception, either of history in general or of the working class in particular, is fragmentary at best, and must be set against the significant evidence of his explicit rejection of such ideas, both in *The German Ideology* and other writings of the mid-1840s.[7] That being the case, the only other explanation of this conviction is that Marx simply thought of it as some kind of empirical generalization. In other words, he simply read the evidence of European working-class activity—between, say, 1845 and 1883—as showing that its class politics was implicitly or explicitly socialist in both spirit and tendency. And he probably based this conviction on the (equally empirical) view that the class struggle against capitalism was revealing to the workers that they could have no lasting success without a socialist revolution.

If this is the case, then the most that can be said, retrospectively, is that this was a remarkably one-sided or wish-laden reading of working-class politics, even in the mid-nineteenth century. But this is perhaps not surpris-

---

6. A. Cutler et al., *Marx's "Capital" and Capitalism Today* (London: Routledge and Kegan Paul, 1977), vol. 1, especially chapters 4 and 5. See also P. Q. Hirst, *Marxism and Historical Writing* (London: Routledge and Kegan Paul, 1985), especially chapters 2, 3, and 5.

7. See my *Karl Marx*, chapter 2.

ing, at least psychologically. For if all conceptions of socialism as prescription or vision are rejected as "utopian," and historical teleology and essentialism are also rejected as "idealist," then the psychological pressures toward such an "optimistic" reading of contemporary events and trends will be intense—that is all one has left to support the conviction that the future will be socialist. It is hardly surprising therefore if Marx himself, and many subsequent generations of Marxists, have manifested a continual tendency to see the socialist bottle as already half full rather than as still half empty.

However, although the main political use made of the notion of scientific socialism by Marx and Engels was to juxtapose Marxism in general to utopianism in general, it is clear that in a more specific sense they believed that the scientific heart of Marxism (that which *made* it scientific) was its political economy. For although *Capital* was indeed a "critique of political economy," the central point and purpose of the critique was to render political economy truly scientific. This was to be done by eliminating its ideological elements, most notably its "naturalization" and "eternalization" of the institutions and practices of capitalist society in the ideological form of abstract "principles" of political economy.[8] According to Engels at least, the major scientific "discovery" made by Marx—one that both revealed the inherent ideologicality of even the best bourgeois political economy and rendered political economy properly scientific—was that of surplus value.[9] For at one and the same time this "discovery" revealed the hidden secret of capitalist society and of the capitalist class (its need to exploit the proletariat in order to make profits and accumulate capital) and solved the major scientific problem in David Ricardo's economics (the existence of profit in a system in which all commodities, including labor, exchange at their labor values).[10]

I have argued at length elsewhere that Marx's theory of surplus value is logically flawed, and that in particular he cannot validate its central proposition—that only variable capital produces surplus value—even given his own organizing premises.[11] From the point of view of this chapter, however, the much more interesting question is how far political economy filled the space

8. See Karl Marx, *The Poverty of Philosophy* (New York: International Publishers, 1963), 120–21.

9. Friedrich Engels, "Speech at the Graveside of Karl Marx," *MESW*, 429–30.

10. See, for example, Karl Marx, *Theories of Surplus Value* (London: Lawrence and Wishart, 1969), part 2, chapter 15, especially 400. See also Karl Marx, *Capital*, vol. 1, *A Critical Analysis of Capitalist Production*, trans. (from the third German edition) Samuel Moore and Edward Aveling, ed. Friedrich Engels (Moscow: Progress, 1965) (hereafter *Capital 1*), 80 n. 1.

11. See my *Karl Marx*, chapter 4.

of Hegelian teleology in Marx's mature thought. That is, to what extent did the mature Marx think that political economy demonstrated, or could be used to demonstrate, the necessary breakdown of capitalism and its supersession by socialism and communism?

Again, the evidence for this view is at best ambiguous. *Capital* does contain a number of disparate remarks about the nature and origins of capitalist economic crises (many, though not all, of them stemming from the alleged law of the tendency of the rate of profit to fall). We also know, as a matter of biographical fact, that Marx several times predicted and expected major economic crises in his own lifetime (in 1850, 1852, 1853, and 1855, for example).[12] But there is no evidence that Marx ever supposed that crises of capitalism, no matter how severe, would—in and of themselves—bring about a socialist revolution. At most he seems to have supposed that they would provide propitious circumstances for such a revolution, but circumstances of which only a well-organized working class with a sophisticated communist leadership could take advantage. And he seems further to have supposed, in a sensible enough way, that whether this would happen in any particular case depended upon a host of specific political and other factors determining the balance of power between the working class and the bourgeoisie in that particular case.

We are left to conclude therefore that Marx and Engels distinguished scientific socialism from all forms of utopian socialism primarily on the basis that the former saw socialism and communism as the outcome of the self-activity of the working class, not as some abstract prescription or blueprint brought to that class by outside ideologues as an ideal to be aimed at. There is, however, no convincing evidence that Marx and Engels ever believed that socialism and communism were in any sense the guaranteed outcome of that activity (guaranteed, that is, either by a general philosophy of history or by the scientific predictions of Marxist political economy). Instead, they seem to have supposed that whether the self-activity of the European proletariat would lead to socialism and communism depended upon a political struggle to be fought within that class for the ideas of scientific socialism, a struggle that of course Marx and Engels themselves waged in the First International and elsewhere. The most that can be said is that Marx and Engels read the political and social trends of their own lifetimes as showing that the struggle was being won and that the European proletariat was (just empirically was) moving toward a mass socialist politics and a socialist revolution against capitalism.

---

12. See, for example, McLellan, *Karl Marx*, 240 and 280.

One may therefore (with hindsight and the easy wisdom it gives) convict the founders of Marxism of sustained wishful thinking, but even in making such a judgment both politics and psychology must enter in. Many a historian of the nineteenth century has, even in retrospect, seen enough in its politics and social conflicts to justify him or her in treating the possibility of revolution seriously.[13] Certainly nineteenth-century conservative politicians all over Europe feared such revolutions as much as radicals desired them.[14] It is hardly surprising therefore if Marx and Engels, two of the most radical activists of the age, should have "accentuated the positive" and "eliminated the negative" in their assessments of long-term revolutionary prospects. The real problems for Marxists came, of course, when even the most optimistic reading of actual social and political trends could no longer sustain any reasonable hope of socialist revolution. But fortunately for them, neither Marx nor Engels lived in such a time, which is why it is probably a mistake for those of us who do to look for any political help or guidance in their writings.

However, if scientific socialism was not used by Marx and Engels as any kind of guarantee that the future would be socialist, I nonetheless believe that it enabled them to play a profound psychological trick on themselves, a trick that may have been very politically helpful to them personally but has, in my view, had deeply damaging consequences for the Marxist tradition. Put simply, this trick was to enable them to be bourgeois activists among the working class while they simultaneously denied that in doing so they were imposing any prescriptions or blueprints *of their own* upon the politics of that class. In other words, scientific socialism allowed Marx and Engels to argue that socialism was nothing but the outcome of the self-activity of the working class, while at the same time the political economy which was at the heart of that science supposedly gave the founders of Marxism a scientifically privileged basis upon which they could agitate for a particular conception of what a "real," "authentic" working-class politics should be.[15]

In short, what scientific political economy supposedly provided for Marx and Engels was a privileged insight into the "true" political and material

13. E. J. Hobsbawm, *The Age of Revolution* (London: Weidenfeld and Nicolson, 1962).

14. Ibid., chapter 6. See also Robert Gildea, *Barricades and Borders: Europe, 1800–1914* (Oxford: Oxford University Press, 1987), especially chapters 3, 4, and 8; Carsten Holbraad, *The Concert of Europe: A Study of German and British International Theory, 1815–1914* (London: Longman, 1970), especially part 1, chapter 1, and part 2, chapter 1; and Friedrich Heer, *Europe: Mother of Revolutions* (London: Weidenfeld and Nicolson, 1964).

15. See, for example, Geoghegan, *Utopianism and Marxism*, 30–31; see also Kolakowski, *Main Currents of Marxism*, 1:323–51.

interests of the working class. But (and this is the central point) that insight was not, or was not seen or believed by them to be, *their* insight, *their* particular point of view. On the contrary, they presented it as, and believed it to be, the insight provided or generated by *science,* and thus something far more powerful and authoritative than any personal or purely subjective view. As I shall indicate in a later section of this chapter, this has been a recurrent motif in the history of Marxism as science, and it is probably the most important psychological and emotional factor in the continual efforts of orthodox Marxists to found Marxism unambiguously as a science or to prove conclusively that it is such.

As is well known, the central claim made by Marx and Engels (one repeated often by other orthodox Marxists) was that political economy demonstrated scientifically that the whole development of the forces of production under capitalism depended upon the exploitation of the working class by the bourgeoisie. They also claimed that it demonstrated (with similar scientific rigor) that the working class could not escape this exploitation without a revolutionary overthrow of the capitalist system itself.

However, if the theory of surplus value is logically flawed (and does not in fact successfully demonstrate that the only source of profits in the capitalist system is the exploitation of living labor power), and if exploitation in Marx's sense is in any case perfectly compatible with rapidly and continually rising standards of living among the working class, it quickly becomes problematic how far Marxists can now claim—if indeed they ever could—to have any superior insight into the "true" or "real" interests of the working class.[16] In fact it becomes probable that Marxists have no greater insight into what those interests are than do the workers themselves.

But if this is the case (and that it *is* the case will be a recurrent theme in the remainder of this book and will be argued at greater length) it no longer seems a strength, but a chronic weakness of the Marxist tradition that it has always shunned an overtly prescriptive or "blueprint" approach to socialism. For if Marxists have no privileged insight into the interests of the working class (or those of anybody else), if the science that they claimed gave them such an insight is a "busted flush" (as American poker players say), then the only alternative route to socialism conceivable is via convincing or persuading people of the moral and political *desirability* of socialism as a form of society vis-à-vis capitalism. And one, though only one, element

16. See my *Karl Marx,* chapter 4; see also Kolakowski, *Main Currents of Marxism,* 1:325–34, and A. J. Polan, *Lenin and the End of Politics* (London: Methuen, 1984), especially chapter 5.

in any attempt to "convince of desirability" (a somewhat different practice from "appeal to material interests") is a vision or blueprint of socialism that one can argue is both feasible and more desirable, by a variety of criteria, than capitalism.

In short, then, the crucial psychological trick that scientific socialism pulled off for Marx and Engels (the trick of allowing them to prescribe to the working class in a form—the appeal to "true" interests—that did not look or sound like prescription at all) may well be its most crippling legacy to the modern Marxist tradition. For it has denied to that tradition—in the name of orthodoxy, science, and hostility to abstract utopian dreaming—the element that it now most desperately needs if it is to revitalize itself. I should stress, however (and this too will be a recurrent theme in much of what follows), that this does not mean that Marxists should simply become casters of spells and weavers of (utopian) dreams. On the contrary, one of the elements that modern Marxists must bring to discussions of the desirability of socialism is a deeply critical concern for its practical feasibility. And this is a task in which, suitably modified, the analytical political economy strain within Marxism can be a real strength. Moreover, it is a strength that, even in its most modern forms, utopian socialist thought still conspicuously lacks.[17] There remains that much validity, at least, in the old Marxist skepticism about utopianism.

The Second International

It may well be true that, as I have argued, Marx himself did not believe that Marxist science showed the communist revolution to be inevitable. But it is a commonplace of histories of Marxism that by the time one gets to the Marxism of the Second International, and in particular to the ideas of its leading theoretician, Karl Kautsky, the science of "historical materialism" was indeed understood in this way. In particular it is Kautsky who is usually credited—or more frequently debited—with founding an interpretation of historical materialism as the "science" of an evolutionary sequence of "modes of production," an evolution by which all human societies are led ineluctably from an earliest historical stage of primitive communism (in

17. See Geoghegan, *Utopianism and Marxism*; see also my *Development and Underdevelopment in Historical Perspective* (London: Methuen, 1982), especially chapter 4. For a comprehensive review of socialist writing focusing on its persistent economic naïveté and lack of rigor, see Noel Thompson, *The Market and Its Critics* (London: Routledge, 1988).

several variants) to a postcapitalist communist future. Whether Kautsky deserves the sole or primary credit for this interpretation of Marxism, or whether he simply codified and propagandized what were in fact the views of Friedrich Engels in his old age, is perhaps an issue that can be left to professional historians of Marxism.[18]

What is important for us here is to explore the psychological effects of any belief in the inevitability of communism, an inevitability supposedly guaranteed by science. It is obvious enough of course that tiny Marxist *grupscules* with few or no resources and no popular influence can draw considerable psychological succor from such a belief, which becomes in effect a sort of rationalist millennialism.

For a total economic breakdown of capitalism and an accompanying revolutionary cataclysm plays the same role in the social psychology of such groups as the Day of Judgment does in traditional religious millennialism. Just as the elect of the faithful are singled out for salvation on the Day of Judgment while millions are consigned to the fires of Hell, in Marxist millennialism the impotent *grupscule* is suddenly, in the day or year of revolution, transfigured into the revolutionary leadership of the popular masses, by whom it is swept to power. (The example of the Russian Bolsheviks can always be adduced to give some plausibility to this vision.)

It is certainly possible, both in the history of Marxism and in its contemporary forms, to find groups that do approximate this psychology (the Workers' Revolutionary party and the Socialist party of Great Britain being perhaps the two most obvious cases in present-day Britain).[19] It is equally

18. See, for example, Massimo Salvadori, *Karl Kautsky and the Socialist Revolution, 1880–1938*, trans. Jon Rothschild (London: New Left Books, 1979), chapter 1; see also Gary P. Steenson, *Karl Kautsky, 1854–1938: Marxism in the Classical Years* (Pittsburgh: University of Pittsburgh Press, 1978); 62–66.

19. The world still lacks a good participant-observation "ethnography" of a Marxist-Leninist sect (including Trotskyist sects). Some raw materials for such a history in Britain are to be found in the bibliography of David Widgery's now rather dated *The Left in Britain, 1965–68* (Harmondsworth: Penguin, 1976). For the International Socialists (now the Socialist Workers party), a lot can be gleaned from reading between the lines of Polan's *Lenin and the End of Politics* and, more explicitly, from Sheila Rowbotham, "The Women's Movement and Organising for Socialism," in *Beyond the Fragments,* ed. Sheila Rowbotham, Lynn Segal, and Hilary Wainwright (London: Islington Community Press, 1979). For the British Communist party between the wars, Stuart Macintyre, *A Proletarian Science: Marxism in Britain, 1917–33* (Oxford: Oxford University Press, 1980) is good, but it is very much an outsider's historical reconstruction from written sources and concentrates almost totally on theoretical concerns. In fact, for a "feel" of life in the party (concentrated in the immediate postwar years) I still know nothing better than the early novels of Doris Lessing, especially *Martha Quest*. For Fourth International sects I know nothing, and this is unsurprising. Those who have left such

apparent, however, that this has *not* been the predominant psychological effect of belief in the inevitability of communism within the Marxist tradition as a whole. For, as already noted, this belief probably enjoyed its greatest popular influence in the last decade or so of the nineteenth century and in the first fourteen years of this century, when its principal advocates were the leaders of the German Social Democratic party. The SPD, far from being an impotent Marxist *grupscule*, was at that time the German political party with the largest single group of deputies in the Reichstag and was acknowledged as the most powerful and influential Marxist political party in Europe.

In this situation, the prime psychological effect of a belief in the "guaranteed" inevitability of communism was not to fuel millennial dreams but, as Ignaz Auer remarked cynically to Eduard Bernstein, to do the precise opposite.[20] That is, its prime effect was to provide revolutionary legitimacy for every electoral advance of the SPD and for every cautious social reform enacted with its support. Given the postulate of the inevitability of communism, every such advance, no matter how tiny, could be adduced as another incremental step toward the inevitable revolution. In other words, and as has often been observed, under the Second International the doctrine of the inevitability of communism became a means by which day-to-day reformist politics could be psychologically and intellectually squared with the revolutionary heritage of the SPD. And the scandal of Bernstein's *Evolutionary Socialism* was simply that, by insisting on the importance of the reforms themselves and calling into question both the scientific status of Marxist political economy and the historical inevitability supposedly based upon it, he made it much more difficult, both psychologically and intellectually, to square the circle of reformism in day-to-day practice with ultimate revolution.[21]

The Third International

Finally, we should note that this same doctrine—the historical inevitability of communism—also enjoyed considerable credence within Third International Communist parties, at least from 1917 to the 1960s. But in this case

---

organizations usually wish to forget them as soon as possible; and those who are still within them have other matters on their minds.

20. See A. Callinicos, *Marxism and Philosophy* (Oxford: Oxford University Press, 1983), 65.

21. See Kolakowski, *Main Currents of Marxism*, vol. 2, *The Golden Age*, chapter 4; see also Steenson, *Karl Kautsky, 1854–1938*, chapter 4, and Salvadori, *Karl Kautsky*, chapters 1

we find it playing yet another psychological role, being neither a prop to millennial expectations (except perhaps during the "ultra-left" period of the 1920s) nor a rationalization of incremental reformism. For, in the case of the Third International Communist parties, belief in the inevitability of communism seems to have acted mainly as a psychological compensation for the hardships and disappointments of the day-to-day political struggle. On its basis any temporary setbacks could always be psychologically compensated by the certainty of ultimate triumph, no matter how distant that victory might be ("not for ourselves, but for our grandchildren," etc.).[22] And this is a very old story. Historians have often observed that the paradox of inevitability doctrines (whether religiously or rationalistically based) is that they do not, generally speaking, breed passivity in those who embrace them, as one might logically expect. On the contrary, such doctrines tend in practice to breed a furious activism, psychologically fueled and sustained by the conviction that God or History or Science is "on our side."[23] However logicians may wonder, nothing psychologically sustains a determined activism in the face of continual disappointment better than the conviction that "in the end" one's triumph is assured.

But the problem, of course, is what happens psychologically and emotionally when one no longer believes—can no longer believe—this. What happens when one comes to believe that such a doctrine, far from being underpinned or guaranteed by Marxist science, is both irrational and totally at odds with the requirements of true scientificity? Some insight into these issues can be gleaned from an analysis of the sad and tortured history of Louis Althusser and his followers.

Marxist Science Reborn:
Louis Althusser and Althusserianism

We have seen that Marx and Engels juxtaposed science (or at least scientific socialism) to utopianism, although the element that they took to be at the

and 2. Bernstein, however, expresses his own ideas clearly and simply enough in his *Die Voraussetzungen des Sozialismus und die Aufgaben der Sozialdemokratie* (translated by Edith C. Harvey, as *Evolutionary Socialism: A Criticism and Affirmation* [London: Independent Labour Party, 1909]).

22. See, for example, Stuart Macintyre, *A Proletarian Science;* especially chapter 5.

23. Christopher Hill, *The World Turned Upside Down: Radical Ideas during the English Revolution* (Harmondsworth: Penguin, 1975), especially chapter 6.

center of Marxism as science, the element that sharply distinguished it from all forms of utopianism, was political economy in its Marxist form. In the periods of the Second and Third Internationals, the science of "historical materialism" (sometimes seen as just a part of "dialectical materialism," embracing natural science as well as human history) was made the basis of a theory of historical evolution. In this theory all human societies were supposedly fated to pass from some stage of primitive communism, via various precapitalist modes of production, through capitalism, to communism.[24]

However, in the work of the French philosopher Louis Althusser and his disciples—work dating from the late 1960s onward—"science" in Marxism is juxtaposed to "ideology." In fact, at least in Althusser's earliest work, science becomes the means, the only means, by which ideology in society can be escaped, where "escaped" roughly means "overcome by being seen through or unmasked." Moreover, under the heading of ideology Althusser included a large—indeed, ever-larger—variety of things, some of which would have been classified as ideology in earlier Marxist traditions but some of which certainly would have not. The following is a more or less complete listing of the propositions and beliefs that Althusser classified, at some point or other in his work, as ideology.

(1) *The belief that Marxism rests on any "essentialist" doctrine of human nature,* that is, on any conception of what human beings essentially "are" qua human beings (competitive, selfish, altruistic, creative, etc.). This is *humanism* and is ideological.[25]

(2) *The belief that history has any end or goal* known to Marxists (or anybody else) to which it is heading. This is a form of *historicism* and is ideological.[26]

(3) *The belief that the politics, culture, and intellectual life of any society is just an "expression" of underlying economic interests and forces* (particularly class interests and forces). This is class or economic *reductionism* and is ideological (*FM*, 103–13; *RC*, 201–24).

(4) *Hegelian philosophy and all Hegelian-influenced Marxism.* This is ideo-

24. Nikolay Bukharin and Evgeny Preobrazhensky, *The ABC of Communism* (Harmondsworth: Penguin, 1969), especially chapter 2.

25. Louis Althusser, *For Marx* (London: Allen Lane, 1969) (hereafter *FM*), 158, and 223–47 ("Marxism and Humanism").

26. Louis Althusser and Etienne Balibar, *Reading Capital* (London: New Left Books, 1970) (hereafter *RC*), 99, and chapter 5, 119–41.

logical because, on Althusser's interpretation, it gives rise to the above ideological positions (1, 2, and 3) within Marxism. It is the root of (1) because Hegel is the origin of Marx's early theories of the "alienation" of "Man's" "species being." It is the root of (2) because Hegel's philosophy is overtly teleological and the young Marx inherited this philosophy of history and brought it in a materialist form into Marxism. More subtly, it is the root of (3) because Marx took from Hegel's philosophy of history an "expressive causality" in which every historical period is seen as simply the expression of some stage in the self-development of the Absolute Idea. Althusser sees ideological Marxism as having embodied this in the materialist form of historical modes of production, so that every human society, in all its dimensions, is simply seen as expressing some underlying economic principle ("primitive communism," "feudalism," "capitalism," etc. (*FM*, 73–83).

(5) *Classical political economy and all its successors,* especially modern neoclassical economics. Here Althusser's account is absolutely orthodox and is drawn directly from *Capital,* the *Theories of Surplus Value,* and other writings of the mature Marx in which his critique of classical political economy is to be found. Thus, Althusser just repeats Marx's argument that even the best of classical political economy (e.g., Ricardo) is ideological rather than scientific because it failed to develop the concept—surplus value—that would have solved its central theoretical problem. It failed to do so because this concept would have made classical political economy untenable at the same time as it made it scientific. By showing that capitalism is necessarily exploitative of the working class, it would have made classical political economy revolutionary. It was, however, the very ideologicality of classical political economy— its objective role as the rationalizer and defender of capitalism—that, according to Marx and Althusser, made such a development structurally impossible for it (*RC*, 22–23, 79–82, 145–81).

Of course this view of classical political economy as ideology rests on a total acceptance of the scientific validity of Marx's theory of surplus value and of all the other formulations drawn from it (for example, the law of the declining rate of profit). In fact, in *Reading Capital* Althusser does just assume, rather than demonstrate, the validity of Marx's political economy. This procedure is explicitly defended on the ground that Althusser is providing a philosopher's reading of *Capital* rather than an economist's reading (*RC*, 14–15). But clearly, if one does not hold that Marx's theory of surplus value and its developments are theoretically valid, then Althusser's account of the ideologicality of classical political economy—as, indeed, Marx's own account—becomes highly questionable.

(6) *All conceptions of human societies that see such societies as made up of social or presocial subjects.* Here Althusser, in his later work, takes over and develops some ideas of Marx about how human beings who are, as members of subordinate or oppressed classes under capitalism, in materially unequal relations with members of dominant classes, may yet be conceived, and conceive themselves, as equal individuals because they are treated as juridically or formally equal as voters, citizens, legal plaintiffs and defendants, legal buyers and sellers, and the like. In his later paper on ideological state apparatuses, Althusser terms this the "interpellation" of formally equal subjects by the ideological apparatuses of the capitalist state, among which he includes schools, churches, and the mass media, among others.[27]

But Althusser also goes a lot further than Marx. For he classifies as ideological *all* theories and descriptions of human society that postulate individual human actors as agents of social change, whether this be change in institutions and practices or changes in ideas. Hence for Althusser any theory of science (to take one example) that explains the development of a science or sciences by examining the ideas, actions, and so on of individual scientists is itself ideological rather than scientific (*FM*, 184–88; *RC*, 67–69).

At bottom this implacable hostility to the subject as autonomous historical agent (a hostility that marks all of Althusser's thought, early and late) seems to rest on a form of linguistic determinism. That is, it rests on the view that since individual human beings can only think and act in terms of the linguistic categories—including scientific categories—that are givens for them, handed down to them as part of their socialization, then *all* forms of individual action (including mental action, thought about oneself and the world) are bounded, as it were, by these given categories. In fact, in Althusser's later writing ideology becomes coterminous with linguistic socialization itself.[28] As a result, the later Althusser explicitly concludes that ideology is found in every society, is inescapable even by science (though it may be comprehended

27. Louis Althusser, "Ideology and Ideological State Apparatuses" (hereafter "ISA"), in *Lenin and Philosophy and Other Essays* (London: New Left Books, 1971), 127–36.

28. "ISA," 155–65. See also P. Q. Hirst, "Althusser and the Theory of Ideology," *Economy and Society* 5, no. 4 (1976).

through science), and will therefore be present in communist society just as it is present in capitalist society, although it will, of course, take different forms ("ISA," 151–52).

I consider both this conception of ideology and the view of language and socialization upon which it is based to be profoundly mistaken, and I shall say why later. But for the moment it is only important to note that to all these forms of ideology Althusser juxtaposes "science" or Marxism as science. As I have already noted, this science is conceived as the only tool through which ideology may be penetrated, unmasked, and escaped, or if not escaped (for the later conception of ideology allows for no escape) at least comprehended.

The picture of Marxist science that Althusser juxtaposes to ideology is, I think, very well known. It consists in part of a long and tortured argument to the effect that the scientific works of Marx's maturity are separated from his ideological (that is, Hegelian or quasi-Hegelian) works by an "epistemological break" through which a scientific set of concepts, which Althusser terms a "problematic," are substituted for the more or less ideological concepts of Marx's immature works (*FM*, 31–38, 227–46). Althusser has some difficulty pinning down exactly when this epistemological break occurred in Marx's development (finding ideological residues and formulations even in *Capital*), but his general conclusion is that it is through the "articulated" concepts of "mode of production" and "social formation" that historical materialism finally emerges as a science (*RC*, 148–61).

The second part of Althusser's picture of Marxist science, and its most genuinely pictorial part, is his attempt to give an account of the "structural causality" operative in Marx's mature, scientific concept of a mode of production. This account is supposed to provide for the determination of each mode of production "in the last instance" by the economy while avoiding what are, in Althusser's mind, the closely associated evils of expressive causality, reductionism (of the political or cultural levels of each mode to the economic level), and historicism or teleology (e.g., *RC*, 220–25).

I must confess at this point that, like a number of people, I long looked upon Althusser's ever more byzantine attempts to describe the epistemological basis of a Marxist science and to separate it definitely from all forms of ideology with a fascinated wonder, a wonder mixed with total lack of comprehension. This failure to understand mainly flowed from my view that most, if not all, of the ideological pitfalls that Althusser was trying to avoid by means of his structural causality *were not found in Marx in any case,* so that a great deal of intellectual energy was, to me, simply being wasted in the attempt to exorcise nonexistent demons from Marxism. What I mean by this may become more clear if we simply review the six forms of ideology identified by Althusser. In the case of "ideologies" (1) through (4), my own views are as follows.

Ideology 1 (essentialist view of human nature in Marx). This is a much-debated issue,[29] but my view of Marx's early writings on alienation and species being is that he does possess an essentialist doctrine of human nature. This, broadly, is the view that humans are the only consciously creative beings currently known of in the universe. But (and this is the point) this concept of creativity is morally open-ended. Thus human beings can, in Marx's conception, create gas chambers as well as chamber orchestras, hell on earth as well as heaven on earth, and what they will do will be determined by specific social and political conditions at specific times.[30] In fact, it seems to me to be one of the brilliant successes of Marx's thought that he developed an essentialist account of human nature that is yet not *morally or politically* essentialist. For it does not purport to identify some true moral nature of human beings that only has to be realized in some ahistorical or transhistorical process (as in William Godwin or Jeremy Bentham, for example). I therefore think that insofar as there is a notion of human progress in Marx it is a thoroughly historical notion which postulates that human beings learn and define what progress means in the light of their previous experiences as they live out their species life. It is not a quasi-Hegelian notion of history as the gradual realization of some ahistorically postulated moral essence.

Ideology 2 (historicism or teleology). Here I simply take the view (and have argued at length elsewhere) that Marx himself did not possess a teleological conception of history, and the evidence that he did not far outweighs the evidence that he did. In particular we may point to his explicit disavowals of Hegelian teleology in both *The German Ideology* and *The Holy Family.*[31] Also, as I have argued above, I do not think that his optimistic prognoses about the revolutionary potential of the European proletariat must be read as his conceiving that proletariat as the materialist form of

---

29. See, for example, Norman Geras, *Marx and Human Nature: Refutation of a Legend* (London: Verso, 1983); Erich Fromm, *Marx's Concept of Man* (New York: Frederick Ungar, 1961); Vernon Venable, *Human Nature: The Marxian View* (London: Denis Dobson, 1946); and the Introduction to Sidney Hook, *From Hegel to Marx* (Ann Arbor: University of Michigan Press, 1962).

30. See my *Karl Marx,* 137.

31. Ibid., 38–39.

Hegel's Absolute Idea, à la the early Lukács.[32] It is also not the case (though one or two Althusserians came precious close to arguing this at times) that any historical account that explains present conditions as the outcome of past events is *eo ipso* teleological.[33] It is perfectly possible (and practicing historians do it all the time) to explain the historical origins of current conditions while examining hypothetical questions about whether, if X had happened and not Y, things would have turned out differently.

Ideology 3 (class or economic reductionism). Marx simply was *not* an economic reductionist. He did not believe that all forms of politics, or culture, or social conflict were simply expressions of underlying economic or class interests, and it would be extremely difficult to find any evidence in his writing that he did. The reason is that Marx was, if nothing else, an extremely intelligent man, and economic reductionism is an extremely silly, not to say incoherent, idea in which to believe. Marx was often concerned with those *aspects* of politics, or culture, or social conflict that had class or economic dimensions. But he certainly would not have thought that, for example, all classical Greek culture (which he loved) or all of the politics of the French Second Empire (by which he was fascinated) could be explained by or reduced to economic or class factors. Indeed I doubt whether he could have stated coherently what such an idea might mean—and not surprisingly, since it has no coherent meaning.[34]

What can be said, however, is that Marx and Engels produced an ontological picture of both society and reality that they sometimes presented as capturing the essence of historical materialism—a picture of levels of reality in which economic and material processes are presented as more basic than social or ideological ones. I have argued at length elsewhere that this picture both seriously misdescribed their own method (through a number of very misleading or inadequate metaphors) and that if taken with an extremely unintelligent literalness, as it was by Althusser, it can lead to the postulation of incoherent problems like "economic reductionism" that then have to be "solved" (by, for example, "relative autonomy").[35] To that degree at least, Marx and Engels bear some responsibility for the ideological problems that Althusser foisted upon them. But for the most part economic reductionism

---

32. See Georg Lukács, *History and Class Consciousness* (London: Merlin Press, 1971), especially the essay "Reification and the Consciousness of the Proletariat," 83–222; see also Kolakowski, *Main Currents of Marxism*, vol. 3, chapter 7.

33. See Hirst, *Marxism and Historical Writing*, chapters 2, 3, and 5.

34. See my *Rethinking Socialism* (London: Methuen, 1983), especially the Appendix, 144–65, and also my *Karl Marx*, chapter 7, 186–227.

35. See my *Karl Marx*, chapter 7.

is a problem *produced by* Althusser's structural causality, as is the solution—relative autonomy—which is therefore the nonsolution of a nonexistent problem.

Ideology 4 (Hegel and Hegelian Marxism). Having argued that ideologies (1) through (3) are not present in Marx, these arguments largely cover ideology (4) as well. Just to repeat: I do not believe that a morally essentialist conception of species being is found in Marx. I do not believe that Marx's conception of history was teleological. And I do not believe that his mode-of-product concept involves any expressive or reductionist causality.

Ideology 5 (classical political economy). Here the case is somewhat different. As I have already intimated, Althusser perpetrates here precisely the opposite fallacy to that which he manages in ideologies (1) through (4). There he predicates Marx with a whole series of ideological positions that he never held. Here he predicates Marx with a scientific achievement that, in my view, is equally spurious. Indeed, as I have already said, all that Althusser does is to reproduce Marx's own account of his scientization of classical political economy and then swallow it hook, line, and sinker.

In reality, however, the matter is complex. In a sense Marx's theory of surplus value does solve a major formal problem in Ricardo's economics. (How can there be profit in a formal model of an economy in which all commodities, including labor, exchange at their labor values?) But in and of itself such a solution tells one nothing about the scientific status of the entities, labor values, in terms of which the Ricardian problem and the Marxist solution are expressed. If the argument that these theoretical entities are real has significant, indeed crippling, weaknesses (and I have already argued, in chapter 2, that theoretical realism as an account of social, as against natural, science does indeed have such flaws), then both the Ricardian problem and the Marxist solution can be regarded as metaphysical, or at any rate as having nothing to do with science. This is indeed the view which I hold: that the labor theory of value is not scientific and neither therefore is Marx's supposed great scientific discovery, the theory of surplus value. This does not mean that neither has any *philosophical* worth, but that is another matter, and one that I have discussed elsewhere.[36]

The point to stress here, however, is that Althusser's account in *Reading Capital* of "ideological" classical political economy versus "scientific" Marxist political economy is grossly inaccurate, indeed precisely as inaccurate as Marx's own account was, for it is the same account. In Althusser's terms I

---

36. Ibid., chapter 4, 95–115.

would have to say that both Ricardian political economy and its Marxist development are ideological, but I prefer to avoid this formulation and say rather that neither was, or is, scientific. The reason for this avoidance is that I think (and will argue below) that Althusser's predominant use of the term "ideology," a use that equates it with "falsehood," is a major distortion of Marx's most profound use of the term and of the use that has most analytical utility in the study of any human society.

One final point on this. I think that Marx's most illuminating use of the term "ideology" in regard to classical political economy is not that which one finds in his accounts of his supposed scientific development of Ricardo, but the use that one finds for the first time in *The Poverty of Philosophy*. Here Marx argues that by taking the economic institutions and practices dominant in one society in one historical period (roughly, Britain in the mid-nineteenth century) and turning them into abstract, timeless principles of political economy, the classicals in effect treated capitalism as the final form of economy and as the only rational form of economy that is historically possible. They thus both judged all previous forms of society by capitalism's canons of economic rationality and acted as ideological apologists for it against those who perceived further historical possibilities beyond it.[37]

I think that this critique of political economy is both profound and true and is equally applicable—indeed rather more applicable, if anything—to modern neoclassical economics. However, this critique did not assert in any simple sense (or indeed in any complex sense) that classical political economy was false. It asserts, rather, that it was limited and blind in certain respects, but in respects that can only be perceived by moving to a different perspective or point of view. But that is to tantalize the reader with a glimpse of what will be the predominant concerns of the third part of this book.

Ideology 6 (the subject as social actor). Here we have to deal with a whole maze of interlinked confusions, some of which are in Marx, most of which are in Althusser, and all of which have been compounded by both Althusserian and post-Althusserian writing in the social sciences.

To begin with, Marx does indeed suggest, in some passages in *Capital* and elsewhere, that capitalism gives rise to a realm of appearances in which substantively or materially unequal class subjects appear as formally equal political or juridical subjects. The first question that arises here is, To whom do things appear thus? Marx's answer seems to be "everybody," or at least

---

37. Marx, *The Poverty of Philosophy*, 120–26.

everybody who lives in a capitalist society. The reason for the answer is that this is one area of Marx's work where a significant Hegelian influence is to be found—formal or juridical equality in a class society is, for Marx, a necessary appearance in the Hegelian sense. It is a form of appearance of class relations supposedly analogous to the form of appearance of wood molecules in Eddington's "second table."[38] But in that case the verb "to appear" can perfectly well be substituted by the verb "to be," at least in English. In other words, in the case of necessary appearances the proposition "Individual subjects appear formally equal as citizens, voters, legal plaintiffs, or defendants" can be more simply expressed as "Individual subjects are [just *are*] equal as citizens, voters, legal plaintiffs, and defendants." In fact, in this case it is far less confusing to say that such forms of equality coexist with forms of class inequality and other forms of material inequality (and may indeed be undermined by the latter). Certainly such a proposition is much clearer and much less philosophically problematic than saying, for example, "Juridical equality is the necessary appearance of class inequality."

In short, the Hegelian terminology and the conceptual relationships it enshrines serve Marx, and Althusser, very ill here. For the necessary-appearance concept is used by Hegel, and by Marx, to refer to entities that can be seen by everybody as real from one point of view but as a mere appearance from another. But whereas this can be given some coherent scientific sense in the case of, for example, wood molecules and tables or steel molecules and bridges, it cannot be given any unproblematic sense in the case of class relations and juridical relations. For reasons rehearsed at length in chapter 2, there is no defensible sense in which the former can be regarded as "more real" than the latter. But if that is the case it is clearly far better to drop the "appearance/essence" or "necessary appearance" terminology altogether and simply state, in the terms already outlined, that in democratic capitalist societies juridical and other forms of formal equality among individual subjects coexist with class and other forms of material inequality among such subjects.

Moreover, not merely do they coexist in this way, they are, I would argue, known to coexist in this way by all those who live in democratic capitalist societies, and Marxists qua Marxists have no greater insight into this coexistence than anybody else. Certainly, the necessary-appearance concept does not provide them with such insight. If its essence/appearance

38. See Karl Marx, in Karl Marx and Friedrich Engels, *Collected Works* (hereafter *MECW*) "On the Jewish Question," (London: Lawrence and Wishart, 1975), 3:153–68. See also *Capital 1*, 176, and McLellan, *Karl Marx*, 69–83.

connotations are dropped, then the proposition "Juridical equality is the form of appearance of class inequality" amounts only to the obvious proposition that individuals are equal as (say) voters, but unequal as (say) workers and managers. And while this is true, one does not need to be a Marxist, or a Hegelian, to know it is true. Conversely, however, if the appearance/essence connotations are retained, then such a proposition amounts to saying that the material inequality between workers and managers is "more real" than their juridical equality as voters, a postulate that must simply be regarded as arbitrary.

However, as already noted, Althusser's conception of the subject as ideological goes well beyond anything found in Marx. For Althusser believes, not merely that juridical equality of subjects is an ideological appearance in a society of class divisions, but that the very postulate of such subjects as autonomous social actors is, in itself, ideological. His principal and oft-reiterated reason for this belief is the proposition that under capitalism, at least (and possibly under communism as well), individual subjects are simply "bearers" and "supports" of class relations, or more generally of social relations of production. What this seems to mean is that a worker qua worker, or a manager qua manager, or a bureaucrat qua bureaucrat, simply fits into a predetermined social role with already prescribed norms, rules, and forms of activity (the norms, rules, and forms of activity required for the reproduction of the capitalist system) and then proceeds simply to reproduce this role through his or her individual activity.[39] And, of course, this analysis can be extended to embrace all other social roles seen as necessary for the reproduction of the system—"mother," "father," "son," "daughter," "citizen," "lawyer," and so on.

It has often been noted that all this amounts to a variety of Marxist functionalism, in which various forms of system imperative are first postulated (the reproduction of capitalist relations of production, or the reproduction of class relations, or the reproduction of the capitalist state) and then individuals are simply assigned the task of reproducing these relations by playing a prestructured social role. The principal problem that Althusser and his disciples experienced with this conception of individuals as bearers and supports of an endlessly reproducing system was, of course, the principal problem that functionalists of all types always experience—the problem of explaining how it is that societies change at all. As Paul Hirst noted,

39. See RC, 167–75, and FM, 223–46; see also "ISA," 156–58, and Nicos Poulantzas, Political Power and Social Classes (London: New Left Books, 1973), 64.

the effect of this Marxist functionalism is to make modes of production "eternities" that simply go on reproducing themselves until suddenly, and quite mysteriously, they go through "forms of transition" and become other modes.[40] The linguistic gymnastics that Althusser and his followers had to perform—in particular, the very curious subjects and social actors that they had to invoke to explain social change without *any* reference to human subjects as agents of change—produced some of the most exquisitely tortured passages of Althusserian prose. To cite two examples:

> In the transition period, the forms of law and state policy are not, as hitherto, adapted to the economic structure (articulated with the peculiar limits of the structure of production) but *dislocated* with respect to it: as well as showing force as an economic agent, the analysis of primitive accumulation also reveals the *precession of law* and of the forms of the State with respect to the forms of the capitalist economic structure. This dislocation can be translated by saying that the correspondence appears here too, in the form of a *non-correspondence* between the different levels. In a transition period, there is a "non-correspondence," because the mode of intervention of political practice, instead of conserving the limits and producing its effects within their determination, displaces them and transforms them. (Balibar, in *Reading Capital*, 306–7)

> In the relations between levels of structures, there is a dislocation between the economic, the political and the ideological: at the stage where the CMP [capitalist mode of production] is in the process of attaining domination, the dominant structures of the state and ideology are still feudal. Then again, let us take the levels of struggle of the bourgeois class, disregarding their internal dislocations with respect to the structure. In one and the same period the bourgeoisie's political organisation and political struggle push ahead, while the class of landed nobility (those "in charge" of the feudal state) is in reality only the representative of the political interests of the bourgeoisie. We can see clearly, in this example, that the juridical-political superstructure of the state is dislocated not simply in relation to the level of the political struggle of the bourgeoisie in the field of the class struggle. This is not a feudal state dislocated in relation to the

40. B. Hindess and P. Q. Hirst, *Modes of Production and Social Formation* (London: Routledge and Kegan Paul, 1977), 23.

economic but corresponding to a politically dominant class of landed aristocracy, which is itself in dislocation relative to an economically dominant bourgeoisie. It is rather a set of relations of dislocation between two systems of relations of dislocation. It is precisely this relation of the two systems which in the concrete conjuncture in question [Britain after 1680] brings it about that the form of reflection of the domination of the CMP in a feudal state is the political domination of the bourgeoisie in the field of the class struggle."
(Poulantzas, *Political Power and Social Classes*, 90)

Readers may feel in need of a little help in understanding what Balibar and Poulantzas are telling us, so prolixly, in these passages. (Without such help, perhaps they will feel threatened with severe dislocation!) All that is being said is that in the transition from feudalism to capitalism the coercive powers of the state and various kinds of legal powers were used to change economic conditions in ways that suited the interests of the rising bourgeois class. Yes, that is all. But because, in the Althusserian worldview, it cannot be human subjects who wield the power of the state or who use the legal system for these purposes, some very curious subjects have to be found to do these things instead—"the State," the "juridico-political level," even a very curious creature called "the mode of intervention of political practice."

But why? Why this implacable hostility to the subject? For this is a hostility that extends not merely to banning such subjects from the explanation of social change but also involves banning them from any role in the construction of theories or in the development of sciences. And this leads to yet more extraordinary prose, some of which will be cited below.

The answer appears to be that Althusser thinks that any postulation of the individual human subject as an effective social actor is equivalent to either (a) postulating an essential human nature of which such subjects are bearers but that is not socially conditional or determined (i.e., which is presocial or asocial in some sense), and/or to (b) postulating that human subjects are always privileged knowers of their own nature and motivations, thus ignoring Freudian and other insights into the ways in which human actors can be motivated by factors unknown to them.[41]

But, of course, one can perfectly well acknowledge that individuals, and groups or masses of individuals, can be effective social actors without postulating either that they are acting on the basis of some essential or asocial

41. *FM*, 228–30, "ISA," 152, and Hirst, "Althusser and the Theory of Ideology," 399–401.

human nature, or that they always know either why they are doing what they are doing or even that they know in what their activity will issue (which may be very different from what they intended). For example, to say of a particular mother that in bringing up her children she unconsciously reproduced many of the patterns in the relationship between herself and her own mother is certainly to postulate that she is an effective agent of (in this case familial) history. It was after all she, and nobody else, who unconsciously reproduced the patterns of her own upbringing. But equally in this case, one is not postulating either that she knew what she was doing or even that she could have chosen not to do it if she had known. Or again, it is perfectly possible to say of a person or of a group of people in a particular society at a particular time that they acted out of motives of material self-interest, or out of altruistic motives, without presupposing that human beings are essentially self-interested or altruistic, or even that what "self-interested" or "altruistic" means can be stated abstractly outside of any particular social and cultural context.

All this would be so obvious as to hardly need saying, were it not that these elementary logical distinctions do not seem to have occurred to Althusser. Nor does it appear to have been obvious to him, although it is true and important, that, even when human beings are merely (if they are ever merely) reproducing existing social relations by playing prestructured social roles, this only happens because those human beings *act* to reproduce those social relations. As Philip Abrams correctly remarked, continuity as well as discontinuity, the maintenance of traditions as well as their abandonment, have to be explained, and it is only human activity which explains them.[42] An explanation like "the continuance of tradition" is in fact as question-begging or defective an explanation of historical events as is "the break with tradition," though it is much less frequently perceived as being so. This is perhaps because it more readily strikes one that human beings need motives to change things and that they need to act to change things, than that they must also be motivated and act so as *not* to change things.

So in short, and for all these reasons, I long looked upon the entire Althusserian project, the entire oeuvre, with bemused wonderment. For I considered it neither the evil apotheosis of intellectual Stalinism,[43] nor the shining hope of Marxism's scientific renewal through the eviction of ideo-

---

42. Phillip Abrams, *Historical Sociology* (Ithaca: Cornell University Press, 1982).
43. E. P. Thompson, *The Poverty of Theory and Other Essays* (London: Merlin Press, 1978).

logical excrescences,[44] but as an intellectually hopeless and utterly confused endeavor of virtually no merit, whose only concrete outcome was a body of hideous prose. More recently, however, I have come to believe that this assessment of Althusser's work was, and is, seriously defective. For I now think that it misses both the real target of Althusser's intervention and the source of its significant psychological appeal for many Marxists. The next part of this chapter considers what these might be.

The Politics and Psychology of Althusserianism

To begin with, it seems probable that although Althusser spent a great many words and pages on the analysis of the works of both the young and the mature Marx, the real target of his assaults upon humanism, historicism, reductionism, and other topics may not have been Marx himself at all, or certainly not primarily.

In *Reading Capital* Althusser launches an explicit attack on Antonio Gramsci as a quintessentially historicist Marxist and follows this up with some similarly critical remarks about Lucio Colletti and Jean-Paul Sartre (*RC*, 138–43). In all these cases the thrust of his criticism is that these thinkers threaten the autonomy and specificity of theoretical practice in Marxism. They do so by (a) seeing Marx's own theoretical work, and especially *Capital*, as no more than an empirical generalization from the facts of nineteenth-century British history. They thus understate the importance of the process of theoretical abstraction that allowed Marx to generate insights into capitalism as a mode of production, insights that far transcended, and continue to transcend, the historical realities of nineteenth-century Britain. Althusser particularly criticizes Gramsci for this historicist interpretation of *Capital*. But more generally, (b) all three thinkers threaten the autonomy of theoretical practice by eliding it into a general notion of "praxis" that, Althusser argues, always results in the subordination of theoretical work to political praxis, and especially to the alleged demands of the "class struggle" (*RC*, 142).

And it is this point that, in my view, is at the center of the whole of Althusser's project. It is the point that provides the political driving force and polemical culmination of nearly all his intellectual work and that was

44. See, for example, B. Hindess and P. Q. Hirst, *Pre-Capitalist Modes of Production* (London: Routledge and Kegan Paul, 1975); Poulantzas, *Political Power and Social Classes;* and the journal *Economy and Society* between its founding in 1972 and about 1978.

at the center of his own rather limited political activity. For example, it led Althusser in May 1968 to oppose the demands of radical students for the root-and-branch reform of the curricula in French universities on the grounds that the professoriat was in command of a body of scientific and professional knowledge the teaching of which could not be subordinated to, or sacrificed to, radical political and ideological imperatives.[45]

Similarly, Althusser very clearly believed that there was an institutionalized tendency in Third International Marxism-Leninism (and especially, of course, within the French Communist party of which he was a member) for theoretical work in Marxism to be treated as the mere handmaiden of whatever political strategy or tactics Communist party leaderships happened to be pursuing at any given moment. Thus policies and political lines were first formulated by these leaderships, on some invariably pragmatic or realpolitik basis, and then party intellectuals were trotted out to surround the chosen political line with an aura of theoretical respectability. Althusser seems to have thought that this was how "socialist humanist" ideas were being used in the only partially de-Stalinized USSR of the early 1960s (hence his hostility to humanism in Marxism).[46] In the late 1970s he launched a rather similarly motivated attack on the French CP's abandonment of the concept of the dictatorship of the proletariat in its manifesto. Again, he did so on the primary grounds that this abandonment had occurred for pragmatic political reasons (to improve the party's democratic image in French politics) without an adequate theoretical consideration either of the real meaning of this slogan in the Marxist tradition (which he argued was a popular democratic rather than a Stalinist meaning) or of the long-term political effects of its abandonment.[47]

This is not to say that Althusser erected his massively wordy philosophical defense of Marxism as science in order to obtain for party intellectuals some relative autonomy from the political demands of Communist apparatchiks. Almost certainly the correct explanation is the other way round.

---

45. See Jacques Ranciere, "On the Theory of Ideology," *Radical Philosophy*, no. 7 (Spring 1974). See also "Dr Althusser," *Radical Philosophy*, no. 12 (Winter 1975), 44; K. S. Karol, "The Tragedy of the Althussers," *New Left Review*, no. 124 (1980); and Ted Benton, *The Rise and Fall of Structural Marxism: Althusser and His Influence* (London: Macmillan, 1984), chapter 1.

46. See Althusser's "Marxism and Humanism," in *FM*, 223–47, especially 240; see also "Dr Althusser," and Valentino Gerratana, "Althusser and Stalinism," *New Left Review*, nos. 101–2 (June 1981).

47. Louis Althusser, "On the 22nd Congress of the French Communist Party," *New Left Review*, no. 104 (July–August 1977).

That is, Althusser genuinely believed that Marxism was a science and on that basis made an insistent demand for Marxist intellectuals to be allowed to pursue that science and to draw political implications from it, without the ideological interference of party bureaucrats and bosses. Rather touchingly in fact, Althusser seems to have believed that a "correct" understanding of Marxist science would somehow, in and of itself, aid the process of de-Stalinization in the USSR, or generate the right revolutionary strategy for the French CP at home—a species of rampant idealism to which professional intellectuals (even supposedly materialist ones) are not infrequently prey.[48]

Nonetheless, even if I am right and it is not Marx (or even Gramsci, Colletti, or Sartre) who is the real target of Althusser's assaults on "humanism" or "historicism" or "reductionism," but the 1960s' and 1970s' political leaderships of the French (or Soviet or Italian or East German) Communist parties, then there are still a number of criticisms that can be made of his endeavors. First, he went about the task in the most oblique and timid way possible (which seems in accord with his generally cautious personality) and in a way guaranteed to have almost no effect on hardened and practical politicians. For the latter, even if they did by some chance have a genuine interest in theory, would be unlikely to brave or survive Althusser's prose style. Second, he might have had somewhat more impact had he been willing to draw clear and unambiguous political implications from his theoretical musings, rather than restricting the statement of such implications to brief, and often exceedingly ambiguous, asides. In particular, to drive his attacks on historicism or humanism or reductionism home in a political way Althusser would have had to have named names, and rather different names than the ones that figure so largely in his writings. (For example, "In his well-known pamphlet . . . Maurice Thorez claimed that communism was inevitable because . . ."; or "In a recent speech Georges Marchais claimed that issues such as feminism were mere diversions from the realities of the class struggle . . ."; or "In an address made in 1936 Palmiro Togliatti claimed that the essential cooperative nature of human beings was being corrupted by . . ."; and so forth.) In point of fact, however, it was not until the 1970s, when he made some unusually sharp and polemical attacks on the leadership of the French CP in the pages of *Le Monde*,[49] that Althus-

---

48. This is certainly the view taken by K. S. Karol; see his "Tragedy of the Althussers," 94.
49. The *Le Monde* articles appeared in April 1978. They are translated and summarized in Althusser's "What Must Change in the Party," *New Left Review*, no. 109 (May–June 1978).

ser even attempted to be anything more than the most timid "closet" politician.

The net result of all this timidity and obliqueness, however, was much as one might expect. For, in fact, the only place where Althusser's ideas made any real impact was in the academy, in particular the humanities and social-science academies of France, Britain, and the United States. In the light of my previous analysis, however, this might seem as surprising as Althusser's total lack of impact on Communist apparatchiks is unsurprising. For I have already argued that Marxism is not any kind of natural science and that Althusser's "theoretical realism" cannot, and did not, establish that it is. I have also suggested that Althusser misconstrued Marx's philosophy, revealed a total and woeful ignorance of the problems of Marxist economics, and mounted an assault on the "problematic of the subject" that is as confused on as many levels as it is articulated. Why, then, did his thought enjoy such an effervescent influence, at least for a brief period, in both Britain and France?

In accord with the principal theme of this chapter, I think the answer is primarily psychological. Althusser's oeuvre contained a number of elements that often psychologically fascinate and entrance intellectuals, and it combined these elements in a potent mixture, including:

1. A cult of intellectual rigor, together with an intoxicating idealism about what such rigor can achieve in and of itself
2. A dense, impenetrable, and exceedingly opaque jargon that yet creates a number of fascinating—because perceived but darkly—metaphorical worlds
3. An assault on the problematic of the subject that was so total as to encompass an abolition of the subject, as author or creator, in Marxist writing itself

In other words, Althusser, as much by example as by explicit assertion, called upon Marxist intellectuals to abolish *themselves* as subjects. This latter element in particular has, I believe, an especially deep psychological appeal for many intellectuals, an appeal that I shall try to explain. We may take these three elements in order.

(1) Rigor

[a] The reader should realise that I am doing all I can to give the *concepts* I use a *strict* meaning, and that if he wants to understand

these concepts he will have to pay attention to this rigour, and, in so far as it is not imaginary, he will have to adopt it himself. Need I remind him that without the rigour demanded by its object there can be no question of *theory*, that is, of theoretical practice in the strict sense of the term. (*FM*, 164)

[b] I shall not evade the most burning issue: it seems to me that either the whole logic of "supercession" must be rejected, or we must give up any attempt to explain how the proud and generous Russian people bore Stalin's crimes and repressions with such resignation; how the Bolshevik Party could tolerate them; not to speak of the final question—how a Communist leader could have ordered them. But there is obviously much *theoretical* work needed here as well. By this I mean more than the historical work which has priority—precisely because of this priority, priority is given to one essential of any Marxist historical study: rigour; a rigorous conception of Marxist concepts, their implications and their development; a rigorous conception of what appertains to them in particular, that is, what distinguishes them once and for all from their phantoms. (*FM*, 116)

[c] We can rigorously define Marx's few and as yet inadequate scientific concepts on the absolute condition that we recognise the ideological nature of the philosophical concepts which have usurped their places, in short, on the absolute condition that at the same time we begin to define the concepts of Marxist philosophy adapted to knowing and recognising as ideological the philosophical concepts which mask the weaknesses of the scientific concepts from us. (*RC*, 146)

[d] In contrast to the empiricist practice of theoretical ideologies, the sciences proceed through the explicit theoretical construction of their concepts and the theoretical definition of their objects. This book is a work of Marxist scientific theory. It must be judged in terms of that theory, in terms of the field of concepts and forms of proof specific to its problematic. We attempt to construct the concepts of certain pre-capitalist modes of production. . . . Our constructions and our arguments are theoretical and they can only be evaluated in theoretical terms—in terms, that is to say, of their rigour and theoretical coherence. (Hindess and Hirst, *Pre-Capitalist Modes of Production*, 3)

[e] Our position on *Economy and Society* was based on *progressivism*. By progressivism we mean the policy of attempting to introduce advanced theory and politics in order to create an intelligentsia capable of supporting a genuine theoretical culture and providing the recruiting ground for Marxist theorists and militants. By advanced theory we mean Marxism, psychoanalysis, the sophisticated forms of classical philosophy and avant-garde aesthetics. . . .

. . . It is always possible to create the elements of a school or tendency by exposition and education. What cannot be created by these means are genuine theoretical advances which provide real leadership and offer real programmes of theoretical and political work to those willing to undertake them. In our view it is necessary to give educational work a *secondary* place and to make it a side effect of genuine theoretical and practical work. It is for this reason that we are now committed to the position that the analysis of the present conjuncture and the production of the theoretical work necessary to that analysis is the primary task. (Hindess and Hirst, resignation letter to the Board of *Economy and Society*, in *Economy and Society* 4, no. 2 [May 1975])

These quotations are psychologically fascinating in a number of ways. First, they all appeal to values that any professional intellectual is likely to find hard to resist, since to do so would be in effect to give up one's identity as an intellectual. Thus no intellectual is going to rush to say that she or he does not want her or his concepts given a "strict" or "rigorous" meaning. Nor is she or he likely to gainsay the importance of "theory" or "theoretical work," especially when such work promises "forms of proof" of a scientific kind and when by means of theory all kinds of wonders can, by implication, be performed. These include, apparently, the erasure of Stalin's crimes, the creation of a "genuine theoretical culture," and the attainment of some unspecified positions of "leadership." This is indeed the intellectual as Promethean hero (and heroine).

Second, Althusser himself, and his followers by simple reproduction of his jargon, demonstrate a genius for alliteration, so that the sound of these sentences is as strict as their semantics. Hence, "can be no question of", "rigorous conception of," "rigorous conception and investigation of what appertains," "inadequate scientific concepts," "absolute condition," "explicit theoretical construction," "genuine theoretical and practical work," and "production of the theoretical work." One can almost hear the governess's whip crack with the consonants. And indeed this dense consonantal structure of Althusser's prose becomes even more marked when he comes to describe the structures constructed with his rigorously articulated concepts, as discussed below.

Finally, of course, both the content of Althusser's discourse and its strict-governess's metaphors facilitate a bullying tone, or at least a semipermanent bravado, in which it is continually implied that either one takes the way of "rigor," "theory," and "science" to the light or one is cast into the outer darkness of "empiricism," "positivism," and all-round sloppiness where no intellectual worth his or her salt is going to want to be. Sometimes this is backed up by overt appeals to intellectual snobbery ("advanced theory," "psychoanalysis," "the sophisticated forms of classical philosophy," and "avant-garde aesthetics"). Who would want to miss being in on all this? This is a heady brew, then, which promises much, especially to the marginalized intellectual. What it delivers is, of course, something else.

(2) An Intellectual Landscape (or, Through a Glass Darkly)

[a] Any object or problem situated on the terrain and within the horizon, i.e. in the definite structured field of the theoretical problematic of a given theoretical discipline, is visible. . . . The sighting is thus no longer the act of an individual subject, endowed with the "faculty" of "vision" which he exercises either attentively or distractedly; the sighting is the act of its structural conditions, it is the relation of immanent reflection between the field of the problematic and *its* objects and *its* problems. . . . It is literally no longer the eye (the mind's eye) of a subject which *sees* what exists in the field defined by a theoretical problematic: it is this field itself which sees itself in the objects or problems it defines—sighting being merely the necessary reflection of the field in its objects. (*RC*, 25)

[b] Marx does not present phenomena—to illustrate his thought temporarily with a spatial metaphor—in the infinity of a homogeneous planar space, but rather in a *region* determined by a regional structure and itself inscribed in a site defined by a global structure; therefore as a complex and deep space, itself inscribed in another complex and deep space. But let us abandon this spatial metaphor, since this first opposition exhausts its virtues: everything depends in fact on the nature of this depth, or, more strictly, of this *complexity*. To define economic phenomena by their concept is to define them

by the concept of this complexity, i.e. by the concept of the (global) structure of this mode of production, insofar as it determines the (regional) structure which constitutes as economic objects and determines the phenomena of this defined region located in a defined site in the structure of the whole. (*RC*, 182)

[c] . . . the effects of the structure on the field of the class struggle are reflected here as a class's threshold of existence as a distinct class, as a social force. But these effects are reflected also as an *extension of the ground* which this class can cover according to the stages of specific organisation attainable by it (organisation of power); and this ground extends as far as its objective interests. If we refer in this way to this double limit of the field (every field having a "near side" and a "far side") a class's objective interests do not appear directly as the *threshold* of its existence as a distinct class, as some kind of "situation" of the class "in itself," but as the *horizon* of its action as a social force. (Poulantzas, *Political Power and Social Classes*, 111–12)

[d] . . . the fact that the structure of the whole is determined in the last instance by the economic does not mean that the economic always holds the *dominant role* in the structure. The unity constituted by the structure in dominance implies that every mode of production has a dominant level or instance; but the economic is in fact determinant only in so far as it attributes the dominant role to one instance or another, in so far as it regulates the shift of dominance which results from the decentration of the instances. (Poulantzas, *Political Power and Social Classes*, 14)

[e] . . . the theory of the mode of production dominant in their formation . . . establishes the general character of the state (feudal, capitalist etc) as a function of the specific articulation of instances given by the matrix role of the economy. . . .

It is one thing to assert that primitive communism exists, it is quite another to establish its concept. As we have seen it is the structure of the economy in its matrix role of determination that defines the necessary and specific form of articulation of instances in the concept of the mode of production. In the absence therefore of the elaborated concept of the primitive communist mode of production we have no theoretical basis for differentiating between primitive and advanced communism, two modes of production that have always been distinguished in the Marxist tradition. (Hindess and Hirst, *Pre-Capitalist Modes of Production*, 40, 42)

[f] It is important to remember that a "pure" mode of production consists of an articulation of different instances in which social classes manifest themselves in the examination of this "pure" mode as the effect of the matrix on its supports: for example, in the theoretical examination of the "pure" feudal mode of production, the classes of this mode already manifest themselves as particular economico-political castes. . . .

Classes . . . manifest themselves . . . entirely as the *global effect of the structures in the field of social relations* . . . and they do this to the extent that the social classes determine the place of agents/ supports in relation to the structures of a mode of production and social formation. (Poulantzas, *Political Power and Social Classes*, 71, 64)

[g] . . . it is necessary to begin by proposing some concept other than "context" for thinking the problem of the object and organisation of knowledge. For the immediate purposes of this review, the concept of "terrain" may be proposed. The distance between terrain and context is that while context thinks only the organisation of knowledge in terms of an undefined outside antithesised to an unde-fined inside, terrain thinks the object and organisation of knowledge in terms of a definition of an area of knowledge inside or outside a particular text. The idea here is very simply that knowledge is orga-nised into particular fields unified by an object of inquiry and mode of proof. . . .

With the concept of terrain it becomes possible to trace the conse-quences of a reading which takes revisions for its object. Much revi-sionism could be termed argument on a terrain because the object of inquiry and mode of proof is not at stake. In this case the reading will not focus on the terrain at all; instead the reading will report disembodied revisionist argument and conclusions, for example, that the standard of living was declining in an area "X" from 1870–1890, with a "context" presented as a "debate" on the standard of living or some such vague formula. The terrain itself only enters the histo-rian's reading when revisionism takes the form of an argument for a shift of terrain, as in the early 1960s when both Thompson . . . and

Hobsbawm . . . raised the question of whether material welfare in itself was a worthwhile object for investigation, given that man does not live by bread alone. (Karel Williams, "Problematic History," *Economy and Society* 1, no. 4 [November 1972]: 459–60)

One of the psychologically most fascinating aspects of the Althusserian literature was these various metaphorical landscapes that it created and invited its readers to inhabit, along with—relatedly—the variety of "structures" (i.e., "problematics," "modes of production," and "social formations") that it held up and rotated before its readers' mesmerized gaze. However, there is a sense in which these landscapes and structures were simply two conceptual outcomes of a single cognitive procedure, a procedure that combined and compounded deep philosophical errors and equally deep psychological appeals. Thus, if we are to understand the Althusserian moment—understand, that is to say, both its considerable intellectual attraction and its deepest confusions—we must examine and understand this cognitive procedure.

First, and most important (since everything else flows from it), Althusser himself and all his followers conceived thought as *conceptualization*. Indeed "concept" is probably the most important word in the whole Althusserian lexicon—see, for example, quotations 1(a) and (c) and 2(e) and (g) above, which are just some of a hundred quotations that might be adduced. For Althusser, to think, to analyze, or to explain is first and foremost to conceive, and to conceive is essentially and always *to attach a name to an object*. Indeed, it is significant that all of Athusser's concepts are nouns ("problematic," "knowledge," "theory," "ideology," "science," "the economic," "the political," etc.) or noun phrases ("social formation," "mode of production," "mode of appropriation of surplus labour," "mode of appropriation of nature," "forces of production," "relations of production," etc.).

However, Althusser does not think that concepts—or, more exactly, the process of conceiving—consists in simply attaching names of labels to objects preexisting outside of thought. For this would be a form of his hated empiricism. Rather, he thinks (generalizing perhaps from some of Bachelard's remarks about non-Euclidean geometry and about Einstein's theory of relativity)[50] that the process of conceptualizing an object (i.e., giving it a name) is, at least in part, creative. That is, it actually creates the object

---

50. Bachelard, *La formation de l'esprit scientifique*, chapter 11; see also Balibar, in *RC*, 226.

in question, which, for Althusser, is always and only an "object in thought" or "object of knowledge," not a "real object." In other words, his epistemology is, at least in a certain respect, activist. Human thought does not, for Althusser, passively reflect a real world outside it; it actively appropriates, and thus shapes, the world through theory or, more exactly, through theoretical practice.

But nonetheless, the way in which this appropriation happens in Althusser, how theoretical practice actively appropriates the world in knowledge, is through conceptualization, understood or conceived as a naming process, and hence one that relates nouns to objects. Thus Althusser's "knowledge," his "theory," and his "science" all work by creating a world or worlds of objects. And thus it is that, whether he is describing the structure of science and its relationship to ideology, or the structure of modes of production and their relationship to social formations, Althusser is always describing things and the relationships between things.

However, since nearly all human "thing" vocabulary and nearly all human "object" vocabulary is derived from, or analogically developed from, the vocabulary of physical objects in spatial relationships, Althusser is always led (one might say semantically led) to create quasi-spatial structures and metaphorical landscapes. In fact, the many debates that occurred at the height of his influence about how far Althusser was or was not a structuralist largely missed the point in my view.[51] For Althusser was led, ineluctably, to structural analogies, just as he was led to theoretical landscapes, by his conceptualization of conceptualization, that is, by his total imprisonment in a picture of thought that saw the name-object relationship as the essence of thinking, or at least as the essence of thinking theoretically or scientifically. In fact, Althusser's structures (just like his metaphorical "fields" and "sites" and "levels" and "regions") are simply complex objects themselves, or perhaps complexes of objects, sets of objects in "determinate"—a favorite Althusserian word—"relations" (ditto).

In fact, we can go further and say that *everything in Althusser, or everything of significance in his thought, is indeed a thing, an object*. Knowledge, ideology, science, social formations and modes of production, and forces and relations of production are all objects, as are "the economic" and "the political" (in fact, these latter are quasi-spatial objects—"levels" or

51. See, for example, Miriam Glucksmann, *Structuralist Analysis in Contemporary Social Thought: A Comparison of the Theories of Claude Lévi-Strauss and Louis Althusser* (London: Routledge and Kegan Paul, 1974), especially chapters 4, 5, and 6; see also Keat and Urry, *Social Theory as Science*, chapter 6.

"regions"). Now all objects have the conceptual characteristic of being distinct or indistinct to the vision, as well as being firmly or clearly bounded (like rocks or tables) or unclearly and shiftingly bounded (like clouds of steam or vapor). But science is about clarity, rigor, and exactitude. Hence in this picture knowing scientifically must be about the clear *definition* of concepts and thus of the objects that they define. Indeed, it is by no means accidental that Althusser himself, and most of his followers, were very fond of the terminology of geometry and trigonometry as a quintessentially "rigorous" language ("matrix of the supports," etc.). For, of course, geometry and trigonometry are two abstract techniques for defining spatial objects exactly and for determining their relations equally exactly.

And what is wrong with all this? A route toward being able to see what is wrong with it, a good initial therapy to escape the picture of thought that Althusser paints so insistently and inventively, is simple denial. Knowledge, we can say, is *not* an object, and neither are ideology, science, modes of production, forces or relations of production, social formations, economics, politics, the State, and so on. Rather, we can think of all these things, not as things at all, but as human practices and hence as temporal processes.

But a denial in itself, though a beginning, will hardly suffice as an adequate therapy for the Althusserian picture of thought, because the denial can itself be denied—"But knowledge *is* an object, can be thought of as a (theoretical) object," and the like. Thus a second stage of the therapy must concentrate on the use of the verb "to be" in both the denials above. For it is the "is" in, for example, "Knowledge is (is not) an object" or "Knowledge is (is not) a human practice" that obscures what we must see if we are to truly escape the Althusserian picture. What we must see is that our language allows us to say either that "Knowledge is an object" or that "Knowledge is a practice" and hence that what we say here is indeed what *we* say. In the case of the English language a way to be reminded of this is through one commonplace use of the simple little verb "to treat." That verb reminds us that we can *treat* knowledge as an object, but we can also *treat* it as a practice, and this formulation draws attention to the subject as a user of the language (choosing to treat something "as" something).[52] Conversely, the use of the verb "to be" in this kind of context has precisely the opposite effect, for the proposition "Knowledge is (is not) an object" makes it sound as if the objectivity of knowledge was a *characteristic* (attribute) of knowl-

---

52. For Wittgenstein on "seeing as," see *Philosophical Investigations*, remarks 74 and 228 and pp. 193–208.

edge, rather than being a way in which "we" (the speakers of the English language) can characterize (action) it.

This objectifying use of the verb "to be" has considerable psychological force, and it is particularly effective in obscuring the subject and in focusing attention on an object and on the characteristics of an object, characteristics that, it tries to persuade us, are "there," as it were, irrespective of the activity of we, the perceiving subjects.[53] Althusser and his followers made continuous use of this objectifying force of the verb "to be"; any reader who wishes to confirm this should simply peruse quotations 2(a) to (g) above, all of which are replete with "is's" and "are's" designed to present persuasive assertions or points of view as factlike statements (and thereby of course make them more persuasive). Thus "an object . . . is visible," "it is no longer the mind's eye which sees," "are reflected as a class's threshold of existence," "is determined in the last instance by the economic," "it is the structure of the economy in its matrix role of determination," "the distance between terrain and context is that," and so forth. The effect of these kinds of formulations is to make the reader peer, as it were, at something that is already "there," and that being "there" can only be correctly or incorrectly grasped. And what it obscures almost perfectly is that there is somebody—the Althusserian author—*putting* these things, these objects, "there." And since this action is obscured, no questions about it, about what precisely is being *done* here, can even be posed, let alone answered.

So, the liberating effect of denial, especially if combined with a reminder of the little verb "to treat," is to break the objectlike inertia of the Althusserian picture of concepts and conceptualization and to remind us that it is a picture, and hence only one picture among a number. It also reminds us that, being a picture, it must have a painter and that we can ask questions about him and about why he paints, chooses to paint, this particular picture of concepts. In addition, the alternative assertions "Knowledge is a practice," "Ideology is a practice," "Science is a practice," remind us, in a way that the objectifying picture does not, that practices require practitioners, just as social processes require actors. In this way these formulations reintroduce subjects into society, just as the little verb "to treat" or "to treat as" reintroduces speakers and writers into language.

Another therapy that can be effective in reintroducing the subjects whom Althusser has linguistically abolished is to concentrate on the notion of

---

53. For some further remarks on this point, see P.M.S. Hacker, *Insight and Illusion: Wittgenstein on Philosophy and the Metaphysics of Experience* (Oxford: Oxford University Press, 1972), 128–30.

"aspect." Here the strategy is to say that "economics," "politics," "forces of production," "relations of production" are not "things" but *aspects* of society and of social institutions and processes. Thus, looked at from one point of view, or from one aspect, a factory may be regarded as a technical force of production. However, looked at from another point of view it may be regarded as a set of relations of production. Similarly, a factory may be thought of as a purely economic entity, but it may also be thought of as a political entity (or looked at from a political aspect), both because political struggles go on within it for power and influence and because its owners or managers may be politically active in a wider arena in order to defend what they regard as the factory's interests (vis-à-vis government policy, for example).[54]

A final therapy to escape the Althusserian picture is to combine both aspect and practice (or process) vocabulary with reference to some specific human activities. Thus, for example, Galileo's life's work can be seen as a moment in the history of the science of astronomy. But equally it was (can be seen as) a practice replete with ideological implications (most notably for the power of the Catholic church and the religious cosmology that formed part of its ideological legitimation). Galileo's life's work also had economic aspects (his need for patrons and resources to continue his work) and political aspects (his relationship with the church and of the church with various temporal powers both in Italy and elsewhere).[55]

All these therapies can help us to escape the grip of Althusser's theoretical landscape. For obviously, if one and the same thing (Galileo's life, or any-body's life, any factory, any government, any society) can have scientific, ideological, economic, and political aspects, among others, if those things can be looked at from all these points of view, then what are we now to make of a metaphorical landscape in which "science," "ideology," "poli-tics," "economics," "forces of production," and "relations of production" are separate theoretical things or objects that occupy separate "positions," "sites," or "regions" and have "relations" traced, quasi-spatially, among them?

The answer to this question is precisely that we *may make* quite a bit out of such a picture, but that is something which we (users of English, French, German, or any other language) must do. For, in itself, this meta-phorical landscape does nothing, tells us nothing. It is we who have to

---

54. For Wittgenstein on "aspect," see *Philosophical Investigations*, part 2, 194–96 and 206–8.
55. On Galileo, see Arthur Koestler, *The Sleepwalkers* (Harmondsworth: Penguin, 1964), parts 4 and 5, 357–503.

make use of it.[56] So the point of everything above is not to say that it is wrong, for example, to see the state as a thing, as an object, or as a complex kind of object, for seeing it as an object may have some point or use in some circumstances. The point of what I have said above is, first, to stress that this is what we (and the Althusserians are part of "we" here) are doing. We are seeing things *as* things. We are using the freedom that our language provides us to conceive in a certain way, a way that is only one of a number of alternatives which that language provides. And we often need to be reminded of those alternatives when the verb "to be" threatens to obscure or suppress them. But, second, I want also to stress that in choosing one picture of conceptualization, or in choosing one way of conceptualizing anything, we must be clear, and make clear to others, why we have chosen that way, what is the point or purpose of doing so. For this, of course, is something that neither Althusser nor his followers did. They never stated what the point or purpose of the Althusserian picture of thought was, because they never thought of it as just one "picture" (among others) that they had "chosen" at all. Rather, they thought of it as the "right," the "correct," the "scientific" picture, as indeed the only possible picture, and they wanted their readers to think of it in those "objective" terms too.

Since, therefore, the Althusserians never posed this question, were never able to pose it, we must pose it for them. What is the point or purpose of the Althusserian picture of thinking or conceiving? What is it meant to do to or for us? I think the answer is obvious from everything that has been said above. The point or purpose of the Althusserian picture of thinking is *to abolish thinking subjects.* And this answer brings us to what is perhaps the central contradiction and puzzle in the whole of Althusser's work, a contradiction and puzzle that can perhaps best be approached through reference to the "aspect" picture that we have used as a philosophical therapy above.

"Aspect," like "perspective" and "point of view," is used frequently when analogies are being drawn between thinking and visual perception. One of the advantages and strengths of this analogy (which came out strongly in its therapeutic use above) is that it very directly problematizes the traditional epistemological picture of the subject-object relationship in philosophy. In this picture the subject is taken as a passive or contemplative reflector in

56. See, for example, *Philosophical Investigations*, remarks 140–41, 374, 422–23, and 425; for an important commentary and elucidation, see G. P. Baker and P.M.S. Hacker, *Essays on the "Philosophical Investigations"* (Oxford: Basil Blackwell, 1980), vol. 1, *Wittgenstein: Meaning and Understanding*, especially chapter 1.

thought of an external world, and that world itself is treated as a set of given objects that can only be accurately reflected (i.e., truth) or inaccurately reflected (i.e., falsehood).[57]

As against this traditional epistemological picture, the aspect picture of thinking has the merit of reminding us that all human beings are active subjects. They move physically, of course; but also, by analogy, they move temporally acquiring new knowledge, attitudes, and beliefs as they go. The metaphor of aspect also reminds us that the object is not a given, but is always perceived, actively appropriated, by the subject interacting sensually with it and perceiving it from different points of view. In fact, the sum total of points of view from which human subjects perceive any object just is what the object "is,"since it has no knowers save human ones. In the case, moreover, of nonphysical objects (the kinds of objects named in human language through abstract nouns and noun phrases), this process of the *creation* of the object through its conceptualization is, in general, more unconstrained than in the case of physical objects. For the latter, though they may be seen from different points of view, are rarely seen as different things (though this does happen from time to time, as in Eddington's "two tables").[58]

Now the real paradox of Althusser's whole project is that he sees this last point clearly enough. Indeed, as already noted, it is one of the strengths of his epistemology, and of his conceptions of both theory and science, that he sees human thought as an active intervention in the world ("theoretical practice," etc.) and not as a passive or contemplative reflection of it (e.g., *FM*, 169–92). Yet, at the very same time as he grasps this, his conception of thinking abolishes all active thinkers, theorizers, scientists, perceivers, conceptualizers. Hence he is driven to assert that the active subjects of science, for example, are scientific *concepts*, that the active subjects of theory are theoretical *concepts*, and so on. Quotation 2(a) above brings this out clearly enough, but it is worth emphasizing this point, and the literal seriousness with which Althusser takes it, by further quotations.

(3) The Abolition of the Subject

[a] It is the field of the problematic that defines and structures the invisible as the defined excluded, excluded from the field of visibility and defined as excluded by the existence and peculiar structure of

57. See Cavell, *The Claim of Reason*, especially chapters 6 and 8.
58. See above (p. 27) and note 5 to chapter 2).

the field of its problematic; as what forbids and represses and reflection of the field in its object. (*RC*, 25–26)

[b] . . . the *"thought"* we are discussing here is not a faculty of a transcendental subject or absolute consciousness confronted by the real world as *matter;* nor is this thought a faculty of a psychological subject . . . although human individuals are its agents. This thought is the historically constituted system of an *apparatus of thought* founded on and articulated to natural and social reality. It is defined by the system of real conditions which makes it, if I dare use the phrase, a determinate *mode of production* of knowledges. As such it is constituted by a structure which combines . . . the type of object (raw material) on which it labours, the theoretical means of production available (its theory, its methods and its technique, experimental or otherwise) and the historical relations (both theoretical, ideological and social) in which it produces. This definite system of conditions of theoretical practice is what assigns any given thinking subject (individual) its place and function in the production of knowledges. (*RC*, 41)

[c] . . . the validity of a scientific proposition as a knowledge was ensured in a determinate scientific practice by the action of particular *forms* which ensure the presence of scientificity in the production of knowledge, in other words, by specific forms that confer on knowledge its character as a true knowledge. . . . We can see these specific forms in action in the discourse of scientific proof, i.e. in the phenomenon which imposes on thought categories (or concepts) a *regular order of appearance and disappearance.* We can say then, that the mechanism of production of the knowledge effect lies in the mechanism which underlies the action of the forms of order in the scientific order of the proof. (*RC*, 67)

[d] That this "change of terrain" which produces as its effect this metamorphosis in the gaze, was itself only produced in very specific, complex and often dramatic conditions; that it is absolutely irreducible to the idealist myth of a mental decision to change "viewpoints"; that it brings into play a whole process that the subject's sighting, far from producing, merely reflects in its own place; that in this process of real transformation of the means of production of knowledge, the claims of a "constitutive subject" are as vain as are

the claims of the subject of vision in the production of the visible; that the whole process takes place in the dialectical crisis of the mutation of a theoretical structure in which the "subject" plays, not the part it believes it is playing, but the part which is assigned to it by the mechanism of the process—all these are questions which cannot be studied here. (*RC*, 27)

There is something radically incoherent here. If knowledge, science, and the like are, in some sense or other, active cognitive practices, then they require human actors, and any conception of knowledge or science in which psychological subjects are simply "agents" of an "apparatus of thought" (conceived, essentially, as a set of concepts) simply does not allow for such actors. Indeed it explicitly, even neurotically, disavows them, as indicated in all these quotations. But given an insistence on theory and science as "practices"—which he avows and reavows with the same insistence as he disavows subjects—Althusser is left postulating that "theory," "science," "ideology" (all conceived as sets of concepts) are *themselves* active subjects, with human beings as simply their "supports," "bearers," or "agents."

Such a notion can be given some apparent empirical plausibility by the reflection that all thinkers, and certainly all scientists, work within traditions of scientific theory and practice, traditions that will prescribe broad limits to, and give meaning to, their practice as individual scientists.[59] But as in the case of history and society generally (see pp. 72–73), we must also reflect that scientists do not simply "reproduce" those limits or those meanings. They also break out of them, either suddenly and dramatically (as in the case of Albert Einstein) or, more frequently, in a slow and cumulative way, through the interaction of new forms of conjecture, new forms of experiment, and new forms of theory.[60] So scientists too "make their own science," though not in scientific and theoretical circumstances of their own (individual) choosing.

So Althusser really cannot have it both ways. If he wants an activist epistemology he must have active human subjects as knowers in and of the world. If, however, he wants to treat such subjects as a total irrelevance to knowledge, then he must postulate knowledge, including scientific knowledge, as a process by which the world simply imposes itself on human knowers by, as it were, "forcing," the right concepts, propositions, and the

59. Gerald Holton's work brings this out well; see especially *The Scientific Imagination: Case Studies*, particularly part 1, "On the Thematic Analysis of Science."
60. Ibid., chapter 2 ("Subelectrons, Presuppositions, and the Millikan-Ehrenhaft Dispute").

like on them so that it is simply "reflected"in these forms of thought. Since most contemporary philosophers, including Althusser, consider this notion of the nonhuman world as the active provider of knowledge to humans as utterly incoherent, they must, and generally do, postulate the active element in knowing as supplied only by human beings. And so (on the most minimal grounds of consistency) should Althusser. But he cannot and will not, which leaves him in an arid structural landscape of his own creation in which curious actors like "Theory" and "Science" and "Concepts" and "Problematics" stalk the world like dinosaurs, with human beings clinging haplessly to their ferocious flanks as "bearers" and "supports."

Yet whatever its intellectual problems, I believe that it is this very characteristic of Althusser's thought, this radically incoherent "activist determinism" (in which human knowledge makes the world, but actual human beings are the mere agents of cognitive subject-objects that dwarf and transcend them) that is at the root of its psychological appeal. For its effect, for the intellectuals who embrace Althusserianism, was to allow them to be radical cognitive activists while believing themselves to be, and presenting themselves as, the anonymous agents of a pregiven problematic. Thus at one (psychological) stroke such intellectuals were both absolved of any responsibility for the knowledge claims that they were making (for such claims do not appear, in the Althusserian discourse, as the knowledge claims of *anybody*) and at the same time had such claims guaranteed as "scientific."[61]

In short, the principal psychological appeal of Althusser's work was that through it a whole group of Young Turk intellectuals in 1970s Britain, France, and the United States were able to lay claim to insights not possessed by their elders without having to *lay* claim to those insights at all. For indeed these insights were not "their" insights (What availeth such arrant subjectivism?)—they were the insights of a "theory," of a "problematic," above all of a "science" itself.

I remarked earlier, in the section of this chapter dealing with Marx and Engels themselves (see pp. 57–58), that this has probably been the primary psychological appeal of Marxism as science, for all Marxist intellectuals, since its very beginnings. For perhaps, the one common experience of all Marxist intellectuals, from the middle of the nineteenth century to

61. A text that in its sheer stridency manifests this psychology perfectly is Karel Williams's "Problematic History,' *Economy and Society* 1, no. 4 (November 1972): 459–72. But anyone perusing the pages of any volume of *Economy and Society* between 1972 and 1978, or of *Radical Philosophy* in the same years, or of the journal *Theoretical Practice* throughout its existence, will find a host of other examples.

the present day, has been that of confronting "real" capitalist societies—
with their complex economic and social institutions, their powerful state
organizations, their formidable class supports (among the bourgeoisie and
middle class), and, for the most part, their clear working-class acquies-
cence—armed with nothing much more than (often tiny) revolutionary organizations and a set of beliefs about the future of capitalism and the
possibilities for socialism. In this situation it is small wonder that such
intellectuals have felt an insistent need of psychological supports to those
beliefs that would make them something more than the "mere beliefs" of
either individuals or groups. In this situation the appeal of a Kantian conception of science as a set of absolute transcendental truths that, once discovered, "age cannot wither nor custom stale" is very great, simply because
it provides something of similar psychological stature to pit against the
triumphant, omnipresent actuality of capitalism.

A Wider and Deeper Syndrome

However, one must note that, if only as a jargon, the appeal of Althusserianism in Britain extended beyond the boundaries of self-consciously Marxist intellectuals to embrace, at least for a short while, a much broader group
of scholars in both the social sciences and the humanities. Part of the reason
was, no doubt, its bullying claims to rigor (see pp. 78–82), but far more
important was its very recognizable and sympathetic—to Anglo-Saxon intellectuals—prescriptions about how such rigor was to be achieved. And
here we come to one of the great intellectual ironies of Althusserianism, or
certainly of British Althusserianism. For the primary rhetorical enemy of
Althusser, and of most of his followers, was "empiricism." Althusser's
rendering of this term was rather peculiar, but essentially he used it to refer
to all those philosophical traditions that conceive thought as a process of
abstracting from certain perceptual givens in the world ("given," that is, to
perception), in advance of the process of conceptual abstraction (e.g., RC,
35–37, 113–24). It was perhaps even more noticeable among Althusser's
British disciples than among their French counterparts that the prime target
of their rhetorical attacks, and the primary tradition juxtaposed to their own
attachment to theory, was the dominant tradition of British empiricism, at
times defined so widely as to embrace anybody who showed the slightest

sign of believing that there were factual truths establishable independently of theory.[62]

And yet, if one examines Althusser's own work closely, one sees that his conception of conceptualization (and thus of rigor), and his conceptualization of concepts as the name of objects, are both astonishingly similar to—indeed, identical to—those found in the tradition of logical positivism. This very rigorous current of empiricist philosophy enjoyed its strongest vogue in Britain in the interwar period, having been imported from Vienna, but in modified forms it fed into, and buttressed, the great British empiricist tradition of philosophy for a long time thereafter.

It is true that, unlike Althusser's, the logical positivists' hunt for true "proper names" was conceived as a search for the conceptual equivalents of the most "simple" or "basic" sense-data entities. For, in the classical empiricist tradition, the logical positivists believed that such entities had to constitute the bases of all meaningful propositions about the world. But nonetheless, the logical positivists, just like Althusser, saw language as, in essence, a vast mass of nouns ("names of objects" in the world) connected by logical relations. And we might add here that they analyzed these relations with much more genuine rigor (with the aid of symbolic logic) than Althusser ever managed. Taken as a whole, this network of logical relations among names of objects was supposed to specify all the possible propositions in language (all meaningful propositions, that is), of which some would be verifiable as true and others found to be false. Any proposition that could not be verified or falsified (for example, a self-contradictory proposition, or one that could not be logically "analyzed" into "basic" propositions with sense-data terms) was meaningless or "nonsense."[63]

With the important difference that in Althusser's philosophy there are "real" objects that are not sense-data objects (such "theoretically real" objects as modes of production), Althusser's essential project is identical to that of the logical positivists; that is, to specify all logically possible modes

---

62. See, as some of many examples, the Introduction to Hindess and Hirst, *Pre-Capitalist Modes of Production*, especially 3, and the introduction to chapter 4 ("Asiatic Mode of Production"), especially 179. See also Manuel Castells and Emilio de Ipola, "Epistemological Practices and the Social Sciences," *Economy and Society* 5, no. 2 (1976), and Karel Williams, "Facing Reality: A Critique of Karl Popper's Empiricism," *Economy and Society* 4, no. 3 (August 1975).

63. On logical positivism, see Otto Neurath, *Empiricism and Sociology,* especially the introduction and chapter 9. See also A. J. Ayer, *Language, Truth, and Logic* (1936; Harmondsworth: Penguin, 1971), especially chapter 3, and F. Waissmann, *Wittgenstein and the Vienna Circle,* ed. B. F. McGuiness (London: Basil Blackwell, 1967).

of production, of which only some will be actualized in the real world.[64] It really cannot be said that either he, or Etienne Balibar, or any of their disciples pulled this off very well. For when closely examined the relations between concepts in Althusserian modes of production were not really logical relations at all, but (irony upon irony) simply disguised empirical relations more or less plausibly generalized from actual empirical cases of historical modes of production.[65] But that is not a matter of any great importance in this context. The really important point is that, despite its hysterical hostility to empiricism, Althusserianism was in the grip of precisely the same picture of language as some of the most rigorous empiricist philosophy. It is therefore not surprising that it struck such sympathetic chords among wide circles of British intellectuals, even if only in the form of a fashionable jargon or patois. It is also not surprising that, for precisely the same reason, the most profound and penetrating critique of logical positivism, and indeed of empiricism in general, ever made—that found in Ludwig Wittgenstein's later philosophy—should turn out to be as penetrating of Althusserian misconceptions about language as it was of those found in logical positivism.

In writing about logical positivism (and about his own early philosophy, which, in some ways, was very close to that of the positivists) Wittgenstein coined one of his most famous remarks, one addressed both to them and to himself as a younger philosopher: "A *picture* held us captive and we could not get outside it for it lay in our language and language seemed to repeat it to us inexorably."[66] As becomes clear upon reading the *Philosophical Investigations,* the "picture" that neither the earlier Wittgenstein nor the logical positivists could "get outside" was the picture of language as a *naming device*—that is, as a device whose primary function was to name objects in the world, and that could therefore be made genuinely scientific and rigorous by having its nouns, its names, defined as exactly as possible. For in defining the names tightly and exactly, it was believed by the logical positivists, as by the Althusserians, that one simultaneously defined the objects that the nouns named and that this in its turn was the prerequisite

64. This comes out very clearly, for example, in Balibar's chapter of *Reading Capital* dealing with "Basic Concepts of Historical Materialism," especially 215–16, and in Hindess and Hirst, *Pre-Capitalist Modes of Production.*

65. This is a point well made in "Concepts of Modes of Production," a review of Hindess and Hirst's *Pre-Capitalist Modes of Production,* in *Economy and Society* 5, no. 4 (1976): 484–96.

66. *Philosophical Investigations,* remark 115.

of deciding which of these objects were real and which unreal (or "nonsensical," in the lexicon of the logical positivists).

In short, what these two apparently very different philosophies have in common is their conviction that nouns are the essential building blocks of language and of meaning of which all other parts of speech are essentially ancillary. (Nouns are, as it were, the "bricks" of language, while verbs, adjectives, adverbs, and so on are merely the "mortar" that holds nouns together semantically.) Thus, since propositions in language, or the making of propositions through language, is seen as essentially the marshaling of the right nouns for the right objects—that is, as the choosing of the right labels to "stick" propositionally on the right "things" in the world—it is small wonder that such attention is given to the definitional task, to the job of "cutting out" the labels as carefully and exactly as possible in order to ensure that the boundaries of the label exactly match those of the object upon which it is to be stuck.[67] Since this is a very commonplace conception of language, and therefore a very commonplace conception of what intellectual rigor requires, it is hardly surprising if it reproduces itself over and over again, even if the forms in which it does so are different in other respects.

Nor, as Wittgenstein stressed, is this picture of language simply wrong, for parts of language do indeed function like this.[68] It is, rather, that the picture is *partial*—that it takes as the whole, or at any rate as the epistemological *core* of language, what is in fact only a part of it. In particular, it tends to lead those who are in the grip of such a picture to think that if commonplace and material nouns name commonplace and material objects, then abstract nouns must name abstract objects. In fact, however, abstract nouns often fulfill a rather different function in language, or very many different functions, depending upon the precise context in which they are employed.

Thus, to take a famous example, the function of the proposition "Beauty is truth, truth beauty,—that is all ye know on earth, and all ye need to know" is not to name anything, nor to assert anything, either about truth or about beauty. Its function is rather to *express* something in the form of an exuberant generalization, in this case a poet's sense of wonder and delight

67. Ibid., remarks 15 and 26.
68. Ibid., remarks 15–79, in which there is a lengthy discussion of "naming" and "labelling" as practices and of the misleadingly partial theories of language that are generalized from these practices by empiricist and positivist philosophers. See also the commentary on these paragraphs in G. P. Baker and P.M.S. Hacker, *Essays on the "Philosophical Investigations"* (Oxford: Basil Blackwell,1980), vol. 2, *An Analytical Commentary on Wittgenstein's "Philosophical*

at the eternal freshness of the human figures and themes captured in the decoration of an ancient Greek urn. Read in the context of the rest of Keats's ode, the proposition "Beauty is truth, truth beauty" can be understood, appreciated, and accepted without it seriously being supposed that Keats held that the characteristics of all beautiful things are coterminous with the characteristics of all truthful things. Were, however, such a proposition to serve as the opening line of a lecture by Keats in which he seriously proposed to demonstrate the truth of the proposition that truth and beauty are coterminous, then in that very different context a different kind of validation of the proposition would be required in order for it to be accepted.

In other words (and as chapter 4 will argue in much more detail), the meaning and function of apparently descriptive sentences and propositions that use abstract nouns in conjunction with the verb "to be" may not in fact be descriptive at all, and whether or not it is will emerge clearly enough when their context of use is closely examined. But if due attention is not paid to these subtle shifts of context and such sentences are always understood as simply "abstract" variants of paradigm "truth function" propositions that do describe "objective" states of affairs ("The cat is on the mat," "London is the capital of the United Kingdom," "The lark is not a migratory bird," and so on), then one of two results will follow. Either (a) attempts will be made to "reduce" these "abstract" nouns and propositions to "concrete" nouns and propositions that can then be empirically observed/tested (logical positivism), or (b) a Platonic realm of "abstract" but "real" objects and relations will be posited on the grounds that such a realm must exist in order to give such nouns and propositions meaning (Althusserianism).[69]

Wittgenstein would argue, however, that both these procedures may be unnecessary and misleading since both follow from a fundamental misconstrual of what human beings are doing when they utilize abstract nouns and abstract propositions in language. It is dangerous to overgeneralize here, but it can be said that a most common and important use of such nouns and propositions, which is ignored in both the empiricist and Platonic approaches to them, is a *reflexive* use—that is, to say or express something about the speaker or writer (or about a human community of which she or

---

Investigations," especially 39, and in vol. 1, *Wittgenstein: Meaning and Understanding,* chapter 7.

69. For the reductionist (i.e., logical-empiricist or logical-positivist) approach to "proper names," see the *Philosophical Investigations,* paragraphs 46–64. See also Baker and Hacker,

he is a part or purports to represent) in a linguistic form that is apparently, but only apparently, descriptive of an objective world beyond that speaker or writer.

But in any case, the epistemological syndrome that (a) conceives knowing as a form of perception or observation ("seeing"), that (b) therefore conceives the "knowledge relationship" as analogous to the relationship of an observer to the objects that she or he observes (a position very literally embraced by Wittgenstein in the *Tractatus* as the "picture theory" of the proposition),[70] and that, therefore (c) trades heavily on the analogy between bringing visible objects into sharper definition or focus and the "rigor" to be obtained from the "exact" "definition" of "concepts" (= nouns, whether "concrete" or "abstract") is a syndrome with an enormous intuitive appeal and a deep psychological hold, a hold that derives from its important but partial truth. Knowing as a human practice *is* indeed partially about such "exact" "perceiving." But it is also in important ways different from this, involving practices other than simply observing or perceiving (no matter how "exactly"),[71] and other uses and areas of language show these further dimensions of knowing clearly if they are sensitively examined. Wittgenstein commences such an examination in his later philosophy, and this book endeavors to extend that examination to the language of social science and, most especially, to the language of Marxism.

It is precisely because this syndrome is so widespread, however (embracing far more intellectuals than Marxists, including many non-Marxists and militant anti-Marxists), and so intuitively persuasive that I have devoted such time and space to the critique of its Althusserian form. For this is all that Althusserianism was—a particular form of this syndrome at work in Marxism. Since Althusserianism is now widely deemed passé (even by many of those who once embraced it enthusiastically), it may not seem worth all of this critical attention, certainly not in the year of the Lord 1994 (1975 might have been a different matter!). But, in my view, although the particular *form* may now have been abandoned, the underlying epistemological syndrome to which Althusserianism made such an appeal is still very much

---

An Analytical Commentary, 101–11, and *Wittgenstein: Meaning and Understanding,* chapter 1. For Althusser's Platonism, see, for example, *RC,* 160–64 ("The Structure of the Object of Political Economy").

70. Wittgenstein, *Tractatus Logico-Philosophicus,* trans. D. F. Pears and B. F. McGuiness, Introduction by Bertrand Russell (London: Routledge and Kegan Paul, 1961), sections 2.1–2.225; see also Anthony Kenny, *Wittgenstein* (Harmondsworth: Penguin, 1973), chapter 4.

71. Max Horkheimer made this same argument powerfully in his seminal 1937 critique of logical positivism, "Traditional and Critical Theory" ("Traditionelle und kritische Theorie") translated in his *Critical Theory* (New York: Herder and Herder, 1968).

alive and well. Indeed, I think it is at the heart of a great deal of "Western," particularly Anglo-Saxon, intellectual culture. And so long as the epistemological/psychological syndrome is alive, it will spin off other forms, other variants (I suspect "analytical Marxism" may be another, more recent, variant, for example), with a similar intuitive appeal, a similar capacity to engage and enthrall the next generations of seekers after "rigor." Wittgenstein's later philosophy can be seen as, among other things, an attempt to provide an antidote, an inoculation, a "therapy" (to use the term that he favored)[72] against these oft-repeated temptations and enthusiasms, and this book may be regarded as another attempt at such a therapy, albeit one designed more narrowly for Marxist sufferers from the syndrome.

Whether, however, the inoculation, the therapy, will be effective is another matter. A prerequisite of its being so is an understanding among sufferers from the syndrome that it has such a deep hold not because it is a delusion (were it a pure delusion, it would be much easier to escape) but because it is a partial truth taken as a whole truth. Moreover, that partial truth constantly presents itself as a model for the whole truth by being embodied and endlessly reiterated in some of the most commonplace and frequently employed forms of our language—that is, in all our many and varied descriptions of the world around us, in which we state that so-and-so "is" or "is not" the case.[73]

Much more will be said about all of this in the next and in subsequent chapters. For the moment, I will simply end this chapter with two quotations from the *Philosophical Investigations* that I think will, in the light of the remarks above, speak for themselves.

> We name things and then we can talk about them: can refer to them in talk.—As if what we did were given with the mere act of naming. As if there were only one thing called "talking about a thing." Whereas in fact we do the most various things with our sentences. Think of exclamations alone, with their completely different functions

72. *Philosophical Investigations*, remark 133; see also Baker and Hacker, *Wittgenstein: Meaning and Understanding*, 288–90.

73. Remark 114 of the *Philosophical Investigations* reads:

> (*Tractatus Logico-Philosophicus*, 4.5): "The general form of the propositions is: This is how things are."—That is the kind of proposition that one repeats to oneself countless times. One thinks that one is tracing the outline of the thing's nature over and over again, and one is merely tracing round the frame through which we look at it.

The *Tractatus* of course begins with the famous proposition "The world is all that is the case."

Water!

Away!

Ow!

Help!

Fine!

No!

Are you inclined still to call these words "names of objects"? (*Philosophical Investigations*, remark 27)

One might say that the concept "game" is a concept with blurred edges—"But is a blurred concept a concept at all?"—Is an indistinct photograph a picture of a person at all? Is it always an advantage to replace an indistinct picture by a sharp one? Isn't the indistinct one often *exactly* what we need?

Frege compares a concept to an area and says that an area with vague boundaries cannot be called an area at all. This presumably means that we cannot do anything with it.—But is it senseless to say "Stand roughly there"? Suppose I were standing with someone in a city square and said that. As I say it I do not draw any kind of boundary, but perhaps point with my hand—as if I were indicating a particular spot. And this is how one might explain to someone what a game is. One gives examples and intends them to be taken in a particular way.—I do not however mean by this that he is supposed to see in those examples that common thing which I—for some reason—was unable to express; but that he is now to employ those examples in a particular way. Here giving examples is not an *indirect* means of explaining—in default of a better. For any general definition can be misunderstood too. The point is that *this is how* we play the game. (I mean the language-game with the word "game.") (*Philosophical Investigations*, remark 71).[74]

ADDENDUM:
MARXIST REALISM SINCE ALTHUSSER

The Althusserian moment was one of the strangest episodes in the history of Marxism, and indeed in the history of the Anglo-Saxon social sciences

74. See also *Philosophical Investigations*, remarks 69, 70, 88, 91, 99, 100.

and humanities since World War II. As already noted, Althusserianism enjoyed an extraordinary vogue and popularity in the academies of France, Britain, and the United States from the late 1960s to the late 1970s, and then, almost as rapidly as it had arisen, it disappeared.[75] Its erstwhile advocates deserted it; its jargon or patois, which had been almost hegemonic in radical intellectual circles, was heard no more; journals, books, and academic dissertations no longer bore its imprint. It had gone, completely, washed away by the same tide of intellectual fashion that had previously borne it forward. From the early 1980s onward it was hard even to find Althusserians who would admit to having been such, and even those who would tended to confine themselves to the most sheepish of smiles and silence when the episode was mentioned.

Of course it is easy to explain all this by reference to the rise of the New Right across Anglo-Saxon politics and culture from the late seventies or early eighties onward and to the general decline in the intellectual fashionability of Left radicalism in general and Marxism in particular that set in almost simultaneously. And no doubt there is as much truth in this kind of "sociology of knowledge" explanation in this case as there is in most cases.

But this is far less important for my purposes than another observation, which is that Althusserianism was simply *abandoned;* it was never properly worked through. That is to say, many of its erstwhile advocates concentrated their critical attention on the final inability of Althusser to avoid the economic reductionism against which his structural causality was supposedly pitted. Such critics then went on to abandon Marxism itself, arguing that Althusser had failed to solve the problem because the problem is in fact insoluble within the Marxist problematic.[76] As already noted, I did not draw this conclusion, because it was fairly clear to me that Marx himself was not an economic reductionist. And Marx was not an economic reductionist not because he successfully avoided this problem, but because *there is no such problem outside of the "structural" picture of Marxism that Althusser himself created.*

Another group of former Althusserians (notably Ernesto Laclau and his associates) directed their critical fire primarily at Althusser's attempted abo-

75. I had regarded Benton's *Rise and Fall of Structural Marxism* as the "swan song" statement in English, but very recently there have been one or two more backward glances at Althusser; see, in particular, Michele Barrett, *The Politics of Truth: From Marx to Foucault* (Cambridge: Polity Press, 1991), chapter 5.

76. See, for example, Cutler et al., *Marx's "Capital" and Capitalism Today,* vol. 1, part 3.

lition of the subject and the "objectivist" epistemology to which this led.[77] As will be apparent from the argument in chapter 3, this seems to me altogether closer to the heart of matters. But it still does not adequately grasp the central issue of Althusser's conception of language and the deep (i.e., not apparent or obvious) homology between this conception and empiricist or positivist conceptions, the homology that I have referred to above as the "naming" or "labeling" conception of language with its invariant epistemological privileging of nouns and noun phrases. As I have already stated, Althusserianism may be seen simply as the "Platonic" or idealist variant of this conception and positivism/empiricism as the materialist variant.

The reason this still seems important, at least to me, fifteen or so years after the death of Althusserianism is that if this "naming" or "labeling" picture of language remains predominant in Anglo-Saxon intellectual culture in general (as the necessary concomitant of the domination of positivism/empiricism), and if intellectual Marxism has to make its way in academies dominated by that culture, then the Althusserian/positivist conception of language is likely to remain hegemonic in Marxist intellectual work even if all of Althusser's other claims about the world have been explicitly or implicitly abandoned.

Thus one can abandon the full-blown realist claim that Marxists can discover a realm of causally efficacious unobservables in the social world directly analogous to the causal unobservables of the natural world. One can even rehabilitate the subject and admit that questions about the biography, the "epistemological community," the values, even the emotions of the observing subject are relevant to a consideration of the descriptions and evaluations she or he makes of the world. But this admission is likely to be largely formal so long as any Marxist clings, consciously or unconsciously, to an objectivist conception of language in which the meaning of words is given by the things in the world that they name and the meaning, as well as the truth-value, of propositions is to be determined purely (or even primarily) by comparing these propositions with facts in the world.

77. See E. Laclau and C. Mouffe, *Hegemony and Socialist Strategy: Towards a Radical Democratic Politics* (London: Verso, 1985), especially chapter 3, 114–27. Laclau and Mouffe also have something to say about Althusser's use of language and make reference to Wittgenstein (105–14). But this is all in the context of an attempt to demonstrate that there are no extradiscursive or nondiscursive entities. I regard this view as extremely dangerous, if only because in the hands of others it too often becomes a warrant for reducing meaning to language. This is, of course, the opposite of what is intended, but the trouble is that it is impossible to control the linguistic connotations of the term "discourse" and its derivatives. It is therefore

And it is of the utmost importance to say precisely—as precisely as possible—what is wrong with this. It is not that we do not discover whether propositions are true or false by comparing them with the facts. Of course we do, or of course we do a great deal of the time for a mass of mundane and not-so-mundane factual propositions. It is that what such propositions *mean*, what they *signify*, cannot be determined in this way. Thus, I can discover whether the proposition "The rate of profit in the U.S. economy has fallen continuously in the last five years" is *true* or not by comparing it with the facts as (hopefully) revealed by U.S. national-accounts data. But what such a proposition *means* depends on a host of factors, including: who said it; when and where they said it (It is likely to mean one thing if said in a meeting of the U.S. Department of Commerce and quite another thing if said in a meeting of a radical branch of the AFL-CIO); why they said it; what else they said; and so on.

In short, then, it is highly likely, indeed almost certain, that if Marxists do not, as it were, go to the root of the Althusserian "problematic" (to use its own term), then the attempt to maintain some form of Marxist realism when the full-blown conception has been abandoned will come to little more than a full-scale collapse into positivism. And this, I believe, is what has happened to Marxist realism since the death of Althusserianism, particularly in so-called analytical Marxism.[78] For this form of Marxist realism

---

far better, and far simpler, to say that the realm of meaning incorporates, but is not exhausted by, the realm of language.

78. It would be specious to attempt to demonstrate in one footnote a case that requires a book in itself. Therefore I will restrict myself to two assertions and some references. The assertions are that (1) *whenever someone seeks to demonstrate the worth or validity of Marxism by immediate and direct reference to its "explanatory power" or some such notion* (i.e., by immediate and direct exemplification of Marxism's explaining something in the world) *she or he has already begged the most important philosophical questions*. These are, as I have already said, about what Marx chose to explain and why he chose to explain it. Moreover, (2) *beginning disquisitions on Marx's "method" in this way is also an almost infallible sign that somebody has capitulated to positivism* (much *more* of a sign of this in fact than an allegiance to methodological individualism rather than holism, or to empirically measurable magnitudes rather than "deep structures," or any of the other more conventional criteria that are adduced in polemical debates over positivism).

For some typical failures to problematize either the object of study or the motive for study in Marxist social science, see, for example, E. Olin Wright, A. Levine, and E. Sober, eds., *Reconstructing Marxism: Essays on Explanation and the Theory of History* (London: Verso, 1992), and J. Elster, *An Introduction to Karl Marx* (Cambridge: Cambridge University Press, 1986), and his *Making Sense of Marx* (Cambridge: Cambridge University Press, 1985). See also J. F. Roemer, *Analytical Foundations of Marxian Economic Theory* (Cambridge: Cambridge University Press, 1981); G. A. Cohen, *History, Labour, and Freedom: Themes from Marx* (Oxford: Clarendon, 1988); and E. Olin Wright, ed., *The Debate on Classes* (London: Verso,

essentially defends Marxism as providing "better explanations" of a range of social and economic facts in the world (a better account of what *causes* these facts) than competing explanations. But in no case is any critical attention given to such questions as how the facts to be explained are chosen or selected, and the precise epistemological status of the "causes" or "explanations" adduced (i.e., whether these are seen as real attributes or characteristics of the social world or as cognitive frames of reference of observers)[79]

In other words, the full-blown Althusserian account of these two questions having been abandoned or found to be seriously flawed, contemporary Marxist realism simply deals with these issues by ignoring them or fudging them in a variety of ways. And this is surely a step backward, even in comparison with the Althusserian moment, for confronting the deep epistemological questions and failing, no matter how badly, is surely better than not confronting them at all.

However, the full demonstration of all this must await further work on post-Althusserian Marxist realism, and is in any case beyond the strict scope of this book, which is concerned with Marxist realism in its most full-blown and self-confident forms. But to repeat, what *is* of relevance to the leading themes of this work is my contention that the Althusserian moment

---

1989). For a brilliant, pioneering, and still too-much-ignored discussion of the issues that *all* the above texts overlook, see Hugh Stretton, *The Political Sciences* (London: Routledge and Kegan Paul, 1969), and the much less brilliant attempt in my *Karl Marx*, especially chapter 6 and conclusion. See also my attempt at a "Strettonite" analysis of a particular academic debate, "Politics, Method, and Evidence in the 'Kenya Debate,'" in H. Bernstein and B. K. Campbell, eds., *Contradictions of Accumulation in Africa* (Beverly Hills: Russell Sage, 1985), 115–49.

I do not wish to be misunderstood. The books by Wright, Elster, Roemer, Cohen, and the others are not bad books. Indeed, most of them are extremely good books; Elster, in particular, presents a view of what is of lasting worth in Marx that is very close to my own. It is simply that as accounts of what is definitive of the Marxist point of view they all begin in the wrong place, both logically and epistemologically. For example, in his well-known concluding chapter to *An Introduction to Karl Marx* ("What Is Living and What Is Dead in the Philosophy of Marx?"), Jon Elster ends by noting that "the sheer vitality of Marx's thinking makes it impossible to think of him as anything but alive. His endless curiosity, vast culture, burning commitment, and brilliant intellect combined to create a mind with whom we can still communicate across the century that has passed." And, he adds, "Marx's goals were generous and liberating: self-realization for the individual, equality among individuals" (199–200). All this is absolutely right, but it is the place to *start*, logically and epistemologically, as well as in exposition, not the place to end. Where did Marx *get* his "burning commitment," his value goals, and what were their effects both on what he studied and on how he studied it? Stretton's book explains brilliantly why these *are* the questions with which to begin.

79. See, for example, Daniel Little, *The Scientific Marx* (Minneapolis: University of Minnesota Press, 1986), who hovers incoherently somewhere between these two alternatives without seeming to realize that he is doing so. See, for example, the very confused discussion of Marx's "Abstractive Method," chapter 4, 101–6.

has never been adequately confronted by Marxists—not by its proponents or former proponents, not by its most violent opponents at the time or since. And one result of the failure to confront that moment deeply enough is that its deepest misconceptions and confusions live on, even in modern forms of realism that claim to have transcended it.

4

An Alternative Conception
of Language

Introduction

Having argued that Marxism is not a science and having examined the various political and psychological advantages that have accrued to Marxists, since Marx himself, from the belief that it is, I will shortly present an alternative picture of Marxism as a "point of view." It is implicit in what has been said to this point, and needs now to be made explicit, that while this conception of Marxism has, in my view, many advantages over the scientific conception, it also has a major disadvantage. Quite simply, this is that it takes away the psychological and political comfort of the belief that Marxism is undergirded by any scientifically guaranteed certainties, whether these be certainties about the future of capitalism (as against the views of non-Marxists) or about the necessity or inevitability of socialism.

I shall argue that Marxists do not possess, and indeed have never possessed, any privileged means of foreseeing the future of capitalism as a form of economy and society; it is even doubtful if they have any better understanding of its development trends than other well-informed observers (such as Wall Street analysts or *Financial Times* journalists). I shall also argue that the traditional Marxist view that capitalism is inherently exploitative and ought, on these grounds, to be abolished is not one whit more scientific than the view that sees the "free-enterprise system" as the most dynamic form of economy yet discovered, one that has improved the material welfare of a considerable section of the human race more significantly than any other form of economy and that ought, therefore, to be lauded, defended, and extended to the rest of humanity as quickly as possible.

Marxists have no warrant, I shall argue, for regarding such views as "ideo-logical" (at least where "ideological" means "false"), let alone as any species of "false consciousness." Nor do they have any warrant for regarding the more commonly encountered view that "this system may not be perfect but it is better than anything else" as false consciousness.

None of this leads to the conclusion, though, that Marxists simply have to accept such views, or that they cannot criticize them or argue against them. It simply means that before criticizing them or arguing against them Marxists must first acknowledge such views as legitimate, and as fair, hon-est, and perfectly valid accounts of what one sees if one looks at capitalism from a certain perspective. In the account which I shall present in later chapters, the task of Marxists is to get people to change their point of view on capitalism. That, as one might expect, involves moving them from the position that they currently occupy (and from which they see what they see) to a Marxist position from which they will be able to see other things about capitalism that they cannot currently see. The most that Marxists might be able to claim, I will suggest, is that from the Marxist perspective it is possible to explain why others hold the point of view that they do about capitalism, but that it is not possible until one has held the Marxist point of view, to explain why Marxists see what they see in capitalism.

This does not mean, however, that once having held the Marxist point of view one cannot abandon it and move elsewhere. The large number of conservative or reactionary former Marxists in the world is enough, in itself, to invalidate such a claim. It only means that having occupied the Marxist position one understands it in a way in which one cannot understand it if one has never occupied it. The reason for this explanatory imbalance be-tween Marxist and non-Marxist views of capitalism is simply that most people do not become Marxists until they are young adults (at least), so that they will normally have held non-Marxist views of capitalist economies and societies before they come to hold Marxist ones. It is, however, alto-gether rarer (although not entirely unknown) for persons to hold Marxist views of the world in their youth and non-Marxist ones in their adult life. Hence most Marxists know what it is like to be a non-Marxist, whereas most non-Marxists—as against ex-Marxists—do not know what it is like to be a Marxist.

Finally, I shall argue in the following chapters that there is no warrant for believing that socialism is a necessary or inevitable outcome of the con-tradictions of capitalism. Indeed there is as much, if not more, plausibility in the view that the world's currently socialist societies will have a capitalist future as there is in the view that the world's currently capitalist societies will have a socialist future. The most that can be said, I shall argue, is that when things are looked at from a Marxist point of view, socialism may be a desirable and possible development of capitalism. However, the experience of the actually existing socialist societies has shown, conclusively I think, that some traditional Marxist conceptions of socialism and communism are not merely flawed but so flawed as to be unrealizable in any currently conceivable form of human society. This being the case, the choice between capitalism and socialism is a much more complex and indeterminate matter than Marxists have usually conceived it to be. I think, for example, that if the world does turn out to have a socialist future, that future will not, contrary to traditional expectations, be one in which all forms of inequality, or of economic competition, or of governmental power have been abolished. And if that is the case, then socialism's desirability vis-à-vis capitalism will need to be, and will be, assessed by rather different criteria than those that have predominated (at least until very recently) in the Marxist literature.

Language

However, before I proceed to the detailed presentation of Marxism as a point of view, and as a prolegomenon to doing so, I must say something explicit about the conception of language underlying the thesis that I shall develop. This conception takes it as axiomatic that language (just like science, or ideology, or modes of production, as discussed earlier) is for many purposes far better conceived as a *practice* than as an *object*. In particular, conceiving language as a practice has the considerable merit that it is not thereby conceived as a prison of pregiven meanings that determine the limits of what is thinkable and sayable.

It has been a hallmark of linguistics, and in particular of structuralist linguistics since Saussure, to treat language as a system of "significations" in which arbitrarily developed signs are given their meanings by their place in a total system of signs. So far as words are concerned, their meanings are, in this conception, those found in any standard dictionary of the language in question, and they constitute the total stock of meanings available to any speaker of that language. Such speakers may combine words in a huge number of ways (ways specified by the system of possible meaning combinations in the language), but there is a limit to what they can think or say given by this stock of available meanings.[1]

Both structural linguistics and modern linguistics in general arrive at this notion of pregiven meanings in language by making a strict distinction between what is commonly termed the *semantics* and *pragmatics* of language. Broadly speaking, the former is its stock of meanings given in the lexicographical or dictionary definitions of its words. Its pragmatics, however, is the whole *pattern of use* of words in that language, which pattern of use may produce a much wider range of meaning both for individual words and for any combination of words than is found in their semantics.[2]

An example may make this clearer. Let us imagine two scenarios with one variable change. In both cases we must imagine two people walking together through a rather run-down area of an inner city.

First Scenario (The two people are acquaintances or relative strangers, out for a walk from a business meeting.)

1. Ferdinand de Saussure, *Course in General Linguistics,* trans. Wade Baskin, ed. Charles Bally and Albert Sechehaye, with Albert Reidlinger (London: Peter Owen, 1960), especially part 1, chapters 1 and 3, and part 2, chapters 1–3.
2. On the pragmatics/semantics distinction, see Charles Morris, "Foundations of the Theory of Signs," in *Foundations of the Unity of Science: Towards an International Encyclopedia of Unified Science,* ed. O. Neurath, R. Carnap, and C. Morris (Chicago: University of Chicago Press, 1955), 1:73–137; see also the discussion in Pitkin, *Wittgenstein and Justice,* 80–85. For important critiques of Saussurian linguistics, see Roy Harris, *Reading Saussure: A Critical Commentary on the "Cours de linguistique générale"* (London: Duckworth, 1987), especially chapter 3, 219–37. See also Raymond Williams, "Marxism, Structuralism, and Literary Analysis," *New Left Review,* no. 129 (September–October 1981); Terry Eagleton, "Wittgenstein's Friends," *New Left Review,* no. 135 (September 1982); and, above all, V. N. Volosinov, *Marxism and the Philosophy of Language* (Cambridge, Mass.: Harvard University Press, 1973), especially part 2, chapter 2. Volosinov's pathbreaking work is, in essence, an appreciation and critique of Saussurian linguistics from a Marxist perspective. Originally published in 1929, it was intended as a counterweight to the first French edition of the *Cours,* which had quickly become an important influence upon linguistics in Russia. I came across it relatively late in this study. Had I discovered it earlier, it might have saved me a great deal of work and agonized journeying. Finding it was both heartening and depressing. Heartening, in that for the first time I found a forerunner of the ideas developed in this book in a text that situates itself firmly and unself-consciously in the Marxist tradition. Depressing, however, in that I was forced once again to reflect on the intellectual damage done to that tradition by Stalinist philistinism and dogmatism and the time that it has taken for Marxist intellectual work to truly recover from the Stalinist closure. Certainly if one wants an index of the intellectual decline of Marxism in the twentieth century, one need only compare *Marxism and the Philosophy of Language* with Maurice Cornforth's *Marxism and the Linguistic Philosophy* (London: Lawrence and Wishart, 1965). Published thirty-six years after Volosinov's text, it is still, intellectually, light years behind it.

A—"I don't like this part of town."

B—"Oh, I don't know. I rather like these old Victorian terraces, though admittedly these are not in very good condition."

Second Scenario (The two people are good and old friends, and one of them—A—was physically assaulted in the area only a few weeks ago. His friend knows this.)

A—"I don't like this part of town."

B—"I know, don't worry. We'll be all right."

In terms of the distinction outlined above, we can say that in the first scenario B is responding to the *semantics* of the sentence "I don't like this part of town." As only a recent acquaintance of A, he may well be guessing at what precisely the sentence is referring to, but the immediately surrounding architecture is a good guess (he might have asked "What do you mean?" rather than guessed), and A would no doubt correct him if he had guessed wrongly.

In the second scenario, however, B, as a close friend, is responding to the *pragmatics* of the sentence "I don't like this part of town." He is using some highly specific information about the *context* in which the sentence is spoken (knowledge both of the speaker's personal history and of the significance of the place in which he is speaking) to take its meaning to be something like "I'm nervous" or even "I'm frightened" or "I'm scared." Now of course no dictionary of the English language would reveal the meaning of the sentence "I don't like this part of town" to be "I'm frightened." This would be so no matter how closely one scrutinized the definitions of, for example, the verbs "to be" or "to like," the negative "not," or the nouns "part" or "town," and no matter how encyclopedic the dictionary one consulted. Nevertheless, in the context of this second scenario, the sentence "I don't like this part of town" *did* mean "I'm frightened"—that was its meaning.

Because consideration of context (in the most ramified sense—historical, interpersonal, geographical, psychological, emotional) in speech acts does complicate meaning in language so enormously, professional linguists, especially those seeking structures or patterns of meaning in language, have generally opted to assign pragmatics a very secondary place in the analysis of language. They have done this by making an absolute methodological distinction between the meaning of words and their use. As a result, most modern linguists would deal with the example above by saying that the words in the sentence "I don't like this part of town" have a range of meanings (given lexicographically), and so, therefore, does the sentence that these words compose. A negative appraisal of some houses while one is walking past them is, allowing for some looseness of reference, one such meaning. However, although, as scenario 2 shows, the sentence "I don't like this part of town" may be *used* to mean "I'm frightened," in some very specific (and relatively rare) sets of circumstances, that usage is, on this view, no part of its meaning, no part of its semantics, strictly conceived.

It is a hallmark of Wittgenstein's later philosophy that it is based, implicitly and explicitly, on a rejection of this distinction between semantics and pragmatics on the grounds that the distinction leads to a theory of meaning in language that is wholly arbitrary. For it insists on a distinction that certainly makes things easier for linguists (by assigning a myriad of complexities to limbo), but that obscures a fundamental feature of human language—that it is both a practice and a practice among, and within, other practices.[3]

By this I mean that human beings do not merely speak (and think) or write, they also walk and talk (agitatedly or calmly), make facial expressions or are determinedly "deadpan," assault and get assaulted, love and are loved, hate and are hated, move from one place to another, have a personal and familial history, and so on. Thus the meaning of what they say (and think, and write) is deeply affected by all these other practices. In other words, the later Wittgenstein's philosophy of language insists repeatedly that *meaning in language is not just a matter of language* but of "language used in context" or "language used in circumstances." This is the deepest implication of his famous assertion that "the meaning of a word is its use in the language," which not only denies any hard-and-fast semantics/pragmatics distinction but that in fact subordinates semantics to pragmatics. For in Wittgenstein's view the lexicographical meaning of words changes (slowly) through (usually very slow) changes in their pragmatics of use, that is, by words being used in different ways in changed contexts. The most common, and certainly the most important, way in which this happens is by the metaphorical and/or analogical extension or projection of the meanings of words.[4]

3. See Garth Hallett, *Wittgenstein's Definition of Meaning as Use* (New York: Fordham University Press, 1967), especially 156–59, and Pitkin, *Wittgenstein and Justice*, 80–85.

4. See Gill, *Wittgenstein and Metaphor*, especially 153–58; Pitkin, *Wittgenstein and Justice*, 49, 58, 61–63, 149; and Cavell, *The Claim of Reason*, 180–90.

It is this theory of meaning on which the whole of what follows is based, and its implication is that the meaning of words, or (therefore) of sentences, is not rigidly fixed or determined for all time and for all language users by "structural relations" or by anything else. On the contrary, the meaning of all words is a matter of their context(s) of use, and the greater the variety of its contexts of use the greater the play or variability in the meaning of a word. This play or variability of meaning may be employed by the users of any language (especially, perhaps, the most creative and inventive of such users) to *create* new meanings or shades of meaning.

Once again, though, it is easier to bring out the meaning and importance of this conception of language-as-a-practice through a specific example. I will therefore now examine Marx's discussion of the relationship between "abstract" and "concrete" concepts in his oft-quoted 1857 Introduction to the *Grundrisse*. Many Marxists have spent much time and energy trying to explicate and unravel the complexities of this text,[5] but I will concentrate particularly on Rafael Echevarria's analysis.[6] For his discussion has the great merit, from my perspective, of trying to clarify Marx's views on abstraction while remaining trapped in the very same misconceptions about language found in the text that it is supposedly clarifying.

Echevarria begins by noting, quite rightly, that there is a central ambiguity in Marx's discussion of abstraction in the 1857 Introduction. For a number of concepts, such as "population," "production," and "labour," are considered by Marx as "concrete totalities," as apparent "concrete" starting points of his critique of political economy. They are all quickly rejected, however, on the grounds that they are, in reality, only "abstractions" that are themselves merely the product of particular "concrete determinations." Marx does not resolve this dilemma in the 1857 Introduction, and Echevarria suggests that throughout the period from 1857 to 1859 he continued to be obsessed with the question of a correct conceptual starting point for his

5. See, for example, L. Harris, "The Science of the Economy"; Martin Nicolaus, Foreword to Karl Marx, *Grundrisse: Foundations of the Critique of Political Economy* (Harmondsworth: Penguin, 1973); A. Sayer, "Abstraction: A Realist Interpretation"; and D. Sayer, *Marx's Method* (Brighton: Harvester, 1979). See also D. H. Ruben, *Marxism and Materialism* (Brighton: Harvester, 1977); most of the contributions to J. Mepham and D. H. Ruben, eds., *Issues in Marxist Philosophy*, 3 vols. (Brighton: Harvester, 1979); and Keat and Urry, *Social Theory as Science*. See also the entry by Roy Bhaskar, "Realism," in *A Dictionary of Marxist Thought*, ed. L. Harris, V. G. Kiernan, and R. Miliband (Oxford: Basil Blackwell, 1983), 407–9, which summarizes and expresses what is probably now the dominant view of Marx's epistemology, certainly in the English-speaking world.

6. Rafael Echevarria, "Critique of Marx's 1857 Introduction," *Economy and Society* 7, no. 4 (November 1978): 340–60.

critique, moving gradually from "labour" to "value" and finally to "the commodity." (The latter formed the starting point of both analysis and exposition in what became the first volume of *Capital*.)

What is interesting, however, is how Echevarria interprets this movement, an interpretation that, being based on a most careful analysis of a number of Marx's texts on political economy written between 1857 and 1859, does capture the problem well, and captures it as Marx himself thought it through. The slow change that took place between 1857 and 1859 in Marx's understanding of the correct conceptual starting point for his critique of political economy is perhaps best captured diagrammatically (Diagram 1).

Diagram 1. Marx: Abstraction and the Concrete, 1857–59

1857 (Introduction to *Grundrisse*)	1859
"Concrete totality"—"population" only an "apparent" not "real" starting point because a "simple abstraction"—the product of many "concrete determinations"	"Concrete totality" (e.g., population) a simple abstraction, the product of many "concrete determinations"

f   e

o   x

r   a

m

p

l

e

f   e

o   x

r   a

m

p

l

e

"labour," "production," "consumption"—but these themselves are abstractions	"labour," "production," "consumption," *and* "value"— *but* these themselves are abstractions
to be analyzed and explained by _____?	to be analyzed and explained by THE COMMODITY—a "simple concrete"—the real starting point.

The problem here may appear obvious from the diagram alone. It centers on the criterion, or criteria, that Echevarria and Marx are using to distinguish "abstract" from "concrete" concepts. For example, according to

Echevarria, by 1859 Marx had ended his search for a correct starting point of his analysis with "the commodity," which could act as such a starting point because it was, according to Echevarria, a "simple concrete" and therefore not an "abstraction" like the concrete totalities ("population," etc.) previously rejected.[7] And he quotes Marx's own description of the commodity as "the simplest economic concretum" (in his *Notes on Adolph Wagner*) in support of this view.[8] But at the same time Echevarria is forced to admit that other interpreters of Marx have seen the commodity as *itself* an "abstraction," as itself a product of "concrete determinations." For example, "the commodity in general," which opens Marx's analysis in the first volume of *Capital*, can itself be regarded as the product of the multifarious forms of concrete labor, from which Marx abstracts in producing the concepts of "abstract labour" and the "commodity in general."[9]

The reason that Echevarria's and Marx's stopping point (the commodity—the stopping point that is the supposedly correct starting point) appears so arbitrary, even to a somewhat worried Echevarria, is of course that *any stopping point* on this conceptual merry-go-round is arbitrary. For any concept may be regarded as, or treated as, abstract from some point of view, and any concept may, simultaneously, be regarded or treated as concrete from some other point of view. Similarly, any thing or object in the world may be treated as simple from some perspective and as complex or composite from another.

Is "population" a concrete concept or an abstraction? Well, you may be tempted to give one answer to this question if you are (for example) pushing your way through the crowded streets of Calcutta and quite another if you are trying to work out a statistical formula for the rate of growth of a human population with a precisely known age and fertility structure and a high and precisely known epidemiology of infant mortality. Is "society" an abstraction? We are tempted to think that it is, and to contrast it with the concrete reality of individual persons. But our concept of a person is by no means coterminous with that of his or her physical body. It also includes abstractions like his or her personality, disposition, energy level, possessiveness, and so on.[10]

So is "the commodity" an abstraction or a "concretum"? Well, this shirt certainly seems concrete enough as I pull it off and note that its collar is

7. Ibid., 354.
8. Ibid., 355.
9. Ibid., 357.
10. Pitkin, *Wittgenstein and Justice*, 195.

dirty. But at the same time I can think of it as the embodiment of a given amount of human labor, as one of millions of commodities produced under capitalist relations of production, as the equivalent of a certain sum or sums of money (its price of production, sales price, etc). We are apt to distinguish abstract from realist or representational painting. But even the most impeccably realist portrait or landscape or still life is as much an abstraction from reality as any of Picasso's work; anyone doubting this should try to cuddle one of Rembrandt's nudes, or eat one of Cézanne's apples, or ride one of Lanseer's horses.

In short, even if we accept the formulation that everything we are dealing with here is "in thought," so that Marx's "concrete" is the "concrete in thought,"[11] it is still true that whether one thinks or conceives of something as abstract or concrete depends crucially on what one conceives oneself *doing* with it. I may think of Picasso's *Guernica* as abstract as I picture its forms in my mind's eye, but I am apt to think of it as rather concrete if I conceive myself trying to steal it! (Another reminder that language is a practice among other practices.)

The matter is even clearer in the case of "simple" and "complex" (or "composite"), and again there are interesting parellels in the history of empiricism. At the time when he was most influenced by British empiricism and logical positivism, Wittgenstein held in the *Tractatus* that there had to be "absolute simples," absolutely simple entities in the world to which all basic "elementary propositions" referred. It is not clear whether, in Wittgenstein's case, these "absolute simples" were sense-data entities, but he certainly held that all the ordinary descriptive propositions in language that were true had to be logically analyzable into "elementary propositions" that "pictured" "atomic facts" (the paradigm of such a proposition being "This is/is not the case"). He also held that, at a still deeper level of logical analysis, there had (logically *had*) to be "absolute simples" in the world, which in their turn composed the various "states of affairs" pictured in the elementary propositions. These entities were absolutely simple because they could not be analyzed into anything simpler (i.e., they were "absolutely simple" objects to which "completely analysed" names corresponded).[12]

---

11. A point much belabored by Althusser; see, for example, *RC*, 73, 108–9, 125, 156, and 186–92.

12. See Wittgenstein, *Tractatus Logico-Philosophicus*, remarks 2.02, 3.2, 3.201, 3.202, and 3.21–3.24. A good commentary on this aspect of Wittgenstein's early philosophy can be found in Kenny, *Wittgenstein*, especially chapter 5, 72–102; see also K. T. Fann, *Wittgenstein's Conception of Philosophy* (Oxford: Basil Blackwell, 1969), chapter 1.

This was one of many philosophical beliefs that Wittgenstein gradually abandoned. One might say that he came to the conclusion that the notion of an "absolute simple" was itself absolutely simple! And, as always, he says why he abandoned this notion in a very clear and humorous way. Remark 47 of the *Philosophical Investigations* reads:

> But what are the simple constituent parts of which reality is composed? What are the simple constituent parts of a chair? The bits of wood of which it is made? Or the molecules or the atoms?—"Simple" means: not composite. And here the point is: in what sense "composite"? It makes no sense to speak absolutely of "the simple parts of a chair." . . . If I tell someone without further explanation: "What I see before me now is composite—he will have the right to ask: "What do you mean by composite? For there are all sorts of things that can mean!"—The question "Is what you see composite?" makes good sense if it is established what kind of complexity—that is, which particular use of the word—is in question. If it had been laid down that the visual image of a tree was also to be called "composite," if one saw not just a single trunk, but also branches, then the question "Is the visual image of the tree simple or composite?" and the question "What are its simple component parts?" would have a clear sense, clear use. And of course the answer to the second question is not "The branches" (that would be an answer to the *grammatical* question "What are here called 'simple component parts'?") but rather a description of the individual branches.
>
> But isn't a chessboard, for instance, obviously, and absolutely, composite?—You are probably thinking of the composition out of thirty-two white and thirty-two black squares. But could we not also say, for instance, that it was composed of the colours black and white and the schema of squares? And if there are quite different ways of looking at it, do you still want to say that the chessboard is absolutely "composite?"—Asking "Is this object composite?" *outside* a particular language-game is like what a boy once did, who had to say whether the verbs in certain sentences were in the active or passive voice, and who racked his brains over the question whether the verb "to sleep" meant something active or passive.
>
> We use the word "composite" (and therefore the word "simple") in an enormous number of different and differently related ways. (Is the colour of a square on a chessboard simple, or does it consist of pure white and pure yellow? And is white simple, or does it consist

of the colours of the rainbow? Is this length of 2cm. simple, or does it consist of two parts each of 1cm. long? But why not of one bit 3cm. long and one bit 1cm. long measured in the opposite direction?) To the *philosophical* question: "Is the visual image of this tree composite and what are its component parts?" the correct answer is "That depends on what you understand by 'composite.'" (And that is of course not an answer but a rejection of the question.)

What Wittgenstein says here about the question "Is this object composite?" is equally applicable to such questions as "Is this object simple?" (or complex) or "Is this concept abstract?" (or concrete). For all these questions have only two possible answers. One is a list of examples of all the "enormous number of different and differently related ways" in which we use the adjectives "simple," "complex," "abstract," "concrete" (and their associated noun and verb forms); the second is the specification of a rule for using these words in a particular case for a particular purpose.

But the important point to note is that neither Marx nor Echevarria do either of these things in their discussions of abstraction and concreteness. That is, they are not content simply to make use of these words in the various and subtly different ways in which they can be used, but neither do they come out and specify a definitional rule of the form "I am using the word 'abstraction' here to mean . . ." or "When I use the word 'abstraction' I intend it to refer to . . ." together with a stated analytical purpose that this definition is meant to serve. And the reason why they do neither of these things is that both are in the grip of the same picture of language. (In fact, of course, it is Marx who is in the grip of this picture and Echevarria who simply reproduces it.) The essence of the picture holding them in thrall is that simplicity and complexity are *attributes or characteristics of the world* that are simply "reflected" in language, and that "abstractness" and "concreteness" are similarly *attributes or characteristics of concepts* per se, attributes or characteristics of which their users simply "take advantage" when they use them. But if Wittgenstein's alternative picture of languge is right, and I think that it is, then neither of these propositions is adequate, because both understate the creative role of language users in *deciding* what is simple and what complex, what is abstract and what concrete.

However, while language provides freedom for its users to decide and determine what is simple and what is complex, what is abstract and what

is concrete, this freedom is by no means total. It is freedom within limits.[13]
Thus almost anything can be looked on as simple from some point of view,
and almost anything can be seen as complex. (I thought that it would be a
simple matter to write this book, but now I see that it is more complex!)
But not everything can be seen as abstract. For example, somebody steps
on my toe and I yell "Ow! That was very abstract!" Here I have stepped
outside any language game playable in English with the word "abstract."
And while probably rather more things can be seen as concrete, it would
probably only be under very extraordinary circumstances that having lis-
tened to a performance of Bach's double violin concerto I would describe
that performance as "very concrete."

But the major constraint on the use of the words "abstract" and "concrete," and the major constraint on the use of the words "simple" and
"complex" (or "composite"), is that nearly all the language games in which
they are used have the rule that one must state *in what respect or for what
purpose* something is being treated as abstract or concrete, simple or complex. Moreover, this same rule applies to a number of other crucial Marxist
words ("material" and "ideal," "apparent" and "real," "equal" and "unequal") and to a number of crucial analytical terms in social science generally
("same" and "different," "exact" and "vague," "general" and "particular,"
"better" and "worse," etc.). One can satisfy this rule either by an explicit
definition or by using the words in a context (of surrounding sentences,
paragraphs, etc.) that "makes it clear" in what respect or for what purpose
something is being treated as abstract or concrete, simple or complex, the
same or different, particular or general.

Thus, "By capitalism I mean simply a market economy" is a perfectly
acceptable definition of capitalism in a particular context. It does not imply
that, in general, one thinks that there is anything simple about a market
economy, or indeed that one thinks that *all* there is to capitalism is a market
economy. The sentence "Patriarchy and class exploitation are very different
forms of oppression" makes perfect sense in a certain context. It is not
in contradiction with the sentence "From the point of view of a woman
experiencing sexual harassment at work, patriarchy and class exploitation
come to much the same thing" because the criteria of "sameness" and "difference" being applied are different in the two cases.[14]

The point of all these examples is to stress that in the use of language as

13. This aspect of Wittgenstein's later philosophy is well discussed in Cavell, *The Claim of
Reason*, chapter 8, and in Pitkin, *Wittgenstein and Justice*, 60–65.
14. In remark 226 of the *Philosophical Investigations* Wittgenstein says:

much as in every other social practice we must postulate a role for active subjects who employ language for their own purposes. Such subjects cannot use language in any way they want (in the sense of trying to realize Humpty Dumpty's project of making words mean "just what I choose [them] to mean"). But if Wittgenstein is right this is a rather silly postulate in any case because a totally "private language" is neither empirically possible nor even conceptually coherent.[15] Human beings can, however, say what they want to say; very occasionally, they can say (and think) new things that nobody has thought before, and they can stretch, develop, or project their language (usually by metaphor or analogy) to allow them to say and think them.

I have argued elsewhere that one of the weaknesses of classical Marxism was that Marx, having developed a philosophy of praxis in his youth, failed to develop a theory of language and of language use to embody the central insights of that philosophy. As a result, in later life both Marx himself and Engels fell back explicitly and implicitly into a conception of language that saw it as a simple mirror or reflector of the world, rather than as a tool that has to be actively used to appropriate the world in knowledge.[16] I also think that this was simply the linguistic analogue of that general movement toward a positivist conception of both knowledge and science that Marx underwent in later life, primarily, I believe, because of his long exposure to classical political economy and to the (generally implicit) positivist epistemology that it embodied.[17]

Suppose someone gets the series of numbers 1, 3, 5, 7 . . . by working out the series $2x+1$ squared. And now he asks himself: "But am I always doing the same thing, or something different every time?"

If from one day to the next you promise: "Tomorrow I will come and see you" are you doing the same thing every day or every day something different?

The point of both these examples, of course, is that they culminate in questions that cannot be answered until it is determined what *criteria* of sameness or difference are being applied. For until such criteria are adduced, it would make equal sense in both cases to say that "the same" thing was being done every time *and* that something "different" was being done every time/day. In other words, it makes no sense to speak of sameness or difference without specifying explicitly or implicitly (by context) the criteria of application of these words. See also *Philosophical Investigations*, remarks 215, 225, 254, 350.

15. See *Philosophical Investigations*, remarks 246–61 and 269–71; see also Kenny, *Wittgenstein*, chapter 10, and Rubinstein, *Marx and Wittgenstein*, especially chapters 1, 2, and 10. For more detailed analyses of Wittgenstein's "private language" thesis, see Saul A. Kripke, *Wittgenstein on Rules and Private Language* (Oxford: Basil Blackwell, 1982), and Colin McGinn, *Wittgenstein on Meaning* (Oxford: Basil Blackwell, 1984).

16. See my *Karl Marx*, chapter 6.

17. "Towards the end of his life Marx moved nearer to the positivism then so fashionable in intellectual circles. This tendency, begun in *Anti-Dühring* and continued by Engels in his

The whole discussion of abstraction and concreteness in the 1857 Introduction to the *Grundrisse* reviewed in this chapter seems to be a perfect example of Marx's falling back into this passive, reflective or positivist conception of language. And as the Echevarria article indicates, it is a falling back that has been reproduced over and over by many modern Marxist scholars following loyally in the footsteps of the master. This reflective conception of language is most especially a hallmark of those scholars smitten with the notion of Marxism as science and with the definitional conceptions of rigor that usually accompany this image of science.

But if the analysis of abstraction and concreteness that I have provided in this chapter has any validity, it makes nonsense of the notion that concepts, and the things or objects that they name/create, are somehow in and of themselves abstract or concrete (rather than being *treated* as such by an analyst or observer). More important, it also makes nonsense of the ontology erected on this conception, whereby a realm of more abstract entities (values, modes of production, etc.) somehow gives rise to or takes the form of appearance of a set of more concrete entities like prices of production, social formations, and the like. Or at any rate it makes nonsense of it insofar as one believes that this most abstract realm is something that is "revealed" by "analysis" rather than a picture that is painted and painted by a painter (Marx), for a certain purpose. Marx chose to treat labor values as "more abstract" than prices of production, just as a painter can choose to paint a background white and a foreground blue, but there is no doubt that it was Marx (and Ricardo, and a few other people) who created labor values. They certainly did this rather than "discovering" them through "analysis."

The crucial issue about labor values or modes of production is not therefore about what they are (to be answered by question-begging formulations like "real abstractions," "concrete abstractions," "the concrete-in-thought," etc.) but about what Marx *does* with them. In other words, these concepts, too, are best conceived not as theoretical things or objects but as *tools to be used.* And the crucial question therefore is, How does Marx use these tools? What propositions or sets of propositions about the world does he construct with them? I have tried to answer this question in my book *Karl*

Ludwig Feuerbach and *Dialectics of Nature,* reached its apogee in Soviet textbooks on dialectical materialism. It was this trend which presented Marxism as a philosophical world-view or *Weltanschauung* consisting of objective laws and particularly laws of the dialectical movement of matter taken in a metaphysical sense as the basic constituent of reality. This was obviously very different from the "unity of theory and practice" as exemplified in, for instance, the *Theses on Feuerbach"* (McLellan, *Karl Marx,* 423).

I agree with this well-known and conventional view, but I think that Marx's movement toward positivism began well before *Anti-Dühring.*

Marx and the Philosophy of Praxis, and I will not repeat that answer here. Suffice it to say that I think some of the propositions that he constructs with these concepts are true, some are false (especially those that make up his theory of surplus value and of labor exploitation), and yet others are subtly but deeply confused.[18] But the more important point in the context with which we are concerned here is that this conception of concepts, their conception as tools of explanatory practice, is both much more accurate generally and much more in tune with Marx's actual explanatory practices than the picture of conceptualization found in the 1857 Introduction.

This latter picture, having been painted by Marx on one of his less in-spired days, has, very unfortunately in my view, attained almost the same iconic status in Marxist scholarship as the 1859 *Preface to A Critique of Political Economy,* and it has been reproduced in a similarly uncritical way by a large number of modern Marxist scholars, of whom Echevarria is only one (see, for example, the quotation from Laurence Harris on pp. 29–30). It is a picture in which concepts appear as objects in a landscape made up of "abstractions" (shadowy figures in the background?) and "concrete realities" (garish figures in the foreground?), with the former in some kind of "causal" or "determinate" "relation" to the latter. So well is it painted that it has drawn the analytical gaze almost totally to its own shadowy and mysterious contours and not to the painter whose work it is and whose purposes it embodies and realizes, albeit rather poorly.[19]

Finally, two further points concerning Wittgenstein. The first may be introduced by a quotation:

> For there seemed to pertain to logic—a universal significance. Logic lay, it seemed, at the bottom of all the sciences.—For logical investi-gation explores the nature of all things. It seeks to see to the bottom of things and is not meant to concern itself whether what actually happens is this or that.—It takes its rise, not from an interest in the facts of nature, nor from a need to grasp causal connexions, but from an urge to understand the basis, or essence, of everything em-pirical. . . .
>
> We feel the need to penetrate phenomena. . . .

---

18. *Karl Marx,* chapter 4.

19. For more on this, see my "Modes of Production: Suggestions for a Fresh Start on an Exhausted Debate," *Canadian Journal of African Studies* 19, no. 1 (1985): 116–26.

But now it may come to look . . . as if our usual forms of expression were, essentially, unanalysed; as if there were something hidden in them that had to be brought to light. . . . This finds expression in questions as to the *essence* of language, of propositions, of thought.—For if we too in these investigations are trying to understand the essence of language—its functions, its structure—yet *this* is not what these questions have in view. For they see in the essence, not something that already lies open to view and that becomes surveyable by a rearrangement, but something that lies within, which we see when we look into the thing, and which an analysis digs out. (*Philosophical Investigations*, remarks 89–92)

This picture of logic, as a structure "at the bottom" of all things, and as a tool for "digging out" the essence of language by an analysis (an essence that would be revealed to be nothing but logic itself), is the picture that both the Viennese logical positivists and—in a slightly different way—Russell, Whitehead, and the logical empiricists of Edwardian England had of their endeavor. It was an endeavor with which Wittgenstein himself was deeply engaged in his early philosophy. In fact, the *Philosophical Investigations* can be viewed as Wittgenstein's definitive settling of accounts with this picture of language and of philosophy and as his brilliant and sustained attempt to say what is wrong with it—"deeply" wrong with it. But from our perspective two points only are of importance.

(1) This picture—of logic as an essence beneath the appearance of language, and as a tool for digging out that essence—was deeply influenced by the logical positivists' and logical empiricists' understandings of natural science, as the second sentence of the quotation above implies. And in the case of logical positivism, just as in the case of Marxism, the sciences of the molecular and submolecular world are the principal source of this picture of what a scientific analysis is.[20] Nor do I think that this terminology (of

20. See Otto Neurath, *Empiricism and Sociology*, especially chapter 9, the manifesto of the Vienna Circle *Wissenschaftliche Weltauffassung: Der Wiener Kreis*). It reads, in part: "The scientific world-conception is marked by a certain method, namely *logical analysis*. The aim of scientific effort is to reach the goal, unified science, by applying logical analysis to the empirical material. Since the meaning of every statement of science must be stateable by a reduction to a statement about the given, likewise the meaning of every concept, whatever branch of science it may belong to, must be stateable by step-wise reduction to other concepts, down to the concepts of the lowest level which refer directly to the given."
The same text states that "physics . . . in regard to precision and refinement of concepts . . . is far ahead of the other branches of science" (312). See, however, Kenny, *Wittgenstein*, chapter 9; Derek L. Phillips, *Wittgenstein and Scientific Knowledge* (London: Macmillan,

essence and appearance, of surface and depth, and of analysis as a digging below the surface) is by any means inappropriate to the practice of these molecular and submolecular sciences. I do think, however, that it is deeply inappropriate to a description of Marxism as an intellectual practice, as inappropriate as Wittgenstein thought it was when applied to the analysis of language.

More important, however, (2) the dominant analogy or metaphor that Wittgenstein employed in his own later analysis of language (an analogy designed, at least in part, to combat the imagery of the "digging out" of "essences") was that of a game. Wittgenstein likened language to a game or to a complex of games ("language games"). I do not want, and there is no need here, to discuss the myriad of issues and debates that have arisen around Wittgenstein's conception of language as a game.[21] But I do wish to bring out what I think was the major point or purpose of this analogy for him, for it is closely related to the central concerns of this chapter.

Wittgenstein likened language to a game to emphasize that it was a rule-bound activity. To speak a language you have to be in command of its grammatical and semantic rules (at least in the sense that you have to be able to obey them or satisfy them), just as to play a game you have to abide by its rules. But in human language, just as in human games, (1) knowing its rules does not in itself mean that you can play the game, and (2) all the rules are open to interpretation, with some of them allowing great latitude for interpretation.

The first point needs little exemplification. That I know and can state the rule for scoring a six in cricket (that the ball must be hit across the boundary line without bouncing on the playing area) does not mean that I can walk out at Lord's Cricket Ground and hit a six off a Caribbean fast bowler, or even that I can walk out onto a village green and hit a six off the bowling of the local blacksmith. Similarly, knowing the rules for conjugating all the 'er' verbs in French does not mean that I can hold a conversation in French.

The second point is more important but just as obvious. In baseball there is a rule that a run scored off a pitcher does not count against the pitcher's

1977), 31–34 and 33–39; Gill, *Wittgenstein and Metaphor*, 165–66; David Bloor, *Wittgenstein: A Social Theory of Knowledge* (London: Macmillan, 1983), chapter 3; Baker and Hacker, *Wittgenstein: Meaning and Understanding*, chapter 3; Hacker, *Insight and Illusion*, 167–69; and Pitkin, *Wittgenstein and Justice*, 39–49.

21. For Wittgenstein's language-game concept, see Kenny, *Wittgenstein*, chapter 9; Pitkin, *Wittgenstein and Justice*, 36–49; and Baker and Hacker, *Wittgenstein: Meaning and Understanding*, chapter 3. For a critical discussion, see A. C. Grayling, *Wittgenstein* (Oxford: Oxford University Press, 1988), chapter 3.

ERA (earned run average per game pitched) if the run resulted from a fielder's error. Thus, if a batter gets to first base on an error by a fielder and subsequently scores a run (i.e., crosses home plate) as a result of a hit made off the same pitcher by a teammate, this run does not count against the pitcher's ERA. Since the error statistics of fielders and the ERAs of pitchers are routinely used in negotiating players' contracts and salary levels, it will be seen that this rule can be of great material importance to professional baseball players. The very considerable latitude for interpretation comes in the determination of what exactly *is* an error. Everybody (players, spectators, officials) might agree that it is an error if a fielder fails to catch a ball hit softly and directly to him. But what if the ball is hit very hard somewhat to the side of the fielder and then bounces wildly as he tries to catch it? If the fielder misses the ball and the runner gets on base, is this an error or a legitimate base hit? The reader will not be surprised to learn that the official scorers, who call errors, are not infrequently confronted after the game by players disagreeing with an interpretation of this rule.

Similarly, the *Concise Oxford Dictionary* defines "abstract" as "separated from matter, practice, or particular examples." From this I might be able to formulate a rule for the use of the word "abstract" of the following form: "Only use the word 'abstract' when referring to something separated from matter, practice, or particular examples." But it is fairly clear, I think, that if this is a "rule" at all, it is one that leaves very considerable scope for its interpretation and application.

In short, then, Wittgenstein likens language to a game in an attempt to grasp, and to help others grasp, the way in which language allows for considerable individual adaptation and inventiveness in its use, but at the same time constrains that inventiveness sufficiently to allow human beings to communicate with each other clearly and unproblematically in a trillion different ways on every day of their lives. This homology or coexistence, indeed cofacilitation, of creativity and constraint is perhaps as difficult to grasp in the abstract as it is easy to accomplish concretely (in linguistic practice). I am not sure that the analogy of a game perfectly communicates this miracle,[22] or whether indeed any analogy could "perfectly" do so. For

---

22. The principal problem of the analogy of language with a game, and of different parts of forms of language with different types of games, is simply that (in English, at least) the word "game" carries inescapable connotations of unseriousness or even triviality, whereas the issues that Wittgenstein is trying to address through the use of the concept "language game" are profoundly serious. One may, moreover, "choose" to play a game or refuse to do so, and one may, without any desperate penalty, choose to stop playing a game at any point. However, we do not, as Wittgenstein himself stresses, "choose" to acquire language, and we equally

this combining of individual initiative and social constraint, of creativity amid discipline, is as much a miracle in language as it is a miracle in music (a closely related human practice with which Wittgenstein constantly compares and contrasts it).[23]

But it is nonetheless important that this miraculous duality of language be grasped, and in particular that Marxists grasp it, if their practice is to be reformed. For what Wittgenstein teaches us, essentially, is that language is a subtle, sinewy, and sensuous tool of our individual and collective ("species") purposes, and that it is probably the greatest of all human inventions or developments. It is most certainly not the plonking hulk of an entity that it appears in much modern Marxist theory and writing, any more than it is the tightly bounded logical grid to which the logical positivists tried to reduce it. And the reason that Marxists in particular need to understand how misconceived their view of language has frequently been is that if Marxism is indeed, as I shall argue, a point of view, then, conceptually, it is something of which people need to be persuaded or convinced. And both persuading and convincing require, as necessary but insufficient conditions, the capacity to write and speak clearly and movingly. For a point of view is, after all, a position to which one has to move people.

I believe that Marxists cannot write clearly and movingly—indeed, they can only write obscurely and boringly—within the picture of language to which they have been prey, but this is just part of a whole knot of problems that feed into each other. The view of language as an object, of concepts as objects, of language as a "mirror" or "reflection" of the real, of concepts as nouns or names, of definition as the drawing of conceptual "boundaries," and of boundary drawing as the only means of being "exact" or "rigorous"—all these things not only make many Marxists extremely bad writers, they are also part of an extremely profound confusion about what Marxism is, that is, about the kind of intellectual practice it is, about the kinds of things Marxists can and should *do*. Getting clear about how language works

---

cannot "choose" to cease using language. However, it is not clear to me what other analogy would be more helpful in presenting language as a *rule-bound activity.*

23. For Wittgenstein's comparisons of music and language, see the *Brown Book* (166–67), in Ludwig Wittgenstein, *The Blue and Brown Books: Preliminary Studies for the "Philosophical Investigations"* (Oxford: Basil Blackwell, 1958); see also *Philosophical Investigations*, remarks 341, 527–29, 531, and 536, and *Zettel* (Oxford: Basil Blackwell, 1967), remarks 157–65. Wittgenstein came from an extremely musical family, and his own love of music and musical accomplishments are well described in a number of sources, notably Rush Rhees, ed., *Recollections of Wittgenstein* (Oxford: Oxford University Press, 1984), 69–71, 111–12, 115, 135–36, 163, and 174, and Norman Malcolm, *Wittgenstein: A Memoir* (Oxford: Oxford University Press, 1958) 6 and 21.

is the indispensable key to unraveling this whole knot, and it is the principal reason why this chapter figures as a prelude to my attempted reconstruction of Marxism. For the aesthetics of Marxism is inextricable from its ontology. Marxists will write better prose only when they have a different view of writing as a practice in the world.

PART THREE

5

Marxism as a Point of View: Strengths and Limitations

Having set out the theory of language upon which all of what follows is based, I can now outline my conception of Marxism as a point of view. I will proceed in two stages. I will first take the analogy or metaphor of a "point of view" and unpack it by examining a number of its implications when we return it to the original language game from which it derives, that of visual perception. I will then examine the implications of the phrase when it is used metaphorically in regard to nonvisual forms of perception; here I will give particular attention to how the phrase's visual origins and connotations can cause confusion and obfuscation when it is employed metaphorically. In other words, in the second part of the analysis in this chapter I will examine how and why the metaphor or analogy of a point of view breaks down when it is pushed too far beyond its original visual home.

Visual Points of View

In *The Great American Novel*, Philip Roth wrote:

> Baseball was a game that looked different from every single seat in the ball park, and consequently could never be represented accurately unless one were able to put together into one picture what every single spectator in the park had seen simultaneously moment by moment throughout an entire afternoon: and that included those moments that in fact accounted for half the playing time if not more,

when there was no action whatsoever, those moments of waiting and hesitation, of readiness and recovery, moments in which everything ceased, including the noise of the crowd, but which were as inherent to the appeal of the game as the few climactic seconds when a batted ball sailed over the wall. . . .[1]

Note first that, as a matter of fact, one could not do what Roth postulates. One could not "put together into one picture what every single spectator in the park had seen simultaneously moment by moment throughout an entire afternoon." For example, suppose that all spectators were supplied with video cameras that they held on to their individual line of vision while sitting in their seats and with which they recorded the entire afternoon's proceedings on the field. The film director who wanted, for some reason, to "put together into one picture what every single spectator in the park had seen" would now have just two choices. She or he could simply run each of these videos in their entirety either simultaneously—on some thirty thousand screens—or sequentially in some arbitrarily selected order. In either case the result would be the same; one segment of the total show would be what each spectator saw, but the whole show (which would in any case be unwatchable either because it was too visually massive or because it would be several days long and exhaust the most zealous viewer) would not be what anybody saw.

Alternatively, the director could opt to cut these several miles of video-tape into a much shorter, watchable whole. But again this whole, though it might well capture important or memorable moments in the afternoon's events in visually compelling ways, would still not be the whole that was "what every single spectator in the park had seen simultaneously moment by moment." Note also that there is no other way of doing this. For example, placing a camera operator in a helium balloon suspended above the stadium (so that "all" of the crowd and "all" of the action can be recorded) would still not be the visual whole constituted of "what every single spectator" had seen. In fact it would be a whole that *nobody* in the ballpark had seen, except of course the camera operator in the balloon.

So in short, and fairly obviously, in the language game of visual perception that is its original home a "point of view" is *a point in space*, a point that has the characteristic of being occupiable by any number of people serially but by only one person at any one moment. This being the case, I

1. (Henry Holt and Co., 1991), 90.

can alter my visual point of view by physically moving myself to another point in space, but again I can only do this serially. I can only occupy one point of view at one time, and thus if I take up a new point of view I *simultaneously* give up the old point of view. And what is true of me is true of everybody. Everybody, every human being, can only occupy one visual point of view at one time. This is, in fact, a species limitation.

Technological developments made by human beings can overcome this species limitation, but only to a very limited extent. I could, for example, go to a baseball game and buy four seats, not one, and I could ensure that each of these seats was in a very different part of the park. I could then set up video cameras on three of the seats, and with the aid of a remote control I could activate them when the game started and run them throughout the proceedings. Meanwhile, I would be in the fourth seat with another camera recording what I could see from there. I could then go home and watch four different views of the game, and of each exciting or controversial incident. But even then, only one of these cameras would have recorded what I saw during the game itself. I still could not, even with the aid of video technology, view the game simultaneously from four different points of view while it occurred. And even if I could, I suspect that the species limitations of my visual perception and visual data processing would make this simultaneous "four-point" (or ten-point or hundred-point) view incomprehensible or useless to me.

But there is something else of which the language game of visual perception reminds us, something of philosophical importance and something that Roth is certainly gesturing at in the quotation above. For one of the ways in which one might be tempted to talk about a baseball game is as a thing, an object, which each spectator "saw" from his or her own different "point of view." But what Roth is clearly suggesting is that in some respects this would be an inaccurate way of talking. The baseball game is *not*, he is suggesting, a single thing that is seen ("visually described," if one wants) from thirty thousand different points of view—for there is no way of seeing or describing it while it is going on that is not from a point of view. And this turns out to be equally true of all the tricks that we might use to get a visual picture of "the whole thing." For each of them either involves a particular point of view presenting itself as the whole (for example, the "balloon" view) or involves an *a posteriori* construction (for example, the ten-day-long video show) that certainly includes what everybody saw but that, as a whole, does not add up to what anybody saw.

However, it would be equally misleading and inaccurate to say that there were thirty thousand different baseball games happening on that afternoon. For there was clearly only one (the Mets versus the Dodgers, say) that all the spectators were watching. They were all watching the same game. But the singular terminology here—"only one," "the same"—should not lead us to postulate that there is a single privileged description or point of view that, somehow, captures the object, the game, in a way that the other 29,999 views do not and against which all these other views should be measured for adequacy. This is not what the concept of "the same game" or "the whole game" means here. We can know that all these people were watching the same game from the facts. For example, the Dodgers got four runs in the fifth inning; the first of those runs resulted from a balk and a fielding error, and the second, third, and fourth runs came off a home run with two men on base. Everybody saw that. It could be seen from every point of view in the park, and everybody who was there during the fifth inning saw it happen. (Indeed, that everybody saw it is what *makes* it a fact.) It is facts like these that constitute the meaning of such phrases as "the same game." No privileged guarantee or guarantor of sameness is required here.

Similarly, everybody who was there on 7 July 1984 and stayed for the whole game would, if asked, say that they saw the whole game. And they would be likely to treat with extreme impatience (at least!) anybody who said that they did not see the whole game but only saw it from their point of view. If they were philosophically inclined they would tell such an operator that seeing a baseball game from a point of view is not contradictory with seeing the whole of it, for seeing things from points of view is in fact a species limitation of human beings. There is no view of the whole, or part, of anything that is not a view from a point of view. If they were not philosophically inclined they might give our philosophically minded objector a punch on the nose, especially if they happened to be supporters of the losing team.

Finally, it should be noted that in the case of a baseball game thinking about it as an object probably does not increase clarity about it at all. For when closely examined a baseball game is, like any other game (see chapter 4), a rule-bound collection or series of *activities*. These include the actions of the players on the field (doing such things as pitching, batting, running between the bases, fielding the ball, throwing a runner out, etc.) and the actions of the spectators (doing such things as entering the ballpark, sitting in their seats, talking about the game, cheering, booing, eating popcorn, etc.). In the case of the spectators, many of their activities could be said to be rule bound as well, though perhaps in a looser way than those of the players. Thus, many of the spectators may follow the permissive rule that "spectators may cheer when the team that they support scores a run." And clearly any spectator who cheers when the catcher takes his mask off or boos when a base runner sneezes might be said not to be following the rules for cheering and booing at baseball games. Rather less strainedly, he or she would be said not to "understand baseball," not to know its "meaning" as an activity or collection of activities.

The reason I stress this point is that the English language, among many others, allows us to treat any collection of rule-bound activities (and that they are bound by the same rules is of course what *makes* them a "collection" and gives them their meaning) as an object. Indeed, "it" often forces us to do so. Thus I began the preceding paragraph with the paradoxical proposition that "in the case of a baseball game thinking about it as an object probably does not increase clarity about it at all," where the two "its" seemed precisely to imply that a baseball game *is* an object. Similarly, the "it" in the sentence "Indeed, 'it' often forces us to do so" may seem to imply that language is an object, thus reintroducing a picture that I have just spent a chapter attempting to problematize.[2]

But it is important to problematize those formulations in our language that allow us to treat collections or series of activities as objects because doing so allows us to perceive some subtle, but immensely important, ways in which activities as things are different from physical objects as things. Or, more exactly, it allows us to understand the ways in which human perception of physical objects differs, as a practice or set of practices, from human perception of activities.

For example, it is as true of looking at an immobile physical object (think of a sculpture in an art gallery) as it is of looking at a set of activities that one can only view it from one point of view at a time. However, in the case of a physical object one can also do such things as walking all the way around it, going onto a balcony to see it from above, reaching out and touching it, even stroking it or feeling its outlines. And having done all of these things, or even some of them, one would, if asked, say that one had seen "the whole" of it. Even more important, however, one can sometimes reproduce the physical object that one is observing. For example, if one has the skills one can copy a sculpture to scale (or build an exact copy of

2. Rubinstein, *Marx and Wittgenstein*, describes and analyzes this "objectifying" or "reifying" tendency of language well and draws out its many important implications for sociological theory; see especially chapter 2 ("Objectivism in Social Science") and chapter 6 ("Mind and Action").

a house one has admired, or reproduce a piece of antique furniture one likes, etc.).

But if we now return our attention to the example of a baseball game as a thing that one observes or perceives, we see a complex pattern of analogy and disanalogy between perception of this thing and perception of a physical thing like a sculpture. Thus I could, with some difficulty, walk all the way around a baseball *field* while a game is being played, but I cannot walk all the way around a baseball *game* per se. I can certainly view a baseball game from several different points in the ballpark, but I cannot touch "it" or stroke "it" (although I could, with some risk of physical violence, touch or stroke some or all of the players who were playing it). Most important, perhaps, while I can reproduce a sculpture, I cannot reproduce a ball game, or at least not *that* ball game. If I were rich enough I might just be able to hire all these players to play the same game again for me, even insist that they go through exactly the same sequence of actions as they did in the original game. But even if I were mad enough or egotistical enough to want to do this, it would have to happen at a different *time*. Whereas if I make a perfect mold of Rodin's *The Kiss* and then make a bronze from that mold, I can be said, pretty unambiguously, to have reproduced Rodin's sculpture. Moreover, I have done so without the "time" complication, since, although sculptures take time to make, they do not take time to happen. In fact sculptures, unlike games, do not "happen." "Happening" is not something we predicate of sculptures or of any physical object. "Happening" is what is predicated of *events*, and activities are a species of event. (Note, however: although nobody would deny that I had reproduced Rodin's sculpture, people might well deny that what I had, what I now possessed, was the "same" sculpture. Further complexities of this very puckish little word.)

So, then, even in the language game of visual perception that is its original home, the use of the concept "point of view" is subject to many complexities, complexities that derive from the fact that visual perception as a human practice is itself a lot more complex than we might at first suppose. And to a degree the language of visual perception (of which "point of view" is a part) both obscures those complexities in everyday use and can be used to illuminate them if its subtleties and contradictions are brought out in the detailed analysis of examples. However, to do this we have, as it were, to pause and remind ourselves of the detail of our perceptual practices. This is something that we very seldom do (because we do not need to do it in order to perceive perfectly satisfactorily) and something that seems rather tedious for precisely that reason.

But tedious or not, such exercises have the merit of demonstrating in a very detailed way that what we call visual perception involves a lot more than simply the impact of light waves on the retina of the eye. For example, in the case of "watching" a rule-bound activity like a baseball game we are required to understand its rules; otherwise, what we "see" will be meaningless to us. Such understanding involves a learning process of greater or lesser difficulty, a central part of which will be watching at least several baseball games. But though this is a well-known fact about the perception of human activity and has been commented upon many times by social theorists,[3] it is not unique to the perception of activity. For even the visual perception of physical objects requires a considerable background knowledge into which these objects are fitted and which, in fact, determines what *kind* of things the things that we see are.

This is very obvious in the case of art objects, such as *The Kiss.* To be recognized, Rodin's piece requires a knowledge of what sculpture is, and to be fully appreciated it probably requires possession of other, more specialized information—the history of Rodin's work, his place in the tradition of sculpture, the technicalities of sculpture as a practice, and the like. But even in the case of ordinary physical objects there is a lot more to seeing them than just seeing them (as we might say).

For example, seeing that an electric toaster is an electric toaster requires a whole context of surrounding information that, by the time we can recognize a toaster as a toaster, will seem so mundane as to be hardly worth mentioning. I am referring to such information as that bread can be toasted by exposing its surfaces to a certain level of direct heat, that electricity can be used to make heat, what food is, what the places in houses called "kitchens" are used for, and so on. In addition, however, a close analysis of different examples (like a baseball game and a sculpture) reveals that patterns of perception change through the selection of different but appropriate "packages" of sensory, physical, and cognitive procedures and practices as different kinds of "things" are "perceived." Thus not only does the practice of visual perception shift with the type of object being "seen," but the total process of perception shifts from one kind of object to another depending upon what it is possible for a human subject to *do* in relation to that type

---

3. Pitkin, *Wittgenstein and Justice* (chapter 11, "Action and the Problem of a Social Science"), is an excellent review of the voluminous theoretical and philosophical literature concerning the relationship between observation and meaning in social science. See also Rubinstein, *Marx and Wittgenstein*, chapters 1–3.

of object.[4] This very subtle process of activity selection by the subject in relating to different types of objects tends to be obscured by the similarity of the terminological garb ("seeing," "perceiving," "point of view") in which our language clothes these carefully differentiated practices.

Metaphorical Points of View

So if we find a maze of unsuspected complexities in the activity of visual perception, and thus in the language that describes it and (frequently) accompanies it (including "point of view"), we should not be surprised if those complexities increase even further when we examine the phrase in its overtly metaphorical use as part of the language game of intellectual activity. To begin the analysis of these complexities and to provide a case study for consideration, I will again use a quotation from a book—Steven Lukes's *Marxism and Morality*.

In his fourth chapter, Lukes examines a recent debate among a number of scholars about whether Marx thought that "capitalism, and more particularly the wage relation between capitalist and worker, was unjust." He begins by noting that there are four "logically possible positions" on the issue and that all have been "ably and convincingly defended." Thus it has been argued in this debate that (1) Marx thought the relation between the capitalist and the worker was just; (2) he thought it was unjust; (3) he thought it was both just and unjust—"just in one respect and unjust in another"; and (4) he thought it was neither just nor unjust.[5]

Lukes then reviews the debate in detail, and having done so expresses his own view as follows:

> My suggestion is that Marx's view of capitalism's justice was both internally complex and hierarchically organised. In the first place, he did offer a functional account of the norms by which capitalist exploitation is judged just: the capitalist wage relation is judged just (on average, and apart from fraud, etc) according to prevailing norms, viz juridical norms of contract law, backed by conventions

4. See, for example, S. H. Bartley, *Principles of Perception* (New York: Harper and Row, 1969), chapter 1.

5. Steven Lukes, *Marxism and Morality* (Oxford: Oxford University Press, 1987), 48.

specifying the minimum socially necessary wage from the perspective of the vulgar economists who "translate the singular concepts of the capitalists who are in the thrall of competition, into a seemingly more theoretical and generalised language, and attempt to substantiate the justice of these conceptions." These norms and the perspective prevail because they sanction and stabilise capitalist exploitation and thus the capitalist system. This is the truth in Position (1). Secondly, however, Marx also offered an "internal" or "immanent" critique of those norms and that perspective, as registering the mere appearance of an equivalent exchange of commodities. As Holmstrom has observed, it "views the exchange between capitalist and worker too narrowly, abstracted from its background" . . . failing to see that the worker is not free but "forced" to sell his labour to some capitalist and thereafter under (that capitalist's) control. This is the truth in Position (3). But thirdly, Marx also offered an "external" critique of capitalist exploitation and of the norms and perspective from which it appears just. That critique is in turn made from the perspective of communism's lower phase: capitalist exploitation is from this standpoint unjust because it violates the principle "To each according to his labour contribution" (minus the appropriate deductions). This is the truth in Position (2). And finally, Marx offered a radical critique of capitalist exploitation, and of the norms and perspective from which it appears unjust, from the perspective of communism's higher phase. From that standpoint, the very attribution of justice and injustice is a mark of a class society, a sign that society is still in a prehistorical phase, an archaism eventually to be transcended. This is the truth in Position (4).

And Lukes adds:

This solution to our interpretive puzzle may cause discomfort to someone who wants to know what, in the end, Marx actually thought *in propria persona*. Did he believe capitalism unjust or didn't he? But the answer, I believe, is that Marx maintained all these positions and that he brought all these perspectives to bear at once. So I disagree with Cohen's suggestion that Marx "must have meant that the capitalist steals in some appropriately non-relativist sense," since, for Marx, there was no such sense: all such judgements are perspective-relative. Objectivity, in the sense of perspective-neutrality was, for him, an illusion, indeed an ideological illusion.[6]

This quotation is very useful in two main ways. First, it provides an answer to one obvious question about Marxism as a point of view—"If it is a point of view, what is it a point of view of?" My answer to this is the one simply assumed in the Lukes quotation—capitalism. Marxism is a point of view on or about the form of society that it calls capitalism.

Second, we should note just how saturated the quotation is in the language of visual perception used, metaphorically, to describe a complex process of evaluation. In this passage there are two views, eleven perspectives, five positions, two standpoints, two illusions, and a clearly metaphorical use of the verb "to see" closely linked to a "mere appearance." But from the perspective of the spatial and visual language game some of these entities do very strange things. Thus one of the perspectives "prevails," another "registers" things, and a third "justifies" something, while a fourth is "brought to bear." Of the five positions, four have truth "in" them and all were "maintained" by Marx. Of the two views, one is of "justice" and the other is of an "exchange," but it is a very "narrow" view of this exchange. As for the two standpoints, one is in or on "communism's lower phase," while the other is in or on its "higher phase," although from both of them one views something called "capitalist exploitation."

So what this passage reveals, simply en passant, is a whole myriad of grammatical ways in which the language of visual perception is metaphorically "projected" or "extended" to deal with various nonvisual phenomena and relations in intellectual life. And once such metaphors have become aged and naturalized by continuous use they cease even to be perceived as metaphors. So that a native speaker of English is hardly likely to think of "maintaining a position" or "bringing a perspective to bear" as metaphorical phrases at all unless their metaphoricality is brought out by the kind of literal treatment found in the previous paragraph.

However, let us now consider where, when, and why such metaphors break down. Or, more precisely, let us see how they can mislead by insinuating implications from their original language game of visual perception into the language game of intellectual evaluation in which they are being employed metaphorically. Let us see, in short, where these metaphors help us to think clearly and where they may confuse us.

6. For Lukes's review of the debate, see *Marxism and Morality*, 48–57; the quoted passages are from pp. 58–59 of that book.

Take, for example, the following question: If Marxism is merely a point of view, how can it possibly be objective? Here the visual language game is actually helpful because we can glean some clarifying reminders from it. First, we can remember that, in the language game of visual perception, a view from a particular point or from a particular perspective is not contrasted with a "holistic" perspective that is, as it were, the view from every point of view. For visually the view from "every point of view" is either nobody's point of view or simply one point of view (for example, the "balloon" view of the ballpark) being presented as a view of the whole. Of course, it is not improper to present an aerial view as a view of the whole, but it does serve to remind us what "a view of the whole" means in the visual language game. In that game, "a view of the whole" is *not* the conceptual opposite of "a particular point of view."

Second, in the language game of visual perception it is perfectly coherent to speak of an "objectively best" point of view for seeing something. Given a careful specification of what it is one *desires* to see, it is perfectly possible to occupy a position that is "the best" position for seeing it. For example, if I am at a cricket match and I want to see if a spin bowler is turning the ball, "the best" place to be is "behind the bowler's arm." On the other hand, if I want to check the speed of a fast bowler, then the best position for doing that is roughly at right angles to the wicket. However, it is also the case that if a particular position, point of view, or perspective is the "objectively best" position to see something specific, it is simultaneously a position from which other things cannot be seen. Thus, I can best gauge the height of the Washington Monument by standing close to it and looking straight up, but from that position I will not be able to see that it is intentionally aligned with the Lincoln Memorial at one end of Washington's Mall and with the Capitol at the other. So analogically, it is possible that Marxism is the objectively best point of view to see certain things about capitalism, but, even if it is, it must also be a position, a standpoint, from which other aspects or characteristics of capitalism cannot be seen.

The foregoing is a useful reminder and perhaps an illuminating analogy, but it also has a crucial flaw, one respect in which it is in fact a disanalogy. For in the case of a cricket match I can say where (roughly, but exactly enough) to stand to see whether "the ball is turning." I can also say where (roughly, but exactly enough) to stand if one wants to see the alignment of the Washington Monument with the Lincoln Memorial and the Capitol. But where does one stand to see from a Marxist point of view? This question has no answer because it marks one of the limits of the analogy. One does not, cannot, stand anywhere to see from a Marxist point of view because it has no spatiality, no spatial coordinates. It is not a place at all.

In fact, one of the clearest linguistic signals that the language of visual perception is being used metaphorically is that, when so used, *it tends to focus attention on what is perceived from a perspective, standpoint, point of view, and the like, while being vague or totally silent about the standpoint itself.* Thus, in the Lukes quotation, Marx views capitalist exploitation from two standpoints, one being the lower phase of communist society and the other being its higher phase. (Are these two points on a metaphorical hillside?) Moreover, in the concluding paragraph of the quotation Marx manages the visually mind-blowing (eye-blowing?) feat of perceiving from four different positions "at once," or, at any rate, he "maintains" all four of these metaphorical positions and brings four different perspectives to bear "at once." In short, one of the most common signals that the language of visual perception is being used metaphorically is that it tends to disintegrate or become, from a visual point of view, incoherent about the precise position or perspective of the observer while concentrating the reader's or hearer's attention on his or her observations. And at this point in the analysis case we stumble not only upon a commonplace analogical or metaphorical distortion of visual-perception language, we stumble also upon perhaps the most important philosophical problem in Marxism.

This problem can be approached fairly directly by looking again at one of the central assertions in the Lukes quotation. Lukes tells us that Marx's view of capitalism's justice or injustice is "hierarchically organised"; he means by this that Marx's four positions on the question are arranged in an ascending order of logical and explanatory significance. What this means, apparently, is that Marx's most profound judgment about capitalism is that it is neither just nor unjust when seen "from the perspective" of communism's higher phase. For, from that perspective, the very notions of justice and injustice are "seen" to be requirements only of societies—like capitalism—in which there is (a) material scarcity relative to demands for material goods and (b) inequality of wealth, power, and status. From this, Marx's most radical and profound critique of capitalism, a society in which neither of the above conditions applied would be a society without the need of concepts like justice and injustice or of social institutions meant to enshrine these principles.

I leave aside the merits of this view. (I think that it has almost no merit and is indeed extremely dangerous.) I am, rather, concerned here with what precisely it can mean to say that Marx occupies a "standpoint" (communism's higher phase) from which he can "have this perspective upon" (= make this judgment of) capitalism. On the face of it what seems to be implied is that Marx's "standpoint" here is somewhere *outside of* capitalism. It is located either in an *imagined* (by Marx) form of society ("communism") or in a *predicted* form of future society that will come after capitalism.

In either case there is a formidable philosophical and political problem. For if the logical status of this standpoint called "the higher phase of communism" is that of an imagined society, then Marx is doing what he and Engels so roundly condemned the utopian socialists for doing, that is, setting up some abstract model of a perfect or ideal society and then judging capitalism by reference to this "abstract" standard. On the other hand, if Marx's claim is that communism, in both its lower and higher phases, is some kind of inevitable future outcome of the "natural" development of capitalism, then two further problems arise. First, how is Marx, or any other Marxist, going to demonstrate this inevitability? But second, such a thesis is radically inconsistent with the view, which I share with most other Marxist scholars, that Marx made no attempt to prove the inevitability of communism, since he did not hold an "inevitablist" conception of history of any kind.[7]

In short, then, it is not surprising that Lukes's descriptions of Marx's precise standpoint on capitalism are so typically sketchy or incoherent. For when one does attempt to make the position (one might say logical position) of this standpoint exact or precise, it seems that Marx is revealed either as a utopian socialist in scientific drag or as the historical determinist that I have earlier argued that he was not. However, appearances are deceptive in this case, and it will turn out that this invidious choice is in fact a misleading product of the visual analogy itself. We must now proceed to analyze why this is so.

The best way to begin such an analysis is to remind ourselves of a formulation that I used a few paragraphs ago. I said that, in Lukes's formulations, Marx must be occupying a standpoint "somewhere outside of capitalism" to make his most profound moral and political judgments of it. But, of course, if we think of Marx the man, it is clear that he lived only in capitalist societies from his birth to his death. The same was true of Engels and indeed of nearly all the great Marxist thinkers and theorists, with the only partial exception of Lenin and the Old Bolsheviks. It is certainly true of all

7. See my *Karl Marx*, chapter 2.

the great figures of Western Marxism. It would seem to follow from this that the standards or criteria that Marxists use to make moral and political judgments of capitalism must either be those that they have derived from the observation of capitalism and their life in capitalist societies (in which case how can they purport to be universal standards by which capitalism may be judged from outside?) or they must be those that Marxists arbitrarily derive from some vision of a perfect future society, a vision both the feasibility and desirability of which can be doubted, and have been frequently.

This issue has been at the center of the voluminous social theory of Jürgen Habermas, and he poses it in a particular way that, both because of its popularity and (in my view) because of its deep confusions, needs to be explicitly analyzed. In Habermas the issue is posed in a manner deeply reliant on Hegel and on Hegelian traditions of Marxism (especially the Frankfurt School) as an issue about reason. For Habermas, it is the central philosophical and political claim of Marx and of the entire Marxist tradition that capitalism is an *irrational* form of society that will be/should be (these alternative formulations themselves mark deep divisions among Marxists)[8] replaced by a more rational form—socialism or communism.

But for Habermas this only raises the central philosophical problem of Marxism—the standards or criteria of reason by which capitalism is being judged irrational. For in his view, which is widely shared, either the criteria of reason are timeless and universal and thus can be used to judge forms of society from some perspective "outside" or "above" them, or such criteria are time bound and society specific, in which case Marx's criteria of rationality and irrationality, being derived from and restricted to capitalism, cannot be used to make rational judgments of it. To use the terminology that Habermas himself most frequently adopts, either Marx's criteria of reason are "transcendental" (in a sense originally deriving from Kant but amended by Habermas in important ways) or they are "historical." If they are the first, then they can do the transhistorical evaluative job that Marx requires of them, but only at the cost of defeating his materialist doctrine that all forms of thought are ultimately derivable from specific material and social circumstances. If they are the second, then Marx's philosophical materialism remains intact, but he has no defensible basis for saying that communism is a better or more rational form of society than capitalism, and indeed his whole rationalist critique of capitalism collapses.[9]

8. See, for example, Gouldner, *The Two Marxisms*, especially chapter 2.
9. A good general discussion of Habermas's work focused on this issue is Rick Roderick, *Habermas and the Foundations of Critical Theory* (London: Macmillan, 1986), especially chapters 2 and 5.

In many ways Habermas's entire intellectual project, at least to the present, can be seen as an attempt to solve this, Marx's most fundamental philosophical problem, as he (Habermas) conceives it. And his solution has been to seize one horn of Marx's dilemma and go the "transcendental" route. That is to say, he has spent a great deal of time and intellectual energy trying to find or produce criteria of rationality that are timeless and universal (at least in the sense that they will apply in and to any society composed of human beings). Habermas has formulated and reformulated these criteria several times, but he has moved increasingly to the view that they are criteria that specify the conditions of *rational communication* among human beings. They are thus the criteria that apply to and that, in his view, are implied in any "speech act" in which human beings are endeavoring to rationally persuade or convince other human beings of the truth of propositions (rather than, for example, trying to terrorize them, or cajole them, or browbeat them). They are thus the criteria that determine what the phrases "rational convincing" or "rational persuading" *mean*, and they have mainly to do with the conditions of free and open dialogue among citizens, including: the absence of physical or other coercion, the absence or reduction of inequalities of power and wealth, equality of access to relevant information, equality of access to skills of written and spoken communication, and so on.[10]

I find Habermas's attempt to redefine rationality procedurally, so that the question of whether people are "rational" or not becomes one about how they make decisions about what *is* "rational," "desirable," and the like most interesting; it is certainly important in the effort to make notions about "liberated" or "genuinely democratic" societies more specific. But I do not believe that Habermas's resort to "ideal speech situations" or (more recently) to "communicative rationality" has much merit as a solution to Marx's problem. I think, instead, that Habermas's conception of Marx's "problem" is deeply confused, that it is in fact a problem produced by the way or manner in which Habermas conceives it.

Habermas's formulation of the problem begins where Lukes leaves off, as it were. For Lukes tells us that Marx's most profound judgments of

10. For Habermas's various attempts to found a theory of rationality as a theory of the conditions of rational *communication* among human beings, see Jürgen Habermas, "Towards a Theory of Communicative Competence" and "On Systematically Distorted Communication," *Inquiry* 13 (1970); see also his "What Is Universal Pragmatics?" in *Communication and the Evolution of Society* (Boston: Beacon Press, 1979), 1–68. His most recent and comprehensive attempt is in *The Theory of Communicative Action: Reason and the Rationalization of Society*, 2 vols. (Boston: Beacon Press, 1984 and 1987). See, as well, the excellent discussion in Roderick, *Habermas*, chapters 3 and 4.

capitalism are made from an (unstated) perspective or point of view somewhere "outside" it, and Habermas attempts to tell us "where" this "outside"
point of view is. It is a timeless, placeless perspective based in the universal
criteria of "reason." But as the language of the last sentence implies, in
other respects both Lukes and Habermas are trapped in the same quasi-
spatial or metaphorically spatial world with its deep, insidious tendency to
objectify human practices and processes.

Thus for Habermas Marx's major philosophical problem is how to "re-
late" certain conceptual "entities"—"reason," "history," "capitalism," "socialism," "communism," and the like—entities that as quasi-spatial objects
must, conceptually, have "boundaries" and thus must have "insides" and
"outsides." Thus "reason" is either "inside" history or "outside" it. If it is
"inside" history then it cannot be used to judge it from "outside," but if it
is "outside" history then it is "outside" of time, and what precise sense can
be made of a reason that is outside time? Similarly, the standards of rationality by which capitalism is judged are either inside capitalism ("internal to"
sounds more sophisticated but is not) or they are outside it ("external to,"
ditto). If such standards are internal to capitalism then they cannot be used
to judge it from outside, but if they are outside capitalism then where
precisely are they—inside communism?[11]

11. Habermas first defined this as the central problem of Marxism in his essay "Between
Philosophy and Science: Marxism as Critique," in his *Theory and Practice* (Boston: Beacon
Press, 1963), 195–252; he first engaged with it systematically in his *Knowledge and Human
Interests* (Boston: Beacon Press, 1971). Important criticism of this first attempt (to which
Habermas responded by moving increasingly to the study of the philosophy of language and
of semantics) can be found in Thomas McCarthy, *The Critical Theory of Jürgen Habermas*
(Cambridge, Mass.: Harvard University Press, 1978); the issue is well surveyed in Fred R.
Dallmayr, "Critical Theory Criticised: Habermas's *Knowledge and Human Interests* and Its
Aftermath," *Philosophy of the Social Sciences* 2 (1972): 211–29. For a critique of all of Habermas's attempts to provide a "normative foundation" for critical social theory in a theory
of "undistorted," "rational" communication among human beings in society, see Roderick,
Habermas, chapter 5, especially 157–66. Here Roderick properly remarks that even in Habermas's most recent attempts to provide such a foundation (in the concept of "communicative
rationality" developed in his *Theory of Communicative Action*) a central problem that has
dogged all his previous attempts reappears:

> From his earliest attempts to justify the normative dimensions of critical theory to
> his latest, Habermas has avoided an approach that treats norms as simply "external"
> (conceptual-transcendental) or "internal" (contextual or immanent). The attempt to go
> between the two approaches in order to avoid both absolutism and relativism produces
> a tension in his work that the concept of communicative rationality does not resolve.
> On the one hand the orientation to understanding, agreement and consensus central to
> the concept is a "universal and unavoidable—in this sense transcendental"presupposi-
> tion of communication which belongs to the development of the "communicative com-

In short, if made graphically crude this whole metaphorically spatial picture looks like Figure 1. Given this cognitive version of the heavenly spheres, it is obvious that one can—Marx can, anybody can—look on history "from the perspective of" reason, on feudalism "from the perspective of" capitalism, on capitalism "from the perspective of" socialism, and on socialism "from the perspective of" communism (or communism's higher phase). But if we erase, through a linguistic therapy, this quasi-spatial world of metaphorical objects, then Marx's problem—or at least Habermas's version of it—disappears as well. For in a world in which these words, these nouns, stand not for conceptual or theoretical objects or places but for different aspects of human practice, then we can pose questions in a very different way. Thus, instead of asking, for example, How can there be universal standards of rationality if that which was regarded as rational under (in) feudalism (the king's healing touch) is regarded as irrational under (in) capitalism? or How can equality be a universal criterion of a rational society when it only emerges as a desirable or conceivable social goal under (in) capitalism? one can ask subtly but crucially different questions. Such questions would include How did an institution—parliament—that began as an institution in which absolute monarchs could negotiate with powerful landlords evolve into an institution of popular control over the executive? or How did demands for the formal or juridical equality of subjects evolve into the demand for greater social and economic equality among subjects? And of course these questions are only relevant to some human societies at specific historical periods, and they will have somewhat different answers from case to case even for those societies to which they are relevant.

More important, however, erasing this quasi-spatial world and the objects and locations within it helps us to see very clearly that there is nowhere for

---

petence" of the human species. On the other hand, communicative rationality is embodied in society and history, but only partially so that it can serve as a goal for action. Habermas' concept of communicative rationality as a critical standard that is both "partially" transcendental and "partially" immanent (both *in and not in* society and history) is a complex and subtle attempt to find a normative foundation for critical social theory of the kind he believes is required. In the end however, Habermas remains trapped in the same dilemma he faced earlier in his theory of "quasi-transcendental" interests. Once one has accepted the "inside"/"outside" dichotomy it is impossible to go down the middle. The "foundation" is either external or internal, it is either in society and history, or it is not. (Roderick, *Habermas*, 164–65)

This is of course true, and as Roderick also sees, the problem is the "inside/outside dichotomy" itself, for it is this conception of the issue that *forces* either "choice" or "compromise" once one has accepted it.

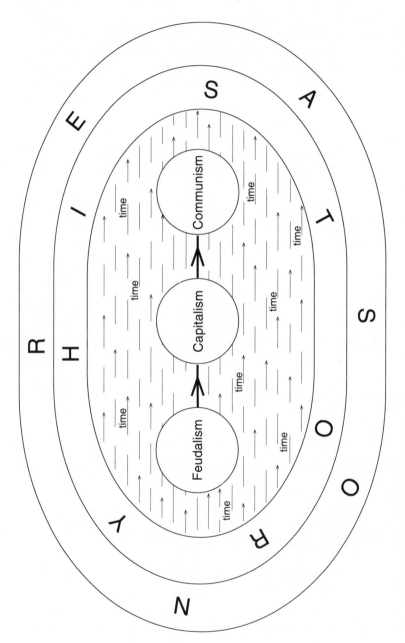

Fig. 1   The universe of intellectual judgment

Marx, or Habermas, or anyone else to stand so that they can perceive history from the point of view of reason, or feudalism from the point of view of capitalism, and so on. There are no standpoints to occupy in our alternative spaceless, relationless world. For in this world none of us can get "outside"; we are all, always, "inside." This just means that we are all "inside" time, living in a particular place at a particular time, thinking in and with a particular language, being influenced by a particular tradition or traditions of thinkers and scholars who have preceded us.[12] And if I may risk a universal statement, that has *always* been true, for *everybody*, since the beginning of time, or more accurately since the beginning of recorded human history. Hence when we move from saying in a particular place at a particular time "That is clearly irrational" (and knowing very precisely what we mean) to saying "But what are the timeless criteria of what is rational and irrational? we move not from the particular to the universal, not from the historical to the transcendental, but from somewhere to nowhere. We become in fact nowhere men.

And yet all that is put badly, for it is a denial trapped in the same picture that it is attempting to deny. When I say that we are all always "inside" history, "inside" traditions, "inside" time; I do not want to say that we are bounded by these metaphorical spaces or trapped inside these hollow objects. Rather, I just mean that "to speak rationally," "to act rationally," "to find a belief irrational," "to find an institution irrational" are *practices* with perfectly well-defined meanings in any human society at any moment, and they obtain that meaning from the total context of other practices in which they are embodied in that place and time. Of course, the meaning of what is rational or irrational changes through time as human practices themselves change, and how and why those changes occur is a question usually answerable in a fairly clear way in any specific case; or at least in cases that have been moderately well documented and recorded. Thus the question, Why in this (x) society was it once regarded as rational to accuse someone of witchcraft, but is now regarded as irrational to do so? is one with a fairly clear historical narrative answer, which may be given in greater or lesser detail.[13] But the answer does not, logically, require any reference to "the

---

12. A firm grasp of this point has always been one of the strengths of the work of Hans-Georg Gadamer on "hermeneutics." In particular, he has always stressed the importance of traditions of thought and culture as the "ever-present" context of human judgment and evaluation; see especially his *Truth and Method* (London: Sheed and Ward, 1981), 245–53. See also R. J. Bernstein, *Beyond Objectivism and Relativism*, especially 129–34.

13. For one such answer, see Keith Thomas, *Religion and the Decline of Magic* (London: Weidenfeld and Nicolson, 1971).

changing nature of reason" or the "changing criteria of rationality," although one could, if one wished, conclude the specific historical account with some generalities of this sort. Offering such generalities is a perfectly harmless practice, provided that it does not lead one to think that in doing so one has simultaneously done something odd, like "applying the criteria of reason to a case study."

Returning now to Marx: from the perspective I am outlining here it is simply inaccurate to say that Marx did something called "judging capitalism to be an irrational form of society," and that for two reasons. The first is that, as I have already noted, "capitalism" is not an object that Marx could view from the "outside" so as to make a judgment of it "as a whole." But second, and in some respects more important, societies are not the kind of things that can be rational or irrational *as a whole*. Hence one does not apply "reason" to "society" any more than one applies shampoo to an oak tree.

So what then *did* Marx do? I suggest that he made certain specific judgments of a type and form that I shall outline below, and in particular that he made three political and moral judgments, *not* of "capitalism" or of "capitalist society," but of certain *activities of people* in the society that he called capitalism. Since these three judgments will form a major point of my analysis not only in the rest of this chapter but in all the chapters that follow, I will now enumerate them carefully.

> *Judgment 1.* "In this (capitalist) society juridical and political equality coexists with, and is significantly undermined by, material inequality among persons, a material inequality that stems mainly from the different roles such persons play in the class structure. Hence a better society would be one that combined juridical and political equality with material equality through the abolition of social classes. A society in which classes had been abolished would be a better society than capitalism because in it the juridical and political equality of citizens would not be compromised and weakened, as it is under capitalism.

> *Judgment 2.* In this (capitalist) society the process of capital investment and economic growth occurs through the market. Hence it is a process that, as a whole, is not controlled by anybody, including the capitalists themselves. These blind,

uncontrolled market forces frequently produce economic crises that cause much human suffering, especially for workers.
Hence a better form of society would be one in which the
processes of capital investment and economic growth were
planned and controlled. In this way economic crises would
be avoided and with them the human suffering that they
cause, and the pattern of production and growth would be
chosen by the members of society as a whole, rather than
being thrust upon them by the blind processes of market competition and profit seeking.

Judgment 3. Human beings have very varied needs, but in
this (capitalist) society the extent to which they can have those
needs fulfilled—or at least those of them that require any
material input to be fulfilled—depends upon their access to
scarce resources. So long as material resources are scarce relative to demand this *must* be the case and there *must* be some
principle or principles that govern this access. In a capitalist
society such principles include ownership or nonownership
of private property, relative scarcity of different skills or abilities, and, to an extent, relative labor contributions. However,
an altogether better form of society would be one in which
there was such material abundance that no rationing principle
of any kind was required. For in such a society the distribution of goods and services would be entirely determined by
the differing needs of human beings, and the possession of
such needs would be the sole qualification for having them
fulfilled.[14]

Now note how one could generalize examples of this sort. One could

14. Marx nowhere states these judgments in these words, but that he made them can, I
think, clearly be seen from an analysis of several of his major works. Thus "Judgment 1" is,
in effect, the central thesis of Marx's "On the Jewish Question" of 1843 (*MECW* 3:146–74)
and is reiterated in his "Introduction to a 'Contribution to the Critique of Hegel's Philosophy
of Right'" of 1843–44 (*MECW* 3:175–87) (but the same thesis also appears in *Capital 1;* see
especially chapter 6, 176). All the elements of "Judgment 2" can be found in *Capital 1,*
especially chapter 1, section 4, 78, and chapter 13, section 9, 486–88, as well as in *Capital,*
vol. 3, *Capitalist Production as a Whole* (Moscow: Progress Publishers, 1972) (hereafter *Capital
3*), especially chapter 15, section 4, 264, and chapter 48, section 3, 818–20. The major text
embodying "Judgment 3" is Marx's "Critique of the Gotha Programme" of 1875 (*MESW,*
315–31), especially 319–21.

generalize them by saying that Marx took the standards or norms of rationality in capitalist society and then, by a critique of such norms, derived his picture or vision of the standards or norms that would operate in a future, better communist society. And indeed this is how what Marx did has often been described, especially within the Frankfurt School tradition of Marxism, where it is usually expressed by saying that Marx provided an "immanent critique" of capitalism that at the same time "transcended" it.

But of course as soon as one makes such a claim in these terms the "deep" problem of Marxism appears to return again. For a skeptic is immediately tempted to ask, But how can an immanent or internal critique of capitalism simultaneously be transcendent of it? And yet when I was rehearsing these three examples in the terms in which I was rehearsing them, no such problem appeared to arise. This is not to say that any or all of these judgments are unproblematic—they certainly are not, and I shall say why at length later—but it is to say that when one writes them or reads them they do not strike one as problematic in this way, in this quasi-spatial "inside"/ "outside" way.

To understand why this is, why this problem of Marxism appears and disappears in this way depending on the terminology one is using, it is helpful to return to the language game of visual perception for a partly illuminating analogy. In the discussion of the view from the helium balloon suspended above the baseball stadium, I noted that such a view could be presented as a view of the whole, since from the balloon, if it is suspended high enough, one can see "the whole" of the ballpark, "the whole" of the crowd, "the whole" of the game. But a moment's reflection reveals just how *partial* this picture of the whole is. For from a balloon suspended half a mile above a baseball stadium there is much that one cannot see, much that one necessarily misses. For example, one cannot see a "breaking ball" break from a position half a mile above the pitcher. One cannot see a batter wince as a pitch "inside" nearly strikes his jaw. One cannot see Larry in row 37f squeeze his girlfriend's hand. One cannot see the small muddy patch just in front of third base on which a runner slipped in the sixth inning, thus denying the Mets an almost certain run.

Analogically, seeing history from the perspective of reason and capitalism and socialism from the perspective of communism is the intellectual equivalent of seeing a baseball game from a half-mile-high balloon. There is much that is going on "down here" (= there is much that is possible for the thinker in a particular place at a particular time, working with the linguistic tools and the intellectual traditions available to him or her) that one cannot see from "up there" (= that one cannot conceive from these high levels of generality). However, there is an interesting reversal in this analogy. For generally speaking one would say that when one is spatially "down here" there is much that looms large in one's vision that disappears when one gets spatially "up there." However, in the language game of intellectual activity, there is much that conceptually looms large "up there" (at high and objectified levels of conception) that disappears when one gets conceptually "down here" (that is, examines some detailed cases of rational argumentation). But this is really only to say that the analogy breaks down at this point. In fact, the myriad of complexly related ways in which analogies do break down is a wonderful and mind-blowing issue in itself. Indeed, to think about such matters is to take a walk in a hall of mirrors (see later) of devilish construction. And yet one can find one's way, though one may be fooled and bump one's nose often.

But even allowing for all this, one may still ask, Are Marx's judgments of capitalism rational? Well, that depends. The three that I outlined above are not *illogical*, but that tells one little about their rationality. For while all illogical propositions are irrational, by no means are all logical propositions rational. (For example, "All dogs are doorknobs. This is a dog. Therefore, this is a doorknob." This is a perfectly logical syllogism, but one would not call it rational.)

To be more exact, Marx's three judgments are made up of (a) some general empirical observations about the capitalist societies that he knew and (b) the identification of possibilities for a better society based upon the postulated elimination of these empirical conditions. Therefore, whether we would regard such judgments as rational or not depends (a) upon whether the empirical generalizations are accurate and, more particularly, (b) upon whether it is in fact possible to produce the better form of society by doing away with the empirical conditions whose elimination he postulates. Concretely, this amounts to the question of whether it is possible to eliminate (1) social classes, (2) market relations, and (3) relative material scarcity in any future form of human society. If it is not in fact possible to do any of these things, or if it is only possible to do so at the cost of creating other economic, social, or political conditions that one might, by applying "reasonable" criteria, regard as worse than the ones eliminated, then Marx's judgments have to be regarded as irrational. Or to express the matter better and somewhat more accurately, they would have to be regarded as "unreasonable" or (even better) "defective."

Another way of generalizing about Marx's three judgments is to say that in them he is identifying certain "possibilities" or "potentialities" of capitalism that could be "realized" but that can only be realized by revolution. This formulation certainly has some advantages over the account of Marx's activity that has him applying the criteria of reason to capitalism, but it has dangers of its own. It also has implications that are not always grasped and that need to be grasped if the full advantages of this picture are to be seen.

Let us take the dangers first. Wittgenstein makes the following observations about some uses of the word "possibility":

> When does one have the thought: the possible movements of a machine are already there in it in some mysterious way?—Well, when one is doing philosophy. And what leads us into thinking that? The kind of way in which we talk about machines. We say, for example, that a machine *has* (possesses) such-and-such possibilities of movement; we speak of the ideally rigid machine which *can* only move in such-and-such a way.—What is this *possibility* of movement? It is not the *movement*, but it does not seem to be the mere physical conditions for moving either—as, that there is play between socket and pin, the pin not fitting too tight in the socket. For while this is the empirical condition for movement, one could also imagine it to be otherwise. The possibility of a movement is, rather, supposed to be like a shadow of the movement itself. But do you know of such a shadow? And by a shadow I do not mean some picture of the movement—for such a picture would not have to be a picture of just *this* movement. But the possibility of this movement must be the possibility of just this movement. (See how high the seas of language run here!)
>
> The waves subside as soon as we ask ourselves: how do we use the phrase "possibility of movement" when we are talking about a given machine?—But then where did our queer ideas come from? Well, I show you the possibility of a movement, say by means of a *picture* of the movement: "so possibility is something which is like reality." We say: "It isn't moving yet, but it already has the possibility of moving"—"so possibility is something very near reality." (*Philosophical Investigations*, remark 194)

Wittgenstein is warning us here that when we replace "it is possible to do" (x) by the apparently synonymous phrase "x possibility exists," or when we speak of any entity—a machine, a society—"having the possibility of" (x) or "having the potentiality for" (y), we make it sound as though a possibility or potentiality were an *attribute or characteristic* of something. And grammatically, conceptually, attributes or characteristics are themselves "things" that can be "perceived." Whereas, Wittgenstein suggests, the verb forms "to attribute," "to characterize" are far less likely to mislead us about what is going on here. For to call something a "possibility" or a "potentiality" is not to perceive it, but to take up a certain *attitude* toward it, very broadly an *active* attitude.

In fact, "potentiality" and "possibility" are two classic examples of what Hanna Pitkin, in an inspired coinage, called *quasi-performatives*. Such words, phrases, and sentences are those parts of language that we use partly to make a factual report and partly to make, as it were, a promise or undertaking. Thus to say, for example, "Capitalism has the potentiality for ending all material deprivation among human beings, a potentiality, however, which is consistently frustrated" is to say "We can *act* in this set of circumstances to end material deprivation" or "This set of circumstances allows us to *act* to end material deprivation." As another little verb reminds us, the thing about possibilities and potentialities is that they must be "realized," and social and political potentialities can usually only be realized by mass human action.

If these quasi-performative uses of language surprise you when your attention is drawn to them, then this is almost certainly because you have been more deeply in thrall to the observer or reflection picture of language than you have realized. You have also perhaps not reflected adequately upon some other mundane uses of language. For example, one classic quasi-performative sentence is the one composed of those three little words "I love you." In saying them to someone we do not merely make a report about our feelings for them (though we do indeed do that). We also make an implied promise or undertaking about our future behavior toward them. A person who has been told "I love you" by someone "has a right" (as we say) to expect certain actions from that person in the future—commitment, loyalty, concern, compassion, and the like. Of course, they may be disappointed. Promises, especially perhaps implied ones, are not always kept. But nonetheless quasi-performatives are a part of language that remind us in powerful and surprising ways that human beings are not just observing or perceiving creatures, they are *active or acting* creatures. And this is a very deep truth. Analysis of our language shows just how unsuspectedly deep it is.

Summary

I shall have more to say about quasi-performatives shortly,[15] for they bring us very close to the heart of what I believe is definitive of the Marxist point of view on capitalism, but for the moment I want to turn aside to summarize my analysis to this point. So far, that analysis allows me to reject or dispose of two popular accounts of what Marx is doing when he is judging capitalist society. On my analysis he is *not* judging capitalism from the perspective of an inevitable future (communism) to which its own developing contradictions will bring it. But neither is he simply arbitrarily imagining some ideal or perfect society by which capitalism is judged and found wanting. He *is*, in the terminology of Habermas and the Frankfurt School, providing an "immanent" critique of capitalism. But this critique does not, on my account, have the deep "inside"/"outside" problem of "reason" attached to it that Habermas identifies—this problem is itself a product of the metaphorical visual-spatial terms in which Habermas, and indeed the whole Hegelian tradition in Marxism, poses it. In fact, it is Hegel who is the main culprit here (for it is his picture of "reason" that is being used in posing Marx's

15. For "performatives," see J. L. Austin, *How to Do Things With Words* (Oxford: Oxford University Press, 1965), especially chapters 1–7; see also his *Philosophical Papers* (Oxford: Clarendon, 1961), 66–67 and 261–62. For "quasi-performatives" see Pitkin, *Wittgenstein and Justice*, 37–39, 60–70, 88, 96, 245, and 261–62. Habermas has also been closely concerned with the performative uses of language; see especially "Towards a Theory" and "What Is Universal Pragmatics?" Austin abandoned the use of "performative" as an analytical category when he realized that forms of speech which state or assert facts (and that he had called "constatives" in contrast to "performatives") were also used to perform actions (precisely the actions of stating, asserting, telling, etc). Austin therefore replaced the performative/constative distinction with a three-fold one among performative utterances—"locutions," "illocutions," and "perlocutions." These distinctions were, in their turn, taken up and further developed by John Searle in his *Speech Acts*. However, such characterizations are not only highly debatable (see, for example, Habermas, "What Is Universal Pragmatics?" 45–46)—by their implicit acknowledgment that *all* uses of language are to a degree performative they only strengthen the points I have made above. In the analysis to this point and in subsequent analysis, however, I will be mainly concerned with what Austin called the "perlocutionary" aspect of speech acts, that is, the intended *effect* of such acts on their hearers—to persuade, convince, frighten, induce doubt, and so on.

"problem"), just as he was the main culprit in Marx's own "essence-appearance" confusions (see chapter 2).

So when we have finally hacked our way through the deep thicket of linguistically generated confusions by which this whole issue is surrounded, what do we find? We find Karl Marx, a brilliant man, living out his life in a particular time and place. We find him using the abundant pregiven (in that time and place) linguistic and intellectual resources available to him in the live traditions of thought and activity on which he was drawing (and that he was both keeping alive and transforming by his own efforts) to engage in some clearly rational activities of analysis, projection, and judgment. We can see that what Marx was doing was rational at that time when we describe it situationally or contextually. But this does not mean that Marx was applying criteria of reason (whether criteria drawn from "within" or "without" history, or capitalism), for there are no such abstract criteria of *reason*. There are abstractly specifiable rules of formal *logic*, but though these rules tell us—in, for the most part, rather obvious ways—what we must do to reason logically, they cannot tell us what to do to reason rationally. And this is so because there is more—infinitely unparaphrasably more, contextually situationally more—to the *activity* of reasoning than mere logic.[16] And now we have seen one particularly fascinating part of this "more." For it turns out that what looks at first sight like the rational or reasonable assertion of the *existence* of something—a possibility or potentiality—is not simply that but is also a promise or undertaking that if certain *actions* are performed, certain consequences will follow.

Marxism as a Point of View: The Problem Revisited and Resolved

So now, at last, we can return to Marxism as a point of view. In returning to this issue we must also return, one more time, to the visual language game that is the original home of the phrase and ask the following question. Is there any equivalent, in its metaphorical use in the language game of judgment or evaluation, of the "objectively best" point of view that, we

---

16. See John R. Searle, "Minds, Brains, and Programs," *Behavioural and Brain Sciences* (1980) and the debate that followed it, which is well reviewed in M. Mitchell Waldrop, *Man-Made Minds* (New York: Walker, 1987), chapter 6.

noted, could be given some coherent meaning in the visual language game? In other words, what sense, if any, can be made of the proposition that Marxism is the objectively best point of view to "perceive" certain things about capitalism?

Everything said to this point should have made us aware of just how complex and multilayered this apparently simple question is likely to be, so we must proceed carefully and by stages here. The first point to note is that Marxists do "perceive" and "observe" things about capitalism. They do, that is to say, make *empirical* observations, of greater and lesser complexity and sophistication, about capitalism as a form of economy and society. For example, there are abundant Marxist analyses of capitalist production, both at a particular time and over extended time spans.[17] There are long-term and short-term analyses of tendencies in the (price) rate of profit on both a national and an international scale.[18] There are analyses of the processes of competition and of the growth of monopoly and oligopoly, analyses both of the "concentration" and "centralization" of capital and of the relationship of these tendencies to capitalist economic crises.[19] There are studies of technological innovation under capitalism and its effects on both employment and the labor process/division of labor.[20] There are Marxist studies of the role of government and other state institutions both in specific capitalist societies and under capitalism generally.[21] There are also

17. For two well-known examples among a host of lesser-known ones, see H. Braverman, *Labor and Monopoly Capital: The Degradation of Work in the Twentieth Century* (New York: Monthly Review Press, 1974), and Michael Aglietta, *A Theory of Capitalist Regulation* (London: New Left Books, 1979). See also H. Beynon, *Working for Ford* (Wakefield: E. P. Publishing, 1975).

18. See Gillman, *The Falling Rate of Profit*, and P. Armstrong, A. Glyn, and J. Harrison, *Capitalism since World War II* (London: Fontana, 1984). See also Hodgson, "Theory of the Falling Rate," 55–82, and P. van Parijs, "The Falling Rate of Profit Theory of Crisis: A Rational Reconstruction by Way of an Obituary," *Review of Radical Political Economics* (Spring 1980).

19. Rudolf Hilferding, *Finance Capital* (1910; London: Routledge and Kegan Paul, 1981); P. Baran and P. Sweezy, *Monopoly Capitalism* (Harmondsworth: Penguin, 1968); H. Radice, ed., *International Firms and Modern Imperialism* (Harmondsworth: Penguin, 1975); and Keith Cowling, *Monopoly Capitalism* (London: Macmillan, 1982).

20. See Braverman, *Labor and Monopoly Capital*, and the voluminous "labor process" literature to which it has led: notably, T. Elger, "Valorization and Deskilling: A Critique of Braverman," *Capital and Class*, no. 7 (1979), and Theo Nichols, *Capital and Labour: Studies in the Capitalist Labour Process* (London: Fontana, 1980). See also Martin Fransman, *Technology and Economic Development* (Brighton: Wheatsheaf, 1986).

21. See R. Jessop, *The Capitalist State* (London: Martin Robertson, 1982); R. Milliband, *The State in Capitalist Society* (London: Weidenfeld and Nicolson, 1969), and *Marxism and Politics* (Oxford: Oxford University Press, 1977); Poulantzas, *Political Power and Social*

Marxist studies of other capitalist social institutions—the family, the mass media, educational institutions, and so on.[22]

All these studies can be, and have been, criticized on both theoretical and empirical grounds by other Marxists and by non-Marxist scholars. However, in my view none of these empirical studies are from a specifically Marxist point of view, or more precisely *none of these studies are, in and of themselves, definitive of what the Marxist point of view is*. I have two closely related reasons for thinking this. The first is that non-Marxist scholars can, and frequently do, undertake empirical studies of many of the same phenomena. Thus there are plenty of non-Marxist studies of capitalist production, of tendencies in the profit rate, of monopolies and oligopolies and the consequences of "imperfect competition," of the short-term "business cycles" of capitalism and of its "long waves" and other longer cycles of expansion and recession.[23] Similarly, there are lots of non-Marxist studies of technological innovation, the state, the family, the mass media, and the like.[24] And indeed Marxist scholars frequently borrow from and are influ-

Classes; and, for an overview of the literature, David A. Gold, Clarence Y. H. Lo, and Erik Olin Wright, "Recent Developments in Marxist Theories of the State," *Monthly Review* 27, nos. 5–6 (1975).

22. See, for example, Raymond Williams, *Television: Technology and Cultural Form* (London: Fontana, 1974), and Glasgow University Media Group, *Bad News* and *More Bad News* (London: Routledge and Kegan Paul, 1976 and 1980). Marxist studies of education in capitalist societies include Brian Simon, *Two Nations and the Educational Structure* (London: Lawrence and Wishart, 1974) and *Education and the Labour Movement, 1870–1920* (London: Lawrence and Wishart, 1965). See also M. W. Appel, *Ideology and Curriculum* (London: Routledge and Kegan Paul, 1979); S. Bowles and H. Gintis, *Schooling in Capitalist America* (London: Routledge & Kegan Paul, 1976); J. Jaurès, *Le socialisme et l'enseignement* (Paris: G. Bellais, 1899); and Paul Corrigan, *Schooling the Smash Street Kids* (London: Macmillan, 1979).

23. At random: A. Shonfield, *Modern Capitalism* (Oxford: Oxford University Press, 1965), part 1; E. T. Penrose, *The Growth of the Firm* (Oxford: Basil Blackwell, 1968), especially chapters 6, 7, 8, and 11; and Leslie Hannah, *The Rise of the Corporate Economy* (London: Methuen, 1977). See also J. H. Dunning, *Economic Analysis and the Multinational Enterprise* (London: Allen and Unwin, 1973), chapter 3, and H. J. Golschmid, H. M. Mann, and J. F. Weston, eds., *Industrial Concentration: The New Learning* (Boston: Little, Brown, 1974), especially chapters 2 and 4. This is not to mention the voluminous reports of the British Monopolies and Mergers Commission.

24. On technological innovation under capitalism, see, for example, Dunning, *Economic Analysis,* chapter 6; J. K. Galbraith, *The New Industrial State* (London: Hamish Hamilton, 1967); William Kingston, *The Political Economy of Innovation* (The Hague: Martinus Nijhoff, 1984); L. Nabseth and G. F. Ray, *The Diffusion of New Industrial Process: An International Study* (Cambridge: Cambridge University Press, 1974); and, of course, the still-seminal work on entrepreneurship and innovation, J. A. Schumpeter, *Capitalism, Socialism, and Democracy* (London: Allen and Unwin, 1976). Important non-Marxist examinations of the state include Charles S. Maier, *Recasting Bourgeois Europe: Stabilization in France, Germany, and Italy in the Decade after World War I* (Princeton: Princeton University Press, 1975), an important

enced by non-Marxist studies in constructing their own accounts of these phenomena (and vice versa). Second, it is notable that both Marxist and non-Marxist scholars often agree on specific empirical observations, even on a large number of empirical generalizations, about capitalist society and may even come to very similar conclusions about their implications. So, in short, it does not seem to me that it is the empirical object or objects of their studies that make Marxist studies Marxist or divide them, definitively, from non-Marxist studies, even though there may be some minor differences of terminology in identifying these objects.

An alternative argument, particularly so far as the study of capitalist economies is concerned, is that the crucial difference is "theoretical" or "methodological" and that in particular Marxist economic studies are differentiated from non-Marxist studies by their use of *value analysis*. However, I do not think that this claim survives close scrutiny, either. For it is notable that empirical studies of capitalist economies by Marxists seldom, if ever, rely centrally on value analysis. Rather, what typically happens is that the labor theory of value and the theory of surplus value as found in *Capital* are briefly stated and (impliedly) endorsed at the beginning of a study, and the terminology of value and surplus value may appear from time to time in the text, but any empirical analysis relies on precisely the same price and national-accounting magnitudes that are found in non-Marxist studies of capitalism.[25] The reason for this, of course, is that empirical analyses of capitalist economies cannot be undertaken using value magnitudes, as has

---

study of the rise of corporatism; on the same topic (but restricted to Britain), see K. Middlemas, *Politics in Industrial Society* (London: André Deutsch, 1979); see also Barrington Moore, Jr., *The Social Origins of Dictatorship and Democracy* (Harmondsworth: Penguin, 1966). The non-Marxist literature on the family is voluminous, but see N. W. Bell and E. F. Vogel, *A Modern Introduction to the Family* (New York: Free Press, 1968); M. Anderson, ed., *Sociology of the Family* (Harmondsworth: Penguin, 1971); Faith Robertson Elliot, *The Family: Change or Continuity?* (London: Macmillan, 1986); C. Hall and L. Davidoff, *Family Fortunes: Men and Women of the English Middle Class, 1780–1850* (London: Hutchinson, 1987); and F. Mount, *The Subversive Family: An Alternative History of Love and Marriage* (London: Allen and Unwin, 1983). On the mass media, see, among a host of possible references, Richard P. Adler, *Understanding Television: Essays on Television as a Social and Cultural Force* (New York: Praeger, 1981); Grace Wyndam Goldie, *Facing the Nation: Television and Politics, 1936–76* (London: Bodley Head, 1977); and Roger Silverstone, *The Message of Television: Myth and Narrative in Contemporary Culture* (London: Heinemann Education, 1981).

25. For three examples of what I mean, see: E. Mandel, *Late Capitalism* (London: New Left Books, 1975); A. Gamble and P. Walton, *Capitalism in Crisis* (London: Macmillan, 1976); and Armstrong, Glyn, and Harrison, *Capitalism since World War II*. For a splendid review of Mandel's work focused on just this issue, see A. Hussein, "Crises and Tendencies of Capitalism," *Economy and Society* 6, no. 4 (November 1977).

been demonstrated in many sources. The most that can be done is to use price magnitudes and ratios and then imply value magnitudes and ratios from them. But such implications are always question begging and indeed logically flawed in basic ways.[26]

Finally, it can and has been argued that what is definitive of Marxist studies of capitalism is that they rest, explicitly or implicitly, on the view that socialism and communism are an inevitable outcome of the developmental trends of capitalism and that specifically Marxist studies therefore concentrate on the analysis of these long-term trends. However, this argument seems to me to conflate one restricted proposition that is true with a much broader proposition that is manifestly false.

It is true that Marxist scholars have often produced high-quality empirical work analyzing the long-term development trends of capitalism. One thinks, for example, of Kautsky's *Agrarian Question,* Lenin's *Development of Capitalism in Russia,* or Rudolf Hilferding's *Finance Capital,* as well as *Capital* itself. But I know of no Marxist empirical/theoretical work on the development of capitalism that culminates in assertions about the historical inevitability of socialism (and that includes Kautsky's work). There *are* of course such works in the Marxist tradition, but they are nearly all grand philosophy-of-history works of the "Diamat" sort, not empirical/theoretical works.[27]

To say this is not to deny that Marx, or Kautsky or Hilferding or Lenin, might have personally believed, at some point or points in their lives, that socialism was historically inevitable.[28] It is just to say that no serious Marxist scholar has ever been so unwise (one is tempted to say so stupid) as to try to demonstrate the inevitability of socialism from some direct extrapolation of capitalist development trends. For they have all known that this cannot be done. Even should the worldwide rate of profit fall to zero with accompanying convulsions and crises (the apocalyptic vision), in and of itself this is not going to produce worldwide socialism, and all Marxists have known this. They have differed markedly about what additional factors or elements they thought would be required to produce socialist revolution out of capitalist crisis, but they have *all* agreed that some additional noneconomic factors are required.

26. Hussein, "Crises and Tendencies of Capitalism."
27. M. Cornforth, *Dialectical Materialism: An Introductory Course,* vol. 2 (London: Lawrence and Wishart, 1953), is a good example.
28. See, for example, Salvadori, *Karl Kautsky,* chapter 2, section 3, chapter 4, section 2, and chapter 5, section 3; Steenson, *Karl Kautsky, 1854–1938,* especially 127–31 and 151–53;

So my conclusion to this point is that if we are seeking what is definitive of the Marxist point of view, what makes it Marxist, we will not find it in what Marxists perceive or observe about capitalism from that "point of view." Or at least we will not find it if we concentrate on the *empirical or empirical/theoretical* observations that Marxists have made about capitalism in the 150 or so years in which Marxism has been a living tradition of activism and scholarship.

In my view, to discover what is definitive of the Marxist view of capitalism we have to return to those observations that I made earlier concerning Marx's judgments about the "possibilities" or "potentialities" of capitalism. In offering this generalization of Marx's three judgments I noted that all assertions about potentialities or possibilities are, in Pitkin's terms, quasi-performatives, that is, forms of language that combine in one word or phrase or sentence a *report* about a state of affairs with an active attitude toward what is reported, with an implied *promise* about action, in fact. But the complexities of quasi-performatives are not exhausted simply by noting this combination, because the reporting and promising functions of quasi-performatives do not simply coexist, they are interdependent. That is, in a quasi-performative assertion *the factual accuracy of the report about the existence of a state of affairs depends upon the impliedly promised action actually occurring.* Thus, whether I really do love you as I say I do *depends* upon what I do subsequently. If I say that I love you on Tuesday and on Thursday refuse to help you when you are in dire need of help, you have "every right" (as we say) to doubt the accuracy—the empirical or factual accuracy—of what I said on Tuesday. Similarly, if I assure you that "the machine is now absolutely safe; there is no possibility of anyone's being hurt when using it," but I show a marked disinclination to go anywhere near it when challenged to show that this impossibility is an impossibility, then you have every (rational) reason to infer that I am not nearly so sure about the nonexistence of this possibility as I say I am.

So, when Marx observes that capitalism "provides the potentiality for" or "provides the conditions for" combining substantive material equality with formal or juridical equality, or that it provides the possibility of replacing market forces with planned production and consumption, or that it offers the potential for supplying material wants in proportion to needs and not by any other rationing criterion, what he is saying is that it "has," it

---

and Patrick Goode, ed., *Karl Kautsky: Selected Political Writings* (London: Macmillan, 1983), chapter 2 ("The Revisionist Controversy").

"provides," these potentialities, these possibilities, these conditions, *if we act so as to realize them*. And the *existence* of these possibilities, potentialities, and the like depends—logically depends—on this *action*. Thus in my view what makes a Marxist a Marxist, what is definitive of the Marxist point of view, is *a rational willingness to act to realize these potentialities*.

However, this willingness is not a mere individualistic voluntarism, for it has three other preconditions. It requires three other propositions to be factually true. The first is that those potentialities can be realized if, but only if, *masses* of people so act. The second is the proposition that when such mass action occurs these potentialities *will* be realized. And the third is that when these potentialities are realized this will produce a social state of affairs that is *better* than capitalism in certain defined respects. If any or all of these propositions are false, then the willingness to act would not be rational.

Let us take each of these preconditions in order. The first is by far the most simple to deal with, and some of Emile Durkheim's observations are very helpful in doing so. Durkheim noted that what he termed "social facts" (by which he meant the sum total of existing social institutions and values) had a "thing-like" quality from the point of view of any individual confronting them. By this he meant that they appeared as binding constraints upon the actions of any individual in society irrespective of what she or he might think about them. To that degree, he argued, they are as constraining of the actions of an individual as any material or physical thing is. I can no more stop Italy's being a Catholic country by disapproving of Catholicism than I can walk through a brick wall by imagining that it is not there.

However, although "thing-like," social facts differ from physical things, according to Durkheim, because, though they are not alterable by what any individual thinks, they are (unlike physical things) alterable by what masses of people think. Indeed it is mainly through masses of people changing what they think and (therefore) do that social facts change.[29] This is, in fact, what the phrase "social facts change" *means*. Hence, to put it simply, in realizing the potentialities of capitalism numbers count. The adult population of Britain is about twenty-nine million people. If among them there are ten thousand Marxists who are all convinced of the existence of these potentialities and willing to act in "revolutionary" ways to realize them, this is probably going to make no expletive-deleted difference to anything.

29. Emile Durkheim, *The Rules of Sociological Method*, trans. Sarah A. Solovay and John H. Mueller, ed. George E. F. Catlin (New York: Free Press, 1938), especially chapter 1.

However, if there are ten million Marxists in Britain who are all convinced of the existence of these potentialities and willing to act in revolutionary ways to realize them, this will probably make quite a bit of difference to a lot of things. And this is why, of course, Marx looked to the revolutionary proletariat or working class, and not just to a few revolutionary intellectuals like himself, to realize these potentialities. Whatever one may think about the relevance of this classical notion to late twentieth-century capitalism, it at least solves a problem that is still a problem and that still needs to be solved—the numbers problem. The Marxist or revolutionary masses must indeed be *masses*. Tiny minorities will not do, for the reasons well laid out by Durkheim.

However, it is the second and third of our preconditions of a rational willingness to change capitalism that raise the most difficult issues. Rationally believing that the potentialities of capitalism are realizable by revolutionary action against it depends upon it being the case, as I have already noted, that the alternative form of society postulated by Marx is actually *feasible*. That is, it depends upon it being the case that, to take each of Marx's three judgments in turn, there could be:

(1) A society entirely without material inequalities except those justified by differing needs
(2) A society with totally planned production and consumption and without a market mechanism
(3) A society with absolute material abundance

More important, however, it also depends upon our rationally believing that such a form of society would be *desirable*, and certainly more desirable than capitalism. What can we say about both these issues?

Well, we must first note that desirability and feasibility are interdependent. For example, if I live in a society in which there are great material inequalities between persons I might well come to think that a society without such inequalities would be desirable. If, however, historical experience of the attempt to totally eliminate (as against reduce) such inequalities shows that this cannot be done, then I am likely to revise my view of its desirability. Or, more exactly, if I am rational I will not act to bring about a state of affairs that I regard as desirable but unfeasible. Similarly, even if I believe that the anarchy of the market leads to continual economic crises, I will not, if I am rational, act to eliminate (as against reform) a market economy if I also become convinced that in a complex industrial society production and consumption cannot be totally planned. And finally, I may consider that absolute material abundance would be a desirable state of affairs, but if I subsequently become convinced that it is a conceptually incoherent notion (because human material wants expand endlessly with the supply of material goods) then I will not, if I am rational, act to bring about a society in which such goods are distributed purely according to needs, because I will conclude that such a society cannot be brought about, or at least not by human beings.

What all this shows, of course, is that the word "desirable" is itself a quasi-performative. To call someone or something desirable is to take up an attitude toward it, precisely the attitude of desiring it (or him or her). We may normally expect those who call a state of affairs "desirable" to act to bring that state of affairs about, and if they do not so act we can reasonably doubt whether such persons really do consider it desirable (even though they say they do). However, the qualification "normally" is important here. There are circumstances in which we would believe that people thought something or somebody desirable although, as we say, "they did nothing about it." And these are circumstances where there are impediments of one sort or another to realizing their desires that the desirers believe cannot be, or even should not be, overcome. In such circumstances one may reasonably desire without doing anything about it, but of course such a desire is doomed to be ineffective, unrealized.

So desirability depends on feasibility, at least in the sense that people will not rationally act to bring about a state of affairs that they regard as unfeasible, however desirable they may think it. And here we begin to get a handle on the way in which the Marxist point of view has shifted since Marx's time. For Marx held that the blocked potentialities or possibilities of capitalism were not only realizable by revolutionary action, but that their realization was desirable, and it was desirable precisely because it was historically feasible or possible as well as (abstractly) desirable.[30] However, as I shall argue in chapter 6, the experience of "actually existing socialism" since his death has brought into fundamental question Marx's easy elision of desirability and possibility.

Such experience has also brought into question whether a totally planned economy is, even "abstractly," a better or more desirable form of society than capitalism. It has suggested, for example, that the central planning of

---

30. See, for example, Marx's letter of 1881 to Father Domela-Nieuwenhuis in The Hague, in Karl Marx and Friedrich Engels, *Selected Correspondence* (hereafter *MESC*) (Moscow: Progress Publishers, 1955), 338–39.

an economy is not readily compatible with the democratic forms of economic and political decision making that Marx just assumed would be a fundamental feature of a communist society. Equally it appears that there is some unavoidable trade-off between the reduction of economic inequality and the speed of economic growth, so that the two are not unproblematically complementary as Marx assumed in his postulation of a society of absolute material abundance.[31] In short, it is no longer clear that the change from a capitalist to a communist society is the unambiguously "positive" or "progressive" change which Marx assumed that it would be.

But here it may seem that Habermas's problem about immanent critique and transcendental reason intrudes again. For what does "positive" or "progressive" mean here? And must we not have some timeless criteria of positivity or of progressivity to state either that communism is "more progressive" than capitalism or, for that matter, to state that it is not? Again, the simple answer to this is no.

In my view, which I have defended in detail elsewhere, Marx does have an essentialist conception of what it is to be truly human. That conception is, broadly, that to be truly human is to be a consciously creative actor. However, although human beings are, for Marx, essentially creative actors, and the only consciously creative form of life currently known, what they use this creativity for is, in principle, absolutely open. Human beings can and do create weapons as well as vaccines, germ warfare as well as wars on want, gas chambers as well as chamber orchestras.[32] Hence for Marx human progress consists in human beings' learning to use their creativity in positive rather than negative ways. But, and this is the point, what "positive" and "negative" *mean* here *is both created and learned historically.* Hence human beings learn that using their creativity to build gas chambers is not a positive way to employ it by taking part in, suffering from, and learning from the Holocaust. Human beings learn that democracy provides a better political context for the development of their creativity than absolute monarchy by living under, struggling against, and making retrospective comparative judgments of absolute monarchy from the standpoint of democracy.

But does this not mean that what human beings regard as positive or progressive can change at any time, so that what they once saw as progres-

31. For some reflections on this point and a standard comparison of degrees of income equality in capitalist and communist countries as they were during the central years of the cold war, see H. Chenery et al. *Redistribution with Growth* (Oxford: Oxford University Press, for the World Bank, 1974).

32. See my *Karl Marx,* 137–38.

sive they can come to regard as retrogressive and vice versa? Indeed it does! There is no guarantee of human progress save what human beings do, and no meaning to be given to the term save the one or ones that human beings give it. But of course human beings also *differ*, *disagree* about the meaning of progress (as about much else), and, to use Marx's own phrase, they "fight out" those disagreements. And so they should, and socialists should pick a side in those disagreements. Indeed, to be a socialist is to do exactly this, and we should do our best to see that our side wins.

But to return to Marx. In the manner outlined above Marx learned (or thought he learned) that communist society would be an advance on capitalism—would be "better" than capitalism, would be "more progressive" than capitalism—by living in, struggling against, and critically analyzing the form of society that he called "capitalism." He provided a rational or reasonable account—rational or reasonable *then*—of why he thought these things and of the potentialities for change from capitalism to communism. But we (and by "we" I mean all those who think of themselves as Marxists or socialists in the late twentieth century) now have good reasons, reasons he did not have, for doubting the reasonableness of his account and the existence of the potentialities that he perceived. To repeat what I have said ad nauseam, reasoning as an activity is always a situational, contextual matter. And thus as historical contexts change, so can what human beings, perfectly reasonably, regard as reasonable changes. So we do not have, nor do we need, any "transcendental" criteria of historical progress or improvement, any more than Marx himself either had such criteria or needed them. Indeed the very notion of "criteria" just confuses us here. For conceptually, criteria are always "brought to bear" from "elsewhere" or from "outside" that to which they are "applied," and surely by now we understand both the potency of this quasi-spatial picture and *its* deeply misleading qualities.

So finally, we have an answer to our question. When used in the language game of judgment or evaluation, the Marxist point of view turns out to be a *rationally motivated willingness to act to transform capitalism*. This conclusion suggests two others. First, this is not the conclusion one would have reached on the basis of a cursory glance at the contemplative visual phrase "point of view." Indeed, I think it is a rather surprising conclusion and one that has the merit of challenging the increasingly common conviction that Marxism is simply some sort of empirical/theoretical approach to the *study* of capitalism. In *Karl Marx and the Philosophy of Praxis* I noted the increasing "academicization" of Marxism in the late twentieth century and the retreat from Marxism's philosophy of praxis to which this had led.[33] The analysis in this chapter may be seen as a further deepening and reinforcement of this argument and as another attempt to persuade Marxists to reconceptualize their own activity. For though my conclusion about what Marxism "is" may seem surprising, it is perhaps the very degeneration of Marxism that makes it seem so, for are not Marxists supposed to be "revolutionaries" and "activists"?

But second, my conclusion strongly suggests that in the late twentieth century Marxism is, must be, in deep crisis, insofar as Marxists can no longer believe that communism, as Marx envisaged it, is either feasible or desirable. For then they will not act (and certainly should not act) to change capitalism for such action would be irrational. To put it another way, if what can be seen from the Marxist point of view on capitalism is certain potentialities or possibilities for its revolutionary development into communism, and if this is what cannot be seen from all non-Marxist points of view, then what happens if such potentialities or possibilities do not exist? What happens if they are mirages or illusions? For then those non-Marxists who cannot see these potentialities in capitalism, far from being ideologically blind, would, rather, be those who are genuinely clear-sighted. For from their point of view they see no socialist or communist potentiality in capitalism, and they would be right!

These alarming conclusions set us our next tasks. We must now consider how far, in the late twentieth century, Marxist views of the socialist and communist potentiality of capitalism are purely illusory and how far they retain some substance. But this is a bad way of putting it, a way enforced by pushing the visual analogy beyond its limits. For our next task is far more active, far more *creative*, than this, and can be seen to be so when properly described. For what we must actually do is examine the evidence about contemporary capitalism and about "actually existing socialism" with the aim of redefining rationally what potentiality there may be, what possibility there may be, now in the late twentieth century, for creating a form of socialist society that will be better, more desirable, more progressive than actually existing capitalism and that will also be feasible.

To end this chapter and to reiterate its principal conclusion: Marxism was for a long time the "objectively best" point of view to take on capitalism, not to *empirically* observe or perceive anything about it but *in order to change it into a better form of society.*

33. Ibid., 35.

Hence it follows that it can remain the objectively best point of view to occupy in order to "see" capitalism's revolutionary potentialities if—and only if—Marxists can still specify a form of socialist society that can be created by realizing some blocked potentialities of actually existing capitalism and that can reasonably be judged to be a better form of society than capitalism. If Marxists cannot do this, or do not do it, then Marxism will perish as a living political tradition, and deservedly so. It will perish because, without a realizable vision of a desirable and feasible socialist society, Marxists cannot convince any reasonable person to be a Marxist, to move to the Marxist point of view.

ADDENDUM:
POINTS OF VIEW AND RELATIVISM

Many questions arise from the conception of Marxism as a "point of view" outlined above. One of the most obvious and politically interesting of these questions concerns the relationship between this conception and philosophical relativism. For if Marxism is a point of view on or about capitalism, is it not simply one of many possible views, all (perhaps) of equal validity?

But second, is there not also a further subtle disanalogy between a visual point of view and its intellectual projection, a disanalogy not mentioned in the body of the chapter? For is it not the case that while one can only adopt one *visual* point of view at a time, one can adopt several different *intellectual* points of view at a time? And if one can do that, how does one choose between them? Are not, for example, Marxism, liberalism, and fascism equally valid points of view on capitalism?

Since so much "postmodernist" thought collapses into just this kind of relativism,[34] and since I have no wish to be identified with a current intellectual trend that I find vacuous and, like all relativisms, logically self-defeating, then it is important that I should be able to clearly differentiate my "point of view" conception from relativism. Is this possible?

---

34. See D. Harvey, *The Condition of Postmodernity: An Enquiry into the Origins of Cultural Change* (Oxford: Basil Blackwell, 1989), especially chapter 3. The classical statement of the postmodern thesis is Jean-François Lyotard, *The Postmodern Condition: A Report on Knowledge* (Manchester: Manchester University Press, 1984); see also Fredric Jameson, "Postmodernism; or, The Cultural Critique of Late Capitalism," *New Left Review*, no. 146 (July–August 1984): 53–92.

I believe that it is, and once again conceptions of *praxis* or *life activity* are central to this differentiation. The reason that academics in particular deem it possible to adopt several different intellectual points of view simultaneously is that doing so, or at least appearing to do so, is an integral part of our professional practice.

Thus I give lectures on Marxist thought, but I also give lectures on liberal and conservative thought, on neoclassical economics, even (occasionally) on fascism. In all cases I take it to be my professional duty to describe each current of thought as fairly, and indeed as powerfully and convincingly, as I can. If, from my lectures, my students find it difficult or impossible to tell whether I am a Marxist, a liberal, or even a neofascist, or if their view of my ideological allegiances changes constantly at each stage of a course, I find this professionally pleasing, a sign that I am doing my job as I should.

But—and this is the point—to be a Marxist is not just to be able to summarize the central theories or propositions of Marxism clearly and fairly (whether in speech or writing). To be a liberal is not just to be able to present Mill's argument in *On Liberty* impeccably. To be a fascist is not just to be able to summarize *Mein Kampf* without significant omission or distortion.

On the contrary, to be a Marxist or a liberal or a fascist is to believe certain theories, propositions, ideas *to be true* and to act on that belief. Such is obvious. What is less obvious is how we recognize the presence of such beliefs about what is true, both in ourselves and in others. How do we tell a person who can summarize Marx's theory of surplus value clearly, and outline with eminent balance the arguments for and against it, from a person who believes the theory of surplus value to be true? How do we tell someone who can give a properly balanced account of the concept of consumer sovereignty from someone who actually thinks that consumers *are* sovereign? How do we tell a person who can summarize Hitler's "scientific racism" propositions objectively from someone who believes that Aryans *are* the master race?

Part of the answer to these questions may be that the people involved also express their true beliefs in what they say or write professionally. "Much has been said against the theory of surplus value, but personally I believe . . ." "Although the presence of advertising, fashion, and the like complicates the picture, on balance we can still say . . ." "However much it may be condemned by canting liberals, biological science, when properly understood, clearly demonstrates . . ." And so on and so forth.

But this is only part of the answer, and in a broader social context a rather atypical one. It is mainly academics, journalists, politicians, and members of some other so-called opinion-forming groups who express their truth beliefs primarily, if not solely, in words. A far more socially and politically significant answer (and one that applies to the above groups as well as to most other people in society) is that one tells the difference btween pedagogy and truth belief *by the whole pattern of life activity of an individual*. By "life activity" I mean such things as:

• The political party or sect to which an individual belongs or gives his or her support
• The interest or pressure groups to which an individual belongs or gives his or her support
• The publications and mass-media programs she or he likes or dislikes
• The friends she or he seeks out
• The kind of employment she or he seeks out
• The social groups ("reference groups") with which she or he identifies
• The social groups ("reference groups") that she or he shuns or criticizes[35]

This list is by no means exhaustive. It could be extended almost indefinitely to embrace still more elements of an individual's personal life (e.g., the choice of a partner, of schools for children, etc.) and professional life (e.g., the consultancies one accepts or refuses), as well as other areas of public life in civil society.

In other words, then, the reason that one cannot in reality embrace "several different intellectual points of view on capitalism at one time" is that there is far more to such "embracing" than speaking or writing. While I can speak or write as a Marxist and as a liberal and as a fascist, I cannot *live* as a Marxist and as a liberal and as a fascist. Or at any rate I cannot do so without contradictions that at best would be psychologically and emotionally destabilizing and at worst might be physically threatening. (How long could one remain simultaneously a member of the Socialist Workers party and the National Front and maintain a whole skin?)

Of course it is true that even in areas of society outside the intelligentsia ideological allegiances are formed by reading and hearing *words* (in newspapers and magazines, on television, in the family, down at the pub, etc.) and being intellectually influenced or convinced by such words. But it is

35. For reference groups, see W. G. Runciman, *Relative Deprivation and Social Justice* (London: Routledge and Kegan Paul, 1966).

nonetheless true that ideologies or ideological beliefs only become powerful social forces if they are "lived out," as it were, by masses of individuals in a society. In fact, that such "living out" occurs among many individuals is what the proposition "X belief is a powerful social force" means. It seems to me that academics and professional intellectuals often overlook this obvious but immensely important point. This is so because in the course of their professional lives they frequently encounter ideologies in the form of spoken or written *words* of careful argumentation (books, articles, formally delivered lectures and seminar papers, etc.), rather than (for example) in the form of violent assaults, social shunning or embracing, enthusiastic acclamation, or passionate denunciation.

But even if one accepts this, or accepts it in broad terms, does it not simply drive the relativist argument one step backward rather than eliminating it? For if previously the relativist thought that all written or spoken *arguments* were equal (or that at any rate there were no universally compelling reasons for choosing one rather than another), now she or he has only to say that there are no purely rational ways of choosing between competing *patterns of life activity.* Once again, are not all of equal worth?

One may begin an answer to this question with a factual observation. Some arguments *cease,* and so do the patterns of life activity of which they are a part. For example, during a long period of European history (say, from the beginning of the seventeenth century to the end of the nineteenth century) a continual conflict took place among the aristocracies and gentry of many European societies between supporters of absolute monarchy and supporters of the theory and practice of constitutional monarchy. Both sides in this dispute produced intellectual texts and popular propaganda; both were organized into sects or groups of "friends"; both had their favorite meeting places, which they dominated; and so forth. (Perhaps they even influenced patterns of marriage!)

However, by the late nineteenth century (over most of western Europe, at any rate) one of these points of view—the absolutist—had ceased to exist. The texts that had espoused it were forgotten, its sects and supporters no more, its clubs and pubs given over to other purposes and disputes. And with the collapse of one side in this dispute (which was of course a political as well as an intellectual collapse), with its total defeat, in fact, the other—constitutionalist—side was itself transformed, merging into the mainstream of liberal democratic thought and activity with other allies and other enemies.

But surely this is no answer to the relativist. For all this example shows, it may be said, is that the absolutists lost, not that what they had stood for was wrong. And conversely, all that it shows about the constitutionalists is that they won, not that they were right, not (or not necessarily) that what they said was true.

In itself this is so, but here, it seems to me, is where Jürgen Habermas does have something important to say. For in his most recent work on "communicative rationality" he has, in effect, argued that all those who wish to live in societies in which truth triumphs and falsehood is rooted out should act to create a social and political environment in which only true ideas continue to be socially powerful (and are in fact socially powerful only because they are true) and in which only false ideas cease to have any social resonance (and in fact cease to have such resonance only because they are false).

Habermas has also convincingly argued that the kinds of social and political reforms that would be required even in currently democratic societies to bring such an environment about amount, in effect, to a program of radical political transformation. They include such things, for example, as equal access to the means of mass communication and persuasion, the elimination of all forms of social and economic inequality and of inequality of power that enable coercive persuasion to be substituted for rational persuasion, radical overhauls of education systems (to enable critical skills to be spread universally), and so on. And as Habermas has also stressed, even if such a universe of communicative rationality cannot be completely created anywhere among human beings, the closer that any society comes to its realization, the closer it will come to a state of affairs in which the truth and social power of ideas are homologous, as are their falsehood and social impotence. Or, more simply and exactly, the closer human beings in dispute will then come to being able to say truthfully of themselves and of others, "they/we lost because, and *only* because, their/our ideas were false" and "they/we won because, and *only* because, their/our ideas were true."[36]

In other words, the relativist is right to argue that even in currently existing democratic societies the political or social victory of ideas is no infallible sign of their truth, and that the political or social defeat of ideas is no infallible sign of their falsehood. But in asking why this is so, that is, in exactly specifying what it is about all currently existing societies that makes the relativist's argument true, one also begins to specify both a pro-

---

36. Habermas, *The Theory of Communicative Action*, vol. 1, especially chapter 4; see also Roderick, *Habermas*, chapter 4.

gram of social and political reform and a means by which his or her argument can be rendered false.[37]

And here the vital point to note is that what will or may render the relativist's argument false is not simply another set of *arguments*, some more written or spoken *words*, but a political program, a long-term form or tradition of *social action*. Moreover, this is not a specific but a general philosophical point. The reason relativist arguments so often tempt professional intellectuals is that they seem so validated by our life experience. That is, professional intellectuals soon learn that even good and sound arguments can be brought into doubt by a verbally clever adversary, and that even thin and specious cases can be ingeniously defended by those clever with words.

Yet the great libraries of the world are full of the clever ideas of clever men and women that are now regarded as both false and socially otiose or redundant and that are read, if read at all, only for "antiquarian" reasons. One thinks, for example, of the speculations of the great Aristotle on physics or biology, or of all those serious seventeenth-century attempts to show that absolute monarchs were the direct descendants of Adam.[38] So to repeat, our aim should be to create a world in which only false ideas end up in such dusty basements (or in the trash files of computers!), and creating such a world involves a practice that incorporates but transcends mere argument in or with words. Can such a political program succeed? Probably not, or probably not totally. But even the attempt to create conditions of communicative rationality will itself create a more truthful world, increasing the frequency with which truthful ideas win (= socially triumph) and the frequency with which false ideas lose (= become socially redundant).

And what are the implications of all this for Marxism as a point of view? Well, the obvious ones. In conditions of communicative rationality what is true in the Marxist point of view will socially triumph (become socially and politically powerful), and what is false will become socially redundant or rejected. And in those circumstances one will be able to say that those

---

37. A good discussion of all this is to be found in R. J. Bernstein, ed., *Habermas and Modernity* (Cambridge: Polity Press, 1985); see especially the Introduction by Bernstein, the pieces by Wellmer and Giddens, and the reply to criticisms ("Questions and Counterquestions") by Habermas.

38. The best-known of these was Sir Robert Filmer's *Patriarcha; or, The Natural Power of Kings* (1680), which is still remembered only because it was the subject of a root-and-branch attack in the first of John Locke's *Two Treatises of Government* (1698). For more or less the full story, see the critical edition of Locke's *Two Treatises of Government*, ed. Peter Laslett (Cambridge: Cambridge University Press, 1960), especially the Introduction, 3–145.

elements in Marxism that do become socially powerful are definitely—yes, even absolutely—true (the rejection and overcoming of relativism), while those elements that are rejected will just be the ones that are definitively and absolutely false (the further rejection and overcoming of relativism). Moreover, what is the case for Marxism will be the case for all other social ideologies, that is, they will be "truth tested" definitively in the same way.

There is, however, one particular dialectical point about Marxism and communicative rationality. We have already seen that the political program to create conditions of communicative rationality would involve a very radical reduction of current social and economic inequalities (to eliminate or at least absolutely minimize the "power" dimension that currently influences, and even at times determines, the social acceptance and rejection of ideas). But this itself is of course a part of the current Marxist critique of capitalism and prescription for its transformation, so that, in effect, creating conditions for communicative rationality in capitalist societies already involves an acceptance of part of the present Marxist point of view. However, it seems to me that the argument to the effect that the discovery of truth requires (among other things) the creation of equality among arguers is not an idea restricted to Marxism or Marxists. (It is found in the later Mill, for example.)[39] And, of course, in creating the conditions of communicative rationality one would discover whether *this* idea was true as well!

Moreover, insofar as I have defined the Marxist point of view as "a rationally motivated willingness to act to transform capitalism," then, to be consistent, I must argue that in a capitalist society reformed to be communicatively rational that willingness would be very widespread and indeed would lead to such transformation occurring. However, logical consistency presents no problem to me in this case because this is what I *do* believe would happen, that is, I believe the above proposition to be true. I also (of course) believe that the arguments in favor of such transformation would be widely, if not universally, believed to be true in conditions of communicative rationality. Moreover, they would be believed to be true because, and only because, they are true (absolutely true!).

One further and final thought on all this. In the conflict of ideas and of the patterns of life activity that embody or carry them, winning and losing are not the only options. Certain bodies of ideas that contain large agreed areas of empirical observation and (more important) of value judgment may end their historical lives by mingling and merging with each other. They

---

39. See J. S. Mill, *On Liberty* (1859; London: Dent, Everyman, 1962), chapter 2, 92–95.

may even give rise to new hybrids or combinations of ideas, new ideologies, new political programs, with new names. It is possible that something like this will happen/is happening with Marxism and liberalism. But of course on the argument made above this will or can only happen because the patterns of life activity of liberals and Marxists are not deeply or extremely contradictory. Many readers of this book, in reflecting upon their own lives, may conclude that this is indeed so (although it is often said, on both sides, not to be!).

6

The Marxist Point of View in the Late Twentieth Century: A Reformulation

Introduction

In chapter 5, I concluded that in the language game of judgment or evaluation the meaning of the Marxist point of view was "a rationally motivated willingness to act to transform capitalism." However, I also insisted that what "rationally motivated" means is always a situational or contextual matter. It is a matter of what can reasonably be said and thought at any moment, given the tradition of thought or activity within which one is working and the social and historical context within which one is thinking and speaking. As a result, what may be reasonable and rational to think or believe at one point in human history may not be reasonable or rational at another.

In line with all this, we must now ask what has been the most significant change from Marx's day to our own (significant, that is, for the reconstruction of the Marxist point of view). There seems little doubt about the answer to this question. It is that in the late twentieth century Marxists are thinking, speaking, and writing in the context of some seventy or more years of experience of "actually existing socialism," in the USSR, of course, but also in Eastern Europe generally and in the People's Republic of China, North Korea, Cuba, Vietnam, and the like.

However different the circumstances within which socialism was constructed in these countries may have been from those envisaged by Marx, and however much the exigencies of political survival and of primitive socialist accumulation may have distorted their versions of socialism, Marxists nonetheless now have some considerable empirical evidence at their disposal about the problems of trying to construct actual economies and societies on avowedly Marxist or Marxist-Leninist principles. This experience must and should put Marxists in the late twentieth century in a completely different position from Marx and Engels or even Lenin.

More particularly, Marxists now have available to them a body of empirical data, of interpretable history, from which they can make a reasoned judgment of the feasibility—and therefore the desirability—of Marx's major principles or postulates of communism, postulates that he had to derive entirely from his three major critical judgments of capitalism (see pages 152–53):

1. That juridical and political equality could be made much more meaningful by being combined with absolute material equality, the latter being obtained by abolishing social classes
2. That the unpredictability and human suffering deriving from the anarchy of market forces could be ended by substituting totally planned production and consumption for such forces
3. That in the "highest phase" of communism there could and would be no principles or criteria used to determine the distribution of material goods and services in society save the principle of varying human needs

I have already stated that Marx derived these principles of communism from, and only from, his analysis of capitalism. His point of view was a view only of actually existing capitalism. However, in the later twentieth century the Marxist perspective must be a view of actually existing socialism as well as of actually existing capitalism, and the Marxist vision of a feasible and desirable socialism must be a vision derived from a rational analysis of both these experiences.

It must be said that, at least until very recently, this has not been the case. On the contrary, it has been astonishing how little serious analytical attention has been paid to the experience of actually existing socialism by nearly *all* the twentieth-century traditions of Marxism. This has notoriously been the case with mainstream Third International Marxism or communism, which for a long time was almost completely purblind in this area. Here a deafening analytical silence or, worse, the most craven apologetics and even lies about the socialist experience were the norm for a long period. This situation was produced by time-serving ideological allegiance in eastern Europe and, in western Europe, by a somewhat more honorable unwillingness to betray the socialist fatherland before "bourgeois" critics and propagandists.[1] However politically understandable such a posture may have been, especially at the height of the cold war, it is nonetheless true that its objective effect was for a long time to turn orthodox communist intellectuals and militants in the West into mealy-mouthed, weak-minded, forked-tongued apologists for the Soviet Union, China, or wherever. Often highly intelligent men and women who would pride themselves on their tough-minded skepticism and materialism when analyzing capitalist societies, most orthodox Western communists would suddenly become dewy-eyed idealists when their attention was turned to the socialist countries.

Whereas they would, for example, simply take it as axiomatic, when examining capitalist societies, that a large gap existed between the democratic rhetoric and self-image of these societies and their reality, this sound and wholesome methodological skepticism would suddenly and mysteriously be dropped as the gaze was turned eastward. For here official party positions and policies or formal constitutional descriptions would be swallowed hook, line, and sinker, at least in public pronouncements.[2]

However, while this blind spot about actually existing socialism in the twentieth-century history of orthodox Third International Marxism-Leninism might be politically understandable (even if intellectually damaging and morally reprehensible), what is even more extraordinary is the very similar silences on this subject within other, nonorthodox traditions of twentieth-century Marxism.

For example, in the 1930s Leon Trotsky provided an analysis of the Soviet Union as a "degenerate workers' state."[3] It was "degenerate," according to Trotsky, because power had been taken out of the hands of the working class by a state bureaucracy which used that power, corruptly, for its own interests and aggrandizement. However, Trotsky denied that the Soviet bureaucracy was a new ruling class or bourgeoisie on the impeccably Marxist grounds that since it did not own the means of production, and could not therefore reproduce itself through the intergenerational transmission of private property, it could not be a class in the Marxist sense. Trotsky also believed, until the end of his life, that the Soviet Union should be defended

---

1. To take one sad example among many, see Maurice Dobb's *Soviet Economic Development since 1917* (London: Routledge and Kegan Paul, 1966). The book manages, even in a post–20th Congress edition, to provide a lengthy analysis of Soviet agricultural development in the period of the First Five-Year Plan with only the most minimal references to the human costs of collectivization; see especially 227–29 and 240–48.

2. Lukes, *Marxism and Morality*, is very good on this; see especially chapter 6.

3. Leon Trotsky, *The Revolution Betrayed: What Is the Soviet Union and Where Is It Going?* (London: New Park Publications, 1973), especially chapter 9.

against the attacks of its imperialist enemies. He held steadfastly to this view even as he lambasted the USSR for its degeneracy and exhorted the Soviet working class to reclaim power from the Stalinist bureaucracy that ruled it.[4]

As a result of all this, Trotsky's own schizophrenic analysis of the Soviet Union was for years simply reproduced (along with his "degenerate workers' state" formulations) among the tiny parties of the Fourth International, which he founded. That is, on the political front such parties maintained a continual rhetorical denunciation of the USSR (especially in debates with orthodox communists) schizophrenically combined with a "last instance" defense of it against its "bourgeois" enemies. At the same time, such parties intellectually stagnated on the issue, simply reproducing Trotsky's analysis and prescriptions as the last word on the subject of actually existing socialism.[5]

In the late 1960s, however, one faction of the Fourth International—a faction represented in Britain by the International Socialists (IS), now the Socialist Workers party (SWP)—went beyond Trotsky's "degenerate workers' state" analysis for the first time. It proposed the view that the USSR was not any kind of workers' state, "degenerate" or otherwise, but was a form of capitalist state, a form of state capitalism, in fact. The Soviet bureaucracy's control over the industrial means of production was taken to be analytically equivalent to the ownership of such means in Marx's analysis of capitalism. This being so, it could be maintained that the USSR's bureaucracy exploited the Soviet working class by using its control of the means of production to obtain a surplus product from the workers' labor and by appropriating it for its own benefit and enrichment. This in turn being so, the Soviet Union was no form of socialist state and indeed could only become so by a revolution of its working class, just as in the West.[6]

4. See, for example, Isaac Deutscher, *The Prophet Outcast: Trotsky, 1929–1940* (Oxford: Oxford University Press, 1970), 459–77.

5. Although a significant minority, led by James Burnham and Max Schachtman, were a lot more critical of the USSR than Trotsky himself and from the time of the Hitler-Stalin Pact refused to recognise it as any kind of workers' state. On this see Deutscher, *The Prophet Outcast*, 471–77.

6. On the "state capitalist" thesis of the International Socialists, see Tony Cliff, *State Capitalism in Russia* (London: Pluto, 1974). The notion, however, that the USSR constituted a form of state capitalism has a much older provenance. It originated with the "Workers' Opposition" group within the CPSU in the early 1920s, and it was probably first used as the basis of a serious analysis of the entire Soviet system in the work of a founding member of the Frankfurt School, Friedrich Pollock. See his *Die planwirtschaftlichen Versuche in der Sowjetunion, 1917–27* (Leipzig: C. L. Hirschfeld, 1929); see also Bruno Rizzi, *Le bureaucratisation du monde* (Paris, 1939).

Despite his rhetorical denunciations of the Soviet bureaucracy, Trotsky himself had stopped short at drawing this conclusion. Indeed, he hoped until his death that the Soviet Union could be reformed peacefully through its working class actually claiming and using the rights and powers that it possessed (at least formally) under the Soviet constitution.[7]

This new position therefore represented a much more total analytical and political rejection of the Soviet Union's socialist credentials than anything seen before within the Trotskyist tradition. However, and despite all this,the IS (later SWP) continued in practice to demonstrate much the same schizophrenia in regard to the Soviet Union as had the older Fourth International parties. For, on the one hand, its rhetorical attacks on the USSR and on the orthodox Western communist parties were, if anything, more strident and insistent than those of the other Trotskyists. On the other hand, however, it too, when push came to shove, would often offer a (admittedly very muted) defense of the Soviet Union against what it regarded as the more "shrill" or "reactionary" attacks of the Western mass media and the like.[8]

7. Deutscher, *The Prophet Outcast*, 459–77.

8. A perfect exemplification of this was the response of the International Socialists internationally to the coup attempted against President Gorbachev in August 1991. In its edition for September 1991 (no. 256) *The Socialist*, the newspaper of the Australian branch of the organization, ran a special feature, "Intervening around the Crisis in Russia." It began:

> In the days after the coup in Russia was beaten, thousands of socialists found themselves facing confident right wingers celebrating "the death of communism" eager to rub our noses in the dirt.
> Yet despite this tide of right wing propaganda, the left can go forward out of this crisis. . . . *But if socialists confine ourselves to simply saying the west is horrible too, we will sound like apologists for Stalinism."* (15; emphasis added)

It is unnecessary to go into the complex politics and psychology of this here. Suffice it to say that although the International Socialists used their "state-capitalist" thesis to adopt a firm "plague on both your houses" stand during the cold war, this concept was really far too broadbrush to provide any coherent guidance on positions to be taken in specific political conjunctures. And in particular, as the above quotation makes clear, when the record of actually existing socialist states was used by right-wing forces in the West as a basis for an attack on the socialist idea as such, the IS always had considerable difficulty in preventing some of its own members (let alone members of other Left groups) from ideologically "drifting" into a defense of the USSR, China, or wherever. This is also why the party found it necessary to continually bang home the "state capitalist" message on the USSR, Eastern Europe, China, and other countries, even to its own members. See, for example, Diane Fields, "Why Russia Is Capitalist," *The Socialist*, no. 221 (January 1989); 12–13, and "Turmoil in the USSR: Why It is a Crisis of Capitalism," *The Socialist*, no. 254 (August 1991): 12–13. See also "Ernest Mandel: An Ambiguous Anti-Stalinist," *The Socialist*, no. 253 (July 1991): 14–15, for a rather good example of the sort of "deviation" the International Socialists felt compelled to denounce constantly precisely because the party's own members were continually falling into it.

From the perspective of the late twentieth century, however, what strikes one as most extraordinary about the whole Trotskyist tradition is how utterly unrigorous and question-begging are all its analyses of actually existing socialism—"degenerate workers' state," "state capitalism," or whatever. For the question that both these formulations so manifestly beg is whether a massive state bureaucracy is a *necessary* part of any attempt to construct a real socialist economy and society and, in particular, whether it is a *necessary* outcome of any attempt to substitute "planned" production and consumption for the "anarchy" of market forces. This question was posed and answered in the affirmative by the great German sociologist Max Weber eighty-five years ago, even before the 1917 revolution had created the Soviet Union.[9] And of course, if his answer is correct, then the whole issue of a feasible and desirable socialism becomes infinitely more complex and difficult than is assumed in either the "degenerate workers' state" or "state capitalist" formulations. For these both share the assumption that somehow it is possible to have a totally planned economy in which planning is directly carried out by "the working class" rather than by a bureaucracy supposedly acting on its behalf. From time to time one or two Trotskyist theorists (Charles Bettelheim and Ernest Mandel being the most notable) have attempted to say what, in practice, this might mean.[10] But for the most part their attempts have not got beyond the most vague and question-begging slogans—"workers' control of industry," "popular participation in planning," and so forth.

In fact, of the nonorthodox traditions of twentieth-century Marxism, only one—the briefly effervescent but now effectively defunct Maoist tradition—took the problem of bureaucracy and state power seriously as the central problem of actually existing socialism. Unfortunately, however, the Maoist solution to the problem (spontaneous or militant-led popular uprisings against the state bureaucracy à la the Chinese "Cultural Revolution") is as jejune and question-begging as anything found in Trotskyism. For the Cultural Revolution as a solution to the problem of bureaucracy turns out to be impaled on the horns of a dilemma noted a long time ago by the "elite

9. Weber's thesis on the likely tendency of socialism to give rise to even greater levels of bureaucratization than capitalism can be found in his *Economy and Society: An Outline of Interpretive Sociology*, ed. Guenther Roth and Claus Wittich (New York: Bedminster Press, 1968), vol. 1, chapter 3, 223–26. The original text, written at intervals between 1910 and 1914, was first published in German in 1921.

10. See C. Bettelheim, *The Transition to a Socialist Economy* (Hassocks: Harvester, 1975); see also Alec Nove, *The Economics of Feasible Socialism* (London: Allen and Unwin, 1983), chapter 1.

theorists" of late nineteenth- and early twentieth-century Europe (Vilfredo Pareto, Gaetano Mosca, Robert Michels).[11] In brief, if the Cultural Revolution is going to be an effective technique for the destruction of bureaucratic power, *it must occur frequently*, for unless this happens the militants (like the Red Guards) who led the last revolution will simply settle down into various official posts as a new privileged bureaucracy. If it does occur frequently, however, it is likely to be highly disruptive of both economic production and consumption and of government and state administration. It is also likely to destroy the expertise required to carry out bureaucratic roles efficiently, for ideologically enthusiastic but technically incompetent or ill-trained "Reds" will continually replace bureaucratically corrupted and privileged but technically competent "Experts." In fact, as we now know, the one and only Cultural Revolution that actually occurred in China was highly disruptive in this way, and indeed contributed to much loss of human life.[12]

However, if the Cultural Revolution does not occur frequently, it is almost certain that the process of bureaucratization will begin again and that the very bureaucratic structures against which the revolution was directed, being in fact a necessary part of any centrally planned economy and society, will—indeed, *must*—reassert themselves. In the terminology of the "elite theorists," the Cultural Revolution will be at best simply a means for the "circulation of elites."[13] That is, it will only replace an old bureaucratic elite with a new one, not eliminate bureaucracy per se. Or certainly this will be the case for as long as the Cultural Revolution is occurring in a centrally planned economy and society.

Finally, we may consider the perspective on actually existing socialism offered by the only significant nonparty tradition of twentieth-century Marxism—the almost purely intellectual tradition of the Frankfurt School, sometimes known as the Critical Theory tradition. *A priori*, one might expect to find a much richer vein of analysis here, for the Frankfurt theorists did not, in general, owe an allegiance to any actually existing Marxist state or to any political party line. For the most part of their lives they were classic independent Left intellectuals, free to follow their own predilections

11. For an overview of these theorists, see, for example, James H. Meisel, ed., *Pareto and Mosca* (Englewood Cliffs, N.J.: Prentice-Hall, 1965).

12. See, for example, Maurice Meisner, *Mao's China: A History of the People's Republic* (New York: Free Press, 1977), part 5, and Tony Saich, *China: Politics and Government* (London: Macmillan, 1981), chapter 3.

13. See Vilfredo Pareto, *A Treatise of General Sociology*, vol. 4 (New York: Dover, 1935), 1787–98.

and consciences.[14] However, this *a priori* expectation of better things turns out to be disappointed. For the most part this tradition is as silent on the experience and lessons of actually existing socialism as are the mainstream political traditions of twentieth-century Marxism, though for rather different reasons.

Here the problem seems not to have been a political or psychological unwillingness or inability to face up to the full extent of the problems and difficulties of actually existing socialism. On the contrary, we have here a writing off of the Soviet Union, and of all non-Western socialist experiments, as hopelessly corrupted and doomed to failure by the simple fact that they occurred in economically backward or underdeveloped parts of the world. In the eyes of the Frankfurt theorists all such experiments were simply force-draft industrialization exercises thinly rationalized by an ideological veneer of Marxism-Leninism.[15]

In fact, in their attitudes toward the Soviet Union and toward other Marxist-Leninist states, all the theorists of the Frankfurt School (including, I think, Herbert Marcuse) took a very orthodox "Second International" perspective, one indistinguishable from that of Karl Kautsky (for example) in his later years. That is to say, they all took it as axiomatic that "even if Marx was wrong he was right." Even if Marx's expectations that socialist revolutions would occur first in the most advanced capitalist countries had been empirically defeated, yet for the Frankfurt theorists, as for Kautsky, the forms of society thrown up by Marxist-Leninist revolutions in peripheral countries showed that he was still theoretically correct. For without the material abundance produced by the prior development of the productive forces (through capitalism), actually existing socialism always turned out to be a form of primitive accumulation under authoritarian-state auspices.[16] And as a result, such "socialist" states were totally bereft of that democratic and culturally varied "civil society" that Marx had just assumed

14. For a standard history of the Frankfurt School, see Martin Jay, *The Dialectical Imagination: A History of the Frankfurt School and the Institute of Social Research, 1923–1950* (Boston: Little, Brown, 1973).

15. Ibid., 20 and 152–53.

16. For Kautsky's arguments to this effect, see his *Terrorismus und Kommunismus: Ein Beitrag zur Naturgeschichte der Revolution* (Berlin: E. Berger, 1919), as well as a number of his other writings from the 1920s and 1930s, most of which remain untranslated. Some of these are excerpted, however, in chapter 7 ("The Transition to Socialism") of Goode, *Karl Kautsky;* they are extensively discussed in Salvadori's *Karl Kautsky,* chapters 7 and 8, and in Steenson, *Karl Kautsky, 1854–1938,* chapter 6.

would be both prerequisite to and concomitant of any socialism worth the name.

The problem for the Frankfurt School theorists, however, was that while they could endorse the orthodox Second International perspective on Marxism-Leninism, they could certainly not endorse its optimistic prognostications about the material and cultural development of capitalism. On the contrary, living and writing in the aftermath of fascism and the Holocaust, and in Western societies in which the working class appeared to have been successfully domesticated and integrated not only into capitalist society but into its most materialist and competitive values, they saw no credible social or material basis for the construction of *any* meaningful socialism, either in the West or in the East.[17]

The Frankfurt theorists' responses to this pessimistic analysis varied. Some, like Adorno in his later years, fell into a deep *personal* pessimism, in which the only viable response to the world as it existed was simply a "Great Refusal," that is, a refusal to accept its canons of rationality (and thus of "possibility" and "impossibility"), combined with a cult of the most abstract and avant-garde forms of Art.[18] The latter, in particular, were seen as the only escape from the "totalizing" technocratic rationality of a world in which Max Weber's dream/nightmare of total rationalization had come to pass. Others, like Marcuse, lived valiantly according to Antonio Gramsci's slogan, Pessimism of the Intellect, Optimism of the Will. For Marcuse, intellectual analyses of the totalizing, integrative, and oppressive tendencies of capitalism alternated with sudden fevered hopes placed in the revolutionary potential of some "marginalized" social category in capitalist society—students, youth, women, blacks, and the like.[19]

At any rate, the net result is that this tradition of Marxism, too, displays very little interest in the world's actually existing socialist societies. Indeed, within the entire Frankfurt School oeuvre there is almost no work addressed to the serious analysis of the problems of socialist planning, or socialist economics, or indeed to any aspect of the practicalities of socialist construc-

---

17. See, for example, Jay, *The Dialectical Imagination*, 281–99, and David Held, *Introduction to Critical Theory: Horkheimer to Habermas* (London: Hutchinson, 1980), chapter 2.

18. See, for example, *Minima Moralia* (London: New Left Books, 1973), *Negative Dialectics* (London: Routledge and Kegan Paul, 1973), and (with Max Horkheimer) his *Dialectic of Enlightenment* (New York: Herder and Herder, 1972).

19. See, for example, his *One-Dimensional Man* (London: Routledge and Kegan Paul, 1963) and his *Eros and Civilization* (London: Sphere, 1969).

tion,[20] Marcuse's *Soviet Marxism* being one of only two possible exceptions to this generalization. But even then, it is a work far more concerned with what might be called the elite and mass psychology of Stalinism, and its roots in Soviet material and cultural backwardness, than with anything that could be termed the political economy of socialism.[21]

But this absence simply reflects a more general weakness of the Frankfurt School tradition as a whole—its lack of interest in, and indeed its openly admitted incompetence in regard to, all matters economic or political-economic.[22] In fact, it is in their total lack of interest in economics (a lack of interest that could be perfectly rationalized as a retreat from "economism" and "crude materialism") that the Frankfurt theorists broke most dramatically with all the other traditions of orthodox Marxism that we have considered in this chapter. This break had many positive dimensions. In

---

20. One possible candidate is Pollock's *Planwirtschaftlichen Versuche in der Sowjetunion*, described by Kolakowski (*Main Currents of Marxism*, 3:343) as "the first serious analysis of planned economy in Soviet Russia." Pollock, an economist, was a member of the Institut für Sozialforschung from its earlier years, but he spent most of his later years as a sort of administrative assistant to Max Horkheimer (the Institute's longest-serving director and the major force in its intellectual orientation for nearly four decades). However, although Pollock wrote relatively little, he clearly influenced the thinking of both Horkheimer and Adorno on economic matters, was probably the first non-Soviet theorist to suggest that the USSR was a form of "state-capitalism," and was an early theorist of "monopoly capitalism," influencing Paul Baran among others. For Friedrich Pollock and his influence, see Jay, *The Dialectical Imagination*, 19–21 and 152–53; see also Pollock's "State Capitalism: Its Possibilities and Limitations" (his study of the Nazi economy and state), published in the Institute's American journal, *Studies in Philosophy and Social Science*, in 1941 and reproduced in Andrew Arato and Eike Gephardt, eds., *The Essential Frankfurt School Reader* (Oxford: Basil Blackwell, 1978), 71–94; see also Held, *Introduction to Critical Theory*, chapter 2.

However, despite Pollock's influence and the work of a number of other economists more or less closely connected with the Institute, such as Gerhard Meyer, Kurt Mandelbaum ("Baumann"), and Richard Löwenthal, even the Institute's most sympathetic historian is forced to admit:

> It would . . . be an error to argue that these economic analyses were really integrated into the heart of Critical Theory. Horkheimer and Adorno, however broad the scope of their interests and knowledge, were never really serious students of economics, Marxist or otherwise. In fact, Horkheimer's attempts to discuss economic theory were greeted with considerable skepticism by the more orthodox Marxists in the Institut. Even the non-Marxist economists like Gerhard Meyer remember how uneasy the relationship was between the Institut's leaders and the economic analysts. There seems to have been some residue of the long-standing German philosophers' distaste for the more mundane world of getting and spending[!] (Jay, *The Dialectical Imagination*, 152)

21. H. Marcuse, *Soviet Marxism* (Boston: Beacon Press, 1958).
22. See above, note 20 to chapter 6.

particular, it allowed these theorists to do pioneering work in expanding the psychological and cultural horizons of Marxism and in confronting and synthesizing the Marxist tradition with other intellectual traditions (most notably, of course, that of Freud).[23] But whatever the merits of all this— and it seems to me to possess much merit and to have enriched twentieth-century thought greatly—it certainly handicapped the writers of the Frankfurt School severely as theorists of socialism. For while, on the one hand, they had effectively given up on the possibilities of socialism in the West, on the other hand they were not really equipped to draw any practical lessons for socialism from the experience in the East.

Indeed, one may say that the Frankfurt School's whole analysis of the cultural and psychological integration of the Western working classes into capitalism—an analysis that was carried out through more and more sophisticated and psychologized notions of ideology—is structurally blind, as it were, to one possibility. This is that the Western working classes were loyal to capitalism and rejecting of socialism, not so much because they were rendered ideologically incapable of generating a critical rational account of capitalism, as because *they were unconvinced of either the feasibility or the desirability of socialism.* And here "socialism" was understood (and why should it not reasonably be understood?) as what occurred in actually existing socialist societies in the world. To put it crudely but accurately, it is perhaps not so much that the majority of people in Western societies are, or ever were, ideologically sold on the wonders of capitalism, as that they thought it was, on balance, better than the only alternative practically on offer in the world.

It is extraordinary and yet unextraordinary (I mean perfectly comprehensible) that in the Frankfurt School's entire intellectual output this explanation of the "integration" of the Western working classes into capitalism is never given anything like the same attention as is lavished on increasingly sophisticated developments of its theory of ideology. And this is true despite the Frankfurt theorists' own rational(?) rejection of Marxism-Leninism as a model of socialism.[24]

In short, the Frankfurt School's dark pessimism about socialism and its insistent elitism about the popular masses of the West seem to me to go

23. For one of many accounts of this, see, for example, Held, *Introduction to Critical Theory,* especially chapter 4.

24. For a fine critical discussion of the Frankfurt School's theory (or theories) of ideology, see Raymond Geuss, *The Idea of a Critical Theory: Habermas and the Frankfurt School* (Cambridge: Cambridge University Press, 1981), especially 4–44.

together. For on the one hand the writing off of the Soviet experience by these theorists and their total lack of interest in analyzing that experience closely led to a reified treating of it as a fixed "thing" ("Marxism-Leninism," "totalitarianism") that, impliedly, was never changing, or at least not in any fundamental way.[25] And on the other hand the possibility that, if the reality of actually existing socialism changed, the popular Western understanding of socialism (and therefore attitudes toward capitalism) might also change was totally discounted in the name of ideology. Thus we have two powerful, and mutually reinforcing, reasons for the darkest pessimism about socialism. And this pessimism was further reinforced by an elitist insistence on seeing the popular acceptance of capitalism in the West as some kind of mass psychosis, rather than as, on balance, a perfectly rational and reasonable (but for that reason changeable) attitude.

All in all, then, twentieth-century Marxism has been seriously defective as a point of view because Marxists have not taken full advantage of the information now available about socialism (information that was not available to Marx) to shift or develop that point of view as they should have done. In particular, all the traditions of twentieth-century Marxism have failed to analyze the seventy-plus years of experience of the actually existing socialist societies in any serious or rigorous manner. I mean that this experience has not been analyzed in a way unblinkered by political allegiance, ideological dogmatism, or, in the case of the Frankfurt School, by a kind of cultural elitism. It might be argued that for a long time this failure (if it is admitted to be a failure) was unavoidable for contingent political and historical reasons. But whether or not this was the case, it is the case no longer. For if Marxism is to survive, either intellectually or politically, *now*, in the late twentieth century and into the next century, this failure must be rectified and the experience of actually existing socialism must be examined closely and critically. Moreover, all the implications of this experience for the Marxist view of capitalism and socialism must be fully taken into account.

For there is here both hope and fear. Fear, because unless this is done, and done properly, neither Marxism nor socialism will have a future. I mean by this that they will have no hope or realistic prospect of remaining popularly acceptable and influential views of the world. But hope, because

25. For a rather good specimen of this kind of pessimistic theorizing about "totalitarianism," see Horkheimer and Adorno, "The Culture Industry: Enlightenment as Mass Deception," in their *Dialectic of Enlightenment*, 120–67. See also Held, *Introduction to Critical Theory*, 39–104.

if it is done and if, at the same time and as part of the same process, the actually existing socialist societies change and become more politically democratic and economically dynamic, then Marxism and socialism will have a future, both as bodies of ideas and as effective social institutions and practices.

So what can be said about all this? What implications can be drawn from the experience of actually existing socialism for the reconstruction of the Marxist point of view? To answer this question I will take each of the three postulates that make up Marx's critique of capitalism/conception of communism and consider what can be said about each of them now, in the light of seventy years of real socialist history.

Marx's Revolutionary Postulates and the Experience of Actually Existing Socialism

> Postulate 1. Abolishing social classes will create absolute material equality, and this will both reinforce and realize true juridical and political equality.

The first and most important point here is that the experience of actually existing socialism has shown conclusively that abolishing social classes, in the sense in which Marx intended such abolition, does *not*, in and of itself, end material inequality between persons. After Stalin's collectivization of peasant agriculture in the 1930s there was effectively no private ownership of the "means of production, distribution, and exchange" in the USSR. Therefore, there was no class division between the bourgeoisie and the workers, the class division to which Marx gave primary attention in his work. There were, however, marked material inequalities between persons—not merely between state and party bureaucrats and workers, but between urban and rural workers, skilled, semiskilled, and unskilled workers, and indeed between persons holding different positions within the bureaucratic hierarchies of the state and the Communist party. There have also been similar inequalities in the other states of eastern Europe and in China.[26] And though, in general, the degree of income inequality was less

26. See Alec Nove, *The Soviet Economic System* (London: Allen and Unwin, 1977), especially 212–16; David Lane, *The Socialist Industrial State* (London: Allen and Unwin, 1976),

in most communist states than in the majority of capitalist states, such inequalities were by no means abolished; indeed, they increased during the last years of the Soviet Union and during recent years in China.

However, and more important than the continued existence of income inequalities (since for a variety of reasons in planned economies differences in money income do not translate directly into differences in consumption levels, as in a market economy), a variety of other forms of material inequality have actually been created in socialist states. Almost all of these derive from the use, and abuse, of bureaucratic and state power. To put it simply, people in high state and party positions in state-socialist societies can and do use these positions to gain a variety of material privileges for themselves—access to private transport, more spacious housing, better education for their children, foreign travel, and so on. In addition, some of those who control or have access to scarce resources (resources often made scarce through the workings of the central planning system, as will be discussed below) have used such access corruptly to gain a variety of privileges for themselves. (One thinks of a number of corrupt party and state officials in the USSR dismissed and tried in the late 1980s who were, it was claimed, "ruble billionaires").[27]

Most seriously of all, perhaps, for Marx's first postulate, there is considerable evidence that those in high state and party positions, both in eastern Europe and China, used such positions to obtain other forms of privileged treatment: in judicial disputes, in dealings with the police, and in threatening or silencing political dissenters (or even personal enemies), for example. In addition, the state and party bureaucracy as a whole controlled and censored the state-monopoly mass media to silence effective criticism, and senior state and party officials used the state monopoly of employment to marginalize dissenters or would-be dissenters in a way that has been in many respects far more total than the marginalization of opponents of the system in capitalist societies.[28] As the first postulate indicates, one of Marx's most profound criticisms of class divisions in capitalism was that when they were very extreme they seriously attenuated the effect of juridical or political

especially chapter 7, 177–211; and R. Munting, *The Economic Development of the USSR* (London: Croom Helm, 1982), 178–83.

27. See, for example, Kervyn Matthews, *Privilege in the Soviet Union* (London: Allen and Unwin, 1987).

28. See, for example, Amnesty International, *Prisoners of Conscience in the USSR: Their Treatment and Conditions* (Sydney: Amnesty International, 1980), and Sydney Bloch, *Diagnosis: Political Dissent; An Abridged Version of "Russia's Political Hospitals: The Abuse of Psychiatry in the USSR"* (London: Overseas Publishers, 1981).

equality.[29] So the evidence that juridical, political, or constitutional equality among citizens has probably been far less meaningful in societies where class divisions have been "abolished" than in contemporary capitalist societies (despite its still being highly imperfect there) amounts to a particularly telling criticism of this traditional Marxist position.

As we have already seen, one way to save Marx's original point of view is to argue that in the Soviet Union or China class divisions were *not* abolished. For it can be argued that the division between the state and party bureaucracy on the one hand and the working class and the peasantry on the other *is* a class division of a Marxist type—an exploitative division between those who control (if they do not juridically own) the means of production and those from whom they expropriate a surplus product.

In considering this argument, we may leave aside the technical issue of whether the division between bureaucrats and workers is a form of class division in the Marxist sense, an issue that is in any case complicated by Marx's own acknowledgment, in *Capital*, that in any form of society the working class would not be able to keep the whole product of its labor for itself.[30] For as we have already observed, the most important question, which all "state capitalist" formulations beg, is whether it is in fact possible to abolish the worker/bureaucrat division in any planned economic and social system not relying on market forces to determine the distribution of resources among competing uses. If it is impossible to do this, then we can for the sake of argument allow that the state bureaucracy may be an exploiting class. For whether it is or not hardly matters, since if it is playing a socially necessary or indispensable role in a planned economy then it cannot be abolished without that economy and society falling into total chaos. However, we will deal with this issue explicitly in considering Marx's second postulate of communism.

> Postulate 2. The anarchy of the market leads to periodic crises and considerable human suffering under capitalism. These can be entirely avoided, and production and consumption brought under the conscious control of producers and consumers, by planned production and consumption.

Paradoxically, the experience of seventy years of actually existing social-

29. See, for example, *Capital* 1:155 and 597–98.
30. Ibid., 530.

ism has focused attention on one merit of a market economy to which Marx gave almost no attention and that has indeed received scant attention even in conventional economics. This merit is that a market economy is, relatively speaking (we will see relative to what shortly), *diffused* or *decentralized*. It is a system in which decision-making responsibility (about what is to be produced, how it is to be produced, and what is to be consumed and in what proportions) is divided among a mass of people. These include enterprise owners and managers, wholesalers and retailers, and, of course, the mass of market consumers. More than two centuries ago Adam Smith marveled at how the "invisible hand" of the market coordinated the decisions of those thousands or millions of different decision makers by means of the price mechanism and produced the pattern of production and consumption that was the one most desired by consumers ("most desired," that is, given their different amounts of income or purchasing power).[31] Indeed, throughout the history of capitalism those who have wished to laud or defend the merits of a free-enterprise or market economy have usually focused on the daily miracle of coordination that it produces, the daily miracle that manifests itself above all in the variety of commodities available every day in millions of retail outlets for those who have the desire (and the money!) to buy them.

There is little doubt that the more extravagant claims about the wonders performed by the market have always been overdone. Actual market economies contain many imperfections, most notably those arising from the growth of oligopoly and monopoly out of the competitive process itself.[32] In addition, such systems are notoriously prone to breakdown when the wondrous coordinating powers of the price and money-flow mechanisms lead millions of producers and consumers to reduce their levels of production, consumption, and investment, thereby producing recession or depression, mass unemployment, and the like.[33]

However, that such claims for the market do have some considerable objective merit, despite their persistent ideological exaggeration, is (ironically) shown most clearly by the experience of those societies that have

31. Adam Smith, *On the Nature and Causes of the Wealth of Nations*, ed. Edwin Cannan (1776; London: Methuen, 1961), 1:477.

32. Joan Robinson, *The Economics of Imperfect Competition* (London: Macmillan, 1933).

33. For a classical piece of Marxist crisis theory, see Henryk Grossman, *Das Akkumulations und Zusammenbruchgesetz des Kapitalistischen Systems* (Frankfurt: Neue Kritik, 1967). For more modern versions, see, for example, Baran and Sweezy, *Monopoly Capitalism*; A. Glyn and J. Harrison, *The British Economic Disaster* (London: Pluto, 1980); and, most especially, Gamble and Walton, *Capitalism in Crisis*.

attempted to coordinate complex industrial and commercial economies entirely without the use of a market mechanism. For, absolutely without exception, the experience of all the societies that have attempted to substitute central planning for the market in this coordinating task is that it leads to what one can only describe as *massive decision overload* on the central planners.

In other words, when the millions (possibly billions) of detailed decisions that have to be made every day in a complex economy (how much raw material to order, of what quality, how many product lines to develop and maintain, how many machines to scrap or replace, how many new vehicles to order, how many old ones to write off as depreciated, and so on) are divided, not among many millions of "decentralized" decision makers responding to revenue and profit signals, but among several hundred thousand state bureaucrats who have no such signals to rely on—because there is no market mechanism to produce them—then a number of unavoidable consequences seem to follow. Most notably, all decisions are made slowly (most much too slowly for effective economic functioning), millions of wrong decisions are made, and millions more are never made at all.

The net result of all this overload is chronic inefficiency and waste throughout the system. By "inefficiency" I mean nothing vastly technical, but simply the chronic failure of the system to use scarce resources in any manner proportional to their scarcity and its failure to produce the goods that its consumers want and require, either in the appropriate quantities or of the desired quality. By "waste" I mean that too many resources are used in one production process, denying those resources to another process where they are in short supply. I also mean that many resources are never used at all, either because goods are produced that nobody wants, or goods or parts of goods are produced that are useless because the other parts that go with them have not been produced, or have been produced to the wrong specifications, and so on.[34]

In short, if market systems produce periodic dramatic increases in human suffering through economic crises, central-planning systems seem to produce a regular, inescapable, insidious drip of human suffering. They do this primarily by making the acquisition of even basic goods and services (get-

34. See Nove, *The Economics of Feasible Socialism;* J. Kornai, *Economics of Shortage* (Amsterdam: North-Holland, 1980); Peter Gey, Jiri Kosta, and Wolfgang Qualsser, *Crisis and Reform in Socialist Economies* (London: Westview Press, 1987); Abel Aganbegyan, *The Challenge: Economics of Perestroika* (London: Hutchinson, 1988); and M. Ellman, *Socialist Planning* (Cambridge: Cambridge University Press, 1979).

ting eggs, milk, tomatoes, repairing a heating system in the winter, making a telephone call to a sick relative) a constant headache, at least for the mass of ordinary people. Such systems also require most people to spend considerable amounts of their waking hours, when they are not working, waiting in queues. There are queues for commodities that are in very short supply at the official prices. There are queues for commodities that are known to be of above average quality because they are from a particular factory with a good reputation. There are queues for commodities that are in abundant supply and desired but which, for precisely that reason, are likely not to be abundant for very long. There are queues to get one's heating fixed, queues to apply to get a telephone (which is not at all the same thing as actually getting a telephone!)—in fact, there are queues for almost everything at some time or another. For those people (especially women) who work long hours at a job outside the home and who may also have a mass of domestic tasks to perform, such queues are the last thing they need. And this is why, of course, being able to jump queues or avoid them altogether is one of the most desired forms of privilege in state-socialist societies, one that tends to be monopolized by senior state and party officials and their families.

It is fascinating, though rather gruesome, to come to understand precisely how and why all this derives from "decision overload" in central-planning systems lacking revenue and profit signals, but I have neither time nor space to go into details here, and in any case there are plenty of readily available sources that tell this story.[35] Suffice it to say that planned production and consumption, as it has been realized in actually existing socialist societies, *has* created a form of full employment and *has* enabled such societies to avoid many of the economic crises associated with market economies (especially periodic recessions or depressions and mass unemployment). But it has done so only at the cost of a massive amount of economic inefficiency

35. On "decision overload" in central-planning systems and the waste and inefficiency to which it leads, see, for example, Nove, *The Economics of Feasible Socialism*, especially 73–81. See also Kornai, *Economics of Shortage*, 533–60; G. Markus, "Planning the Crisis: Some Remarks on the Economic System of Soviet-type Societies," *Praxis International*, no. 3 (1981); Trevor Buck and John Cole, *Modern Soviet Economic Performance* (Oxford: Basil Blackwell, 1987); Gey, Kosta, and Quaisser, *Crisis and Reform;* and, for the views of a prominent economist closely associated with the Gorbachev reforms, Aganbegyan, *The Challenge.* This central problem of socialist planning was in fact predicted nine years before the Bolshevik Revolution by the Italian economist Eugenio Barone. See E. Barone, "The Ministry of Production in the Collectivist State" (1908), in *Socialist Economics*, ed. A. Nove and D. M. Nuti (Harmondsworth: Penguin, 1972), 52–74; in the same book, see also L. von Mises, "Economic Calculation in the Socialist Commonwealth" (1920), 75–91.

and waste, from which ordinary people—mainly in their role as consumers rather than as producers—have suffered considerably. It has also avoided such crises only at the cost of a much slower growth of real incomes and real consumption levels among the mass of the people than would (almost certainly) have occurred under a market system.[36]

Once again, however, some Marxist theorists who have examined these central-planning systems have denied that they constitute a realization of Marx's vision of planned production and consumption. Their argument here is that Marx envisaged that such planning would be done, not by professional bureaucrats, but by the "associated producers"—broadly, *everybody* in a society, all producers and all consumers, acting together in various democratic planning processes. Trying, valiantly, to fill out Marx's own extremely cryptic remarks about this democratic planning process and how it might operate, contemporary Marxists like Mandel, Bettelheim, and Hillel Ticktin have offered a variety of suggestions. In particular, they have argued that real socialist planning would be much more decentralized than in state-socialist systems. They have come up with various nostrums to ensure this from the decentralization of the state apparatus and the popular accountability of bureaucrats, to workers' control of industries and enterprises to localized, democratic planning procedures. They have even postulated totally computerized socialist economies in which each consumer could inform the planners of his or her desires and preferences through a direct link from his or her own terminal to planners' computers.[37]

All these theorists have, however, stopped short of advocating the restoration of market relations as a part of their decentralization/democratization schemes. They have done so for the impeccably Marxist reason that if market relations were restored then all products, including human labor power, would become commodities again, and all the instabilities and crises associated with markets would return.

However, there is every reason to believe—every rational reason to believe—that one cannot have it both ways here. For it is probable, indeed

36. See A. Bergson, *Planning and Productivity under Soviet Socialism* (Pittsburgh: Carnegie-Mellon University Press, 1968), the discussion in Ellman, *Socialist Planning*, 246–53. However, much of the classical debate on the efficiency of capitalism versus state socialism is now out of date, based as it was on a far-too-uncritical appraisal of Soviet economic data, even among the "pro-capitalist" analysts like Bergson; see, for example, Alec Nove, *Glasnost in Action: Cultural Renaissance in Russia* (London: Unwin Hyman, 1989) chapter 8.

37. See, for example, Bettelheim, *The Transition to Socialist Economy*, especially 117–18 and 226–34, and E. Mandel, *Marxist Economic Theory* (London: Merlin Press, 1971), chapter 17, especially 664–68.

effectively certain, that without the restoration of a market, and thus of an "active" revenue and profit mechanism, most or all of the economic problems that currently afflict bureaucratic central planning would remain, *no matter how decentralized or democratic the planning processes that are envisaged to replace it.* Since it is so important for Marxists and radicals of all persuasions to understand clearly why this is, it is necessary to go into a little exemplary detail here.

One way to make clear what is involved is to imagine two scenarios, one capitalist or free market and the other planned or nonmarket, involving the production and consumption of a single commodity. Let us postulate that the commodity involved is buttons, and that in both scenarios there is one enterprise among several button enterprises whose buttons are particularly desirable. They come, shall we say, in a range of attractive colors and shades, are well designed, and are durable, being made of material that keeps its color and shape extremely well.

In our first, capitalist, scenario the producers of these buttons (both managers and workers) are rewarded for their efforts in making better buttons by the demand for their product rising faster than that for their competitors' products. Since the consumers in this scenario pay for the buttons with money, this increase of demand takes the form of an increase of revenue and profits. The increased revenue can in turn be converted into increased button production because it allows the purchase of more raw materials, more button machinery, and so on. It can also be converted into increased wages and salaries for the management and workers (and perhaps even result in the hiring of more workers). On the other hand, of course, this enterprise's less successful competitors are penalized by the monetary-demand mechanism of the market in a way that is the direct antithesis of the rewards to the more successful enterprise. That is to say, their revenues and profits fall, production is cut, and management and workers receive no wage increases (and may indeed, if the situation is serious enough, either take wage cuts or be laid off).

Now let us consider the same situation in our second, planned-economy, scenario. It is the same in the sense that in this case too there is a button-making enterprise whose products are more desired by consumers than those of other enterprises. The crucial difference, however, is in the way this demand or preference expresses itself in a totally planned economy. Just as in a market economy, it will of course begin by consumers buying more of the favored buttons in the state shops. But there are three crucial differences. First, the increased demand will not affect the price of the buttons. It will not rise, nor will the prices of the less favored buttons fall, because the prices of all buttons, like those of all other products, are set by the central planners and can only be changed by those planners, not by market demand. Second and more important, however ("more important" because in actual capitalist economies many prices, especially of consumer durables, are highly demand inelastic), the greater number of rubles or yuan or whatever paid for these buttons will *not* be converted into increased revenue or profits for the most successful button enterprise. For the amount of money which that enterprise receives (to buy raw materials, install machines, pay workers, etc.) is also set in prior negotiations between the enterprise and the central planners. It is not altered, or at least not directly or immediately, by the success of the buttons. In fact, all that happens in this case is that the state pockets the revenue from the shops and *may*, retroactively, pay the successful managers and workers a bonus for their efforts. Third, and more important, still, however, let us say that the successful buttons are so popular that demand greatly exceeds supply and they are completely sold out in the state shops and even become the object of some black-market dealing. Once again the successful enterprise will not benefit directly from any of this. But more vitally, *it cannot increase production to meet this unsatisfied demand.* For once again, the amount of raw materials it can use, the number of machines it can install and operate, the number of workers it can hire, and so forth have all been "set." They have been set in prior negotiations between the enterprise and the planners concerning the enterprise's output target, a target that is then fixed for a set period (usually at least a year).[38]

As a result, first, the management and workers in the more successful enterprise have no *incentive* to increase production, and in any case, second, they have no *means* to do so, unless of course the planners change the plan and allocate them more raw materials, workers, and so on (or the money to obtain them). However, planners are on the whole reluctant to change plans in midstream, because, of course, allocating more of anything to one enterprise means, at least in the short run, allocating less of that thing or things to another enterprise or perhaps several enterprises. So changing one variable in a plan comes to much the same thing as changing the whole plan, and plans cannot be continually changed without becoming chaotic and, in fact, ceasing to be plans at all.[39]

---

38. See Nove, *The Soviet Economic System*, 26–34, and Alexander Eckstein, *China's Economic Revolution* (Cambridge: Cambridge University Press, 1977), chapter 4.

39. This is a somewhat oversimplified assertion. In the Soviet Union, for example, plans were not often *formally* changed, but a continuous process of negotiation and bluff between planners and directors of enterprises meant that frequent "informal" (and often uncoordinated)

But the problem with complex industrial economies is that "little" changes like the one we have considered above (consumers—and not just final consumers, but the other firms or enterprises that are industrial consumers—deciding that they prefer one line of products to another line or lines) *are happening all the time.* It is probable, indeed almost certain, that no planning mechanism that human beings could devise would be flexible enough and responsive enough to keep up with these continual changes. And the larger and more complex the economy the more formidable this problem becomes. For in any modern industrial economy, for example, demand shifts of the sort considered above probably occur many hundreds of thousands of times every year in thousands of different product lines.

So the question is, What difference would it make to this endemic problem of planning without market money flows if the planning process were as impeccably decentralized and democratic as some Marxists want it to be? Let us suppose, for example, that the demand for buttons has been set, not by a few thousand bureaucratic central planners and enterprise directors, but by all the managers and workers in all the button enterprises and by all the button consumers consulting together in some totally "democratic" way. (I have no idea how this might be done, but let us imagine some computer wizardry.) The output target for buttons thus democratically arrived at is then divided between lines, styles, and colors, which in turn are allocated to particular enterprises, along with matching amounts of raw material, machinery, workers, and so forth. All this happens, shall we say, in 1987. By 1989, however, it is becoming obvious that the buttons produced by one of the enterprises are more popular than those produced by others. At this point, we have the situation as already outlined, with all the ensuing problems we have reviewed.

Which of these problems is going to be diminished by the fact that the planning process is impeccably "popular" and "democratic" rather than "bureaucratic"? I think it is obvious that none of them will be. Indeed, it is probable that a democratic planning process would exacerbate rather than relieve the problems here. For however slow a few thousand bureaucrats might be to change the plan and increase allocations to the more successful enterprise, one can wager that several hundred thousand managers and workers, along with several million button consumers (or even their democratically elected representatives), are going to take even longer. It is not

---

changes were made in practice. See, for example, Nove, *The Soviet Economic System*, especially 41–48.

difficult to imagine, for example, that the managers and workers in the less successful enterprises would use their democratic rights of representation in the plan to oppose larger allocations to their more successful competitor. And such opposition would be difficult, and certainly extremely time-consuming, to overcome democratically.

In short, then, in addition to gross decision overload, planned economies suffer markedly because they have not succeeded in finding an adequate substitute for the market's monetary demand mechanism in performing an absolutely essential threefold task in a complex economy. And we can describe that task very precisely. It is:

1. To signal changes in demand and in preferences from consumers to producers
2. To reward or punish producers for eliciting those signals (positive or negative) by their products
3. To enable or force them to respond to the signals—"enable" in the case of positive signals (expansion), "force" in the case of negative signals (cutbacks)

The point about a market and monetary-demand mechanism (and there is no "active" monetary-demand mechanism without a market) is that it accomplishes all three tasks quickly *because it accomplishes them simultaneously.* For example, in the positive case, an enterprise experiencing a sharp rise in its monetary income or revenue (a) knows that its products are being successful, (b) can reward its management and workers by paying them more, and (c) can take some part of its increased revenue into the market and buy the increased raw materials, increased work force, and other elements needed to produce for the enhanced demand.

Conversely, in a planned economy totally without a market (and whether democratic or not):

1. There *is* a signal of success or failure (decreased or increased stocks in the state shops), but the signal only reaches the enterprise slowly (if at all) because it only reaches it through the decisions of the planners
2. Even when the signal reaches the enterprise there is no reward for eliciting it (or punishment if it is negative) *unless the planners decide that there will be one*
3. The enterprise is not enabled or forced to respond to the signal *unless the planners enable it or force it*

In short, there are very good reasons to believe that, even in the best possible case, a totally planned economy will be one that is much *less* flexible and responsive to the demands of consumers (and that just means to the changing material demands and needs of the people/citizens who depend upon it) than a market economy. Moreover (and this may be the most vital point of all), the *more democratically planned it is the less flexible and responsive it is likely to be.* For, of course, the more democratic any decision-making process is, the longer the time that it takes. It hardly needs to be stressed how destructive these conclusions are for Marx's original vision of a socialist society as one in which production and consumption are planned by the "associated producers" and the market mechanism totally abolished.

This is not to say that the planned economies of actually existing socialist societies proved themselves totally without merit. I have already noted that on the whole they avoided economic recession and mass unemployment, the most destructive forms of capitalist crisis, and this in itself is no mean achievement. It also seems that central planning is capable of laying the foundations of an industrial economy in poor and backward countries very rapidly, if rather wastefully.[40] Moreover, even at more advanced stages of development central planning can be an effective means of concentrating resources on particular sectors or programs that are given top political priority (for example, space programs, the military, or preparing for the Olympics). And this is just what one might expect from the analysis given above. For if planning is an extremely inefficient means of coordinating the millions of mundane but utterly vital decisions that have to be made to keep a complex economy running, it is a much more appropriate tool for hitting a tightly defined and static single target (build this steel complex in three years, have this Olympic village opened by June 1980, etc.). but even these specific successes pass on a considerable cost to the rest of the economy. Thus, the Olympic village is completed on time and looks fine, but this is only done by diverting to it a considerable proportion of the (underestimated) amount of electric cable available for domestic installation in Moscow this year. Hence Olympic athletes are comfortable, but three blocks of workers' flats remain unoccupiable for another eighteen months!

But the main point is, as already noted, that once the foundations of an industrial economy have been laid through central planning that form of

40. See, for example, E. H. Carr and R. W. Davies, *Foundations of a Planned Economy* (Harmondsworth: Penguin, 1974), especially chapter 12, and Eckstein, *China's Economic Revolution*, 50–63 and 120–89.

planning proves itself increasingly incapable of *running* the economy it has created. And the more sophisticated and complex the economy becomes, the more this incapability increases. Hence we can imagine what might have happened had Marx's original vision been realized and the first Marxist revolutions occurred in the most advanced capitalist economies. We would, apparently, have had a recipe for chaos and disaster, not for general liberation.

One possible response to all this (or one partial response, at any rate) is to say that in Marx's vision of socialism a market mechanism is not required to reward producers, because he envisages that they will be responding to other types of incentives, particularly "moral incentives." In response to this, I will simply note in passing that moral incentives have been tried and abandoned in all actually existing socialist societies for the very good reason that they have not worked, at least not as effective economic incentives.[41] However, I will deal with this issue in my examination of Marx's third major postulate about communism.

> Postulate 3. In communism's higher phase, absolute material abundance would allow the distribution of society's material product to be undertaken on the principle "From each according to his abilities, to each according to his needs."

This is one aspect of Marx's point of view on capitalism and communism that remains effectively untouched by the experience of actually existing socialism. For none of the societies that call themselves communist have ever even *claimed* to have got to Marx's "higher phase" of communism, in which Godwin's famous "abilities/needs" principle would apply.[42] However, in discussing this third postulate we can reasonably use the experience of an additional hundred years of capitalist development since Marx's death, as well as reflecting on some experiences from actually existing socialist societies that have implications for the feasibility and desirability of Marx's "lower phase" of communism. For if, as I shall argue, there are now (in the late twentieth century) good reasons for thinking that Marx's vision of

41. Nove, *The Economics of Feasible Socialism*, chapter 1, 50–54.

42. The slogan "From each according to his abilities, to each according to his needs," quoted in Marx's "Critique of the Gotha Programme" as the central slogan of the "higher phase" of communism (*MESW*, 321), originates in William Godwin, *Enquiry concerning Political Justice* (1793); Harmondsworth: Penguin Classics, 1976)—see especially book 2, chapter 2, and book 8, chapters 1–3.

the "higher phase" is radically incoherent—that it is, in fact, the vision of an *impossibility*—then we may have to rest content with the lower phase or some variant of it.

The most powerful and direct way to problematize Marx's vision of the higher phase of communism is to say that the concept of "absolute material abundance" is incoherent, though at first sight it may not appear to be so. The usual way of demonstrating that it is incoherent is simply to state that human desires for material goods and services expand with the supply of those goods and services. Thus there will never be a situation in human societies in which there is no relative economic scarcity, that is, a scarcity of goods and services *relative to the demand for them*. However, although this argument against Marx's vision is most frequently employed by, and convincing to, professional economists or those with some knowledge of neoclassical economics, I have not found it very successful, at least in this general form, in convincing Marxists and radicals that "absolute material abundance" is an incoherent notion. So I will offer a more detailed form of argument in the hope of making the general point clearer.

The reason that the neoclassical economist's peremptory argument does not convince those who do not see its full implications is, I think, that it does not seem impossible to imagine a world whose existence would refute it. That is, it seems perfectly possible to imagine that there might, at some time in the future, be a society so materially productive that every town or city could have a warehouse in which there were so many refrigerators (say) that if anybody needed a refrigerator he or she could just go down and get one "free."

However, while there is nothing incoherent about this imagining in itself, there is something very incoherent about it, says the conventional economist, when it is placed in a wider context. For the economist argues that, in any future world in which something like this could happen, a number of other things would almost certainly have happened that would make this possibility an impossibility. For example, refrigerators today are typically constructed of steel, some other metals, plastic, and various kinds of synthetic rubbers. Thus our economist postulates that in the year 2217 (say) steel, plastics, and synthetic rubbers would not just be used to make refrigerators but would also be used in a mass of other products, many of them as yet unheard of (for household interstellar spacecraft, for example, by then as common as automobiles today). However, this being the case, it is almost certain that the demand for steel or steel alloys, for example, would be pressing hard on the supply. (And this would be true no matter what technical advances we imagine in steel production or in the materials that may have replaced it by 2217.) But if this is the case, then the manufacturers of refrigerators would not be able to make them available free on demand, because they would have to compete for relatively scarce steel with other producers using steel.

Depending upon what else we imagine about the wider context of this situation, this means one of two things. If we imagine that the economy of 2217 is a market economy, it means that a monetary price will have to be charged for the refrigerators, one at least equal to their costs of production. Or, if we imagine that there is no market, then the supply of refrigerators would have to be rationed in some way to ensure that the demand for refrigerators did not outrun the amount of them that the planners could afford to supply, given competing demands for relatively scarce steel and their plan priorities. This rationing could operate on a "first-come, first-served" basis (in which case there would be physical queues of people outside the warehouse, and there would also be times when the warehouse was simply empty). Or it could operate through some formal entitlement mechanism (so that every household would be entitled to renew its fridge every six years, for example) in which case there would be, as it were, a "paper" or "bureaucratic" queue of competing entitlements. Either way, one could *not* simply go and get a fridge "free" from the warehouse as one had imagined. Indeed, if the society in question operated legal-entitlement rationing, it is highly likely that there would be many people who would not be able to get a refrigerator even when they needed it (because, for example, their previous fridge was poorly made and broke down well before their next entitlement). And the "refrigerator" situation would apply to any and all other products that we might imagine existing in this future society.

Of course, this scenario depends upon it being the case that human desires for material goods and services *do* expand with the supply of those goods and services. One cannot prove conclusively that this will always be the case, although it has, very clearly, been the case in all of human history to the present. But one can say that the demand for material goods and services has continued to expand in all capitalist societies since Marx's death, thus maintaining relative scarcity, and this despite a positively awesome increase in the material productivity of those societies since the late nineteenth century.[43] Moreover, Marx himself argued, in *The German Ideology* and else-

43. See, for example, Armstrong, Glyn, and Harrison, *Capitalism since World War II*, especially chapter 8, 167–92.

where, that human history was, in part, the story of the continuous production of new needs by human beings, a generalization that he did not restrict to capitalism.[44] So it is hard to see why he should imagine that this would suddenly cease to be the case when the "higher phase" of communism arrived.

The second, rather less subtle argument for showing that Marx's vision of the higher phase of communism is incoherent is that the principle of distributing goods and services according to "abilities" and "needs" begs the question of how the abilities and needs of widely differing people are to be determined, and, more particularly, of *who* is to determine them.

That people's abilities and needs do vary (and contrary to a widespread myth, Marx just assumed, throughout his life, that there were inequalities of ability among human beings that were probably eradicable in any form of society)[45] means, of course, that a principle of distribution from "abilities" according to "needs" is *not* one of equal distribution, or at least not of "absolutely" equal distribution. Indeed, a principle of absolutely equal distribution of goods and services among human beings in any society would clearly be irrational as well as unjust. Are the needs of a baby the same as those of an adult? Are those of an elderly person the same as those of a teenager? Are the needs of a family or household that enjoys playing music the same as those of a family or household intensely interested in sport? Are the needs of women the same as those of men? Are those of a young mother with three small children the same as those of an unattached woman with no children? One has merely to pose these questions to see that biological maturation and aging *alone* (leaving aside any other considerations of varying interests, preferences, abilities, etc.) are enough to make for considerable inequalities of need among human beings in any society.

Similarly, the fact that people's abilities are also unequal (as Marx explicitly acknowledges in his "Critique of the Gotha Programme") implies that in any society those who have statistically rarer abilities—whether, for example, in physical strength, or in mathematics, or in music—can make contributions, through their labor, to fulfilling the needs of others that those who do not possess such abilities will not be able to make. Hence the principle "From each according to his abilities, to each according to his needs"—a principle that is in fact a principle of *inequality*, both in

---

44. Marx and Engels, *The German Ideology*, 48–49, 62, 86, 115–16.
45. His clearest statements on this matter are probably those in the "Critique of the Gotha Programme," 315–31, especially 319–21.

contributions to producing goods and services and in the distribution of such goods and services.

However, this is certainly not the greatest problem with this principle. In fact, it may not be thought to be a "problem" at all. For the inequality that this principle dictates will probably seem perfectly just to anyone who reflects upon the matter. Is it not, after all, perfectly just that those who have greater abilities should use them to contribute in greater measure to the needs of others, while they, along with everybody else, receive a share of society's material product that varies only as their needs vary from the needs of others?

The greatest problem with the abilities/needs principle is not this. It is that, as it is enunciated by Marx in the "Critique of the Gotha Programme," the principle is totally silent about who or what *decides* what the abilities and needs of each person are, and indeed *how* they decide. Since I have already stated at length the massive questions that are begged in Marx's treatment of this issue, I will simply quote here my comments on the matter in *Karl Marx and the Philosophy of Praxis.*

> "Society", we are told, will inscribe upon its banners "From each according to his abilities to each according to his needs". But who is to decide what an individual's abilities or needs are? Again there are two possible answers to this question. The first is the *individual himself or herself will decide.* Thus, under communism "I" decide what my abilities are and "I" decide what my needs are. But if that is the answer [then] how can it be guaranteed that I will not think that I have abilities which I do not in fact have (and so undertake some role in society to which I am totally unsuited)? Moreover, how is it to be guaranteed that I (or anybody else) will not think that I have needs greatly in excess of everybody else's but which I am entitled to have met if I am to receive "according to" my "needs"?
>
> Suppose, for example, that my needs include two country houses with 200 servants each, three yachts and a private jet aircraft? If these are my "needs" honestly and conscientiously stated after due introspection, then why should I (or anybody else with the same needs) not have them met?
>
> Again Marx has two choices here. He can either say that such needs are "artificial" ones produced by the material acquisitiveness of capitalism and that they will disappear with that mode of production (which I think is what he would have said, though I am not sure).

Or he could set up a distinction between wants and needs, and say that, e.g. country houses and private jet aircraft may be part of my "wants" but they are not part of my "needs". But if he opts for the second alternative then we are back to the same question in a slightly different form. That is *who* is to draw the line, make the distinction, between wants and needs? Clearly now it cannot be *me* for myself (or anybody else for themselves) since I have already defined as part of my needs some things which Marx has assigned to my "mere wants". But if each individual is not to be allowed to make this distinction for themselves, then it follows (and this is the second alternative) *that somebody or something is going to make that distinction for them and enforce it upon them whether they like it or not.* Who or what is this something or somebody?

Marx's answer is "society". "Society", says Marx in *The German Ideology*, "regulates the general production". Each worker, says Marx in the *Critique of the Gotha Programme*, "receives a certificate from society" to show what labour he has provided and to allow him to draw from "the social stock of means of production" that to which he is entitled through his labour input. "Society", he says in the same text, inscribes upon its banners "From each according to his abilities[,] to each according to his needs". But who or what is this "society"? It clearly is not everybody taken *individually*, making their own individual decisions, or at least if it is, we are back to the problem above. So it must be either "everybody" gathered in some *collective* decision-making body, or it must be some *representatives* of society as a whole gathered in such a body.

If it is the first ("everybody" in society gathered in a collective decision-making body or assembly of some sort) then Marx must be conceiving communist society as a whole as made up of *very small* self-governing communities, of a few hundred people at most, otherwise, of course, such an idea would be impracticable.

If it is the second (some representatives or delegates of society gathered in a decision-making body) then we are talking about a *state* (albeit a democratic state) making crucial decisions about production and consumption, about abilities and needs on *behalf* of "society" and Marx ought to say that and not talk obfuscatingly about "society" itself making such decisions. (*Karl Marx*, 143–45)

In other words, if the principle of "From each according to his abilities, to each according to his needs" is to operate in a society in which production and consumption are totally planned and the market abolished, then this principle puts massive—one could properly say totalitarian—powers into the hands of whoever is doing the planning. For it involves nothing less than such planners having the power to decide what the "abilities" and "needs" of every individual in such a society are. This, in turn, implies a degree of power over the most intimate aspects of each person's life (especially on the "needs" side) that planners in actually existing socialist societies have never claimed or obtained, although they have been condemned as totalitarian often enough.

If one adds to this reflection the observations made earlier about the problems and imperatives of central planning in complex industrial societies revealed by seventy years of actually existing socialism, then the full implications of such a vision are surely enough to make one shudder. For those earlier observations suggested that:

1. To be realized in actuality a totally planned economy has to be an economy planned by a specialized and powerful group of state bureaucrats
2. This planning is highly inflexible and inefficient and becomes more so the more economically complex the society being planned
3. None of these features is eradicable by democratic forms of planning, at least if "democratic" means planning by "everybody" for "everybody" (which is what Marx's vision might imply). Indeed it is likely that all the problems of a planned economy and society would, if anything, be worsened by such democracy, even if it were feasible (which it is not)

So we must conclude from all this that if Marx's "higher phase" of communism ever did come into existence the people who were unfortunate enough to "enjoy" it would live lives of continuous and absurd misery. For they would have to spend a large part of their waking hours either in endless planning meetings or in continuous computer contact with each other making a thousand decisions a day on their production and consumption preferences. For a good deal of the rest of the time, they would all be taking part in/being subjected to "democratic" decision-making processes to determine what one another's abilities and needs were and whether these had changed, and how, since the last "democratic" decision. Meanwhile they would almost certainly be continually short of many goods and services (all of which they would presumably "need") because the whole planning process would be so impossibly slow and cumbersome that many or most things would never get produced, or (therefore) consumed. So most of their democratically determined abilities would, in fact, go to waste and their needs would languish. Surely the cynical slogan of such a society would soon be "Man does not live by needs alone," and the planning meetings would be empty and the computer terminals deserted as the demoralized and exasperated citizens of the "higher phase" combed the no doubt flourishing black market in search of potatoes.

I think therefore that we can now conclude, reasonably and rationally, that Marx's higher phase of communism is not only unrealizable but that it is far better left unrealized. And we can rationally conclude that from an analysis of the development of capitalism since Marx's death and from the experience of actually existing socialism in the twentieth century. That being the case, the best that Marxists can and should aim for is the realization of some variant of Marx's lower phase of communism, also outlined in the "Critique of the Gotha Programme." In that phase, we may remember, the distribution of goods and services would not be according to need, but according to *labor performed*. And since Marx explicitly assumes that because of unequal abilities labor performed would also be unequal, he explicitly countenances an (unstated) degree of inequality of real incomes and consumption in this phase.[46]

However, while this lower phase may now seem to us to be infinitely preferable to the higher phase of communism, there are still a whole number of problems with it, at least in the very sketchy form in which it is presented in Marx's text. And again the most fundamental of these problems is Marx's total silence on the issue of how and by whom these unequal performances of labor (and hence unequal rewards for labor) are to be measured and determined.

By now we should not have to rehearse at length what the history of actually existing socialism has taught us about the alternatives here. In a totally planned economy either state bureaucrats will make these measurements and assessments of rewards (in which case they will have enormous power over the rest of the population, and we can expect much delay, crude injustice of decision, and considerable inefficiency) or "everybody" makes these measurements and assessments "democratically" (in which case we can expect interminable delays, probably somewhat less injustice, but even more inefficiency). In either case, it is highly likely that in such a society many workers and citizens would not feel that their labor performed had been accurately or justly assessed or (therefore) that their rewards were proportional to their performance.

46. Ibid., 320.

Indeed, making such measurements of labor performed and of appropriate rewards in a complex economy and society would be—indeed *is*, we now know—such a massive, complex, and in many ways arbitrary task (What precisely is the labor contribution of a ballerina, in comparison with a physicist, in comparison with a cellist, in comparison with a computer programmer, in comparison with a truck driver?)[47] that it is almost certain that *any* planned decision on these matters, no matter how "democratically" arrived at, would leave somebody or many people aggrieved. And if one adds to all this the consideration that even when their rewards had been determined, many of those rewards would not actually be forthcoming (because of production and/or distribution foul-ups), it is almost certain that the level of frustration and grievance in this socialist society would be perennially high, and a continuous sense of injustice would pervade a large part of its citizenry.

We have to conclude, therefore, that if these problems are to be avoided measurement of labor performed and of the appropriate rewards for it *must be left to a labor market*. In a feasible and desirable socialist society there must be market in labor, as well as in many other goods and services. However, it is perfectly possible to make this labor market subject to some constraints or parameters about the highest and lowest rewards to be paid for labor performed. Thus a socialist government could instruct enterprises or employers of labor that their highest paid employees were not to receive more than (say) six times the remuneration of their lowest paid employees. Alternatively, rewards could be taxed by a government with the aim of bringing about the same distributional result. On balance I would prefer this latter course, since although it has potential problems (tax avoidance and evasion, for example), it does not provide a direct incentive for enterprises to evade the regulations at times of labor shortage or labor abundance.[48]

However, these remarks abut on the concerns of the final section of this chapter. For having now completed a rational evaluation of Marx's own point of view on capitalism and communism from a late twentieth-century perspective, I can now proceed beyond this to provide, at least in outline, an alternative picture of a feasible and desirable socialism, feasible and desirable, that is, from the point of view of a contemporary Marxist with a knowledge of both present-day capitalism and of actually existing socialism.

47. See Nove, *The Economics of Feasible Socialism*, 50–54, 127–28, 180, 214–21.
48. Ibid., 216–17.

I will do this only in outline, however, both because to do more would require a separate book in itself and because more detailed treatments of this issue are now beginning to appear and are available for the interested reader to consult.

The Marxist Point of View Reformulated: A Desirable and Feasible Socialism

As will be apparent from everything that has been said above, I believe that now, in the late twentieth century, a rational Marxist must hold that the socialist alternative to capitalism will have to be a "market socialism."[49] That is to say, it will have to be a form of economy and society in which the majority of goods and services are produced by enterprises that compete against each other in a market system, and in which those goods and services are also distributed through a market. This means, of course, that all these goods and services will be produced as commodities and sold for money, that is, there will be an active role for both money and prices. This market would include, as already noted, a market for labor, which means that the rewards of labor would be determined by a market mechanism, and so, therefore, would the access of these workers, as consumers, to other goods and services. Thus, just as under capitalism, the higher one's monetary income the more of the marketed goods and services one could afford, and the lower one's monetary income the less of them one could afford.

However, although a feasible and desirable socialist economy would be, in good part, a market economy, this does *not* mean that it would be an economy in which there would be private ownership of the means of production, distribution, and exchange. On the contrary, all the enterprises in this economy, large and small, could be socially owned in various ways. For example, some of the larger ones could be socially owned by joint collectives of workers, managers, and perhaps the representatives of the local communities in which the enterprises were based. Others, perhaps the smaller ones, would be cooperatives of various kinds, made up either of

49. On market socialism, see W. Brus, *The Market in a Socialist Economy* (London: Routledge and Kegan Paul, 1972), and O. Sik, *The Third Way* (London: Wildwood House, 1976). Oscar Lange was one of the first theorists of market socialism; see his "On the Economic Theory of Socialism" (1936), in Nove and Nuti, *Socialist Economics*, 92–110.

workers or of workers, consumers, and local community members. All these enterprises would require management structures, but whereas in the larger concerns managers could be appointed or elected by occasional general assemblies of the collective, and be responsible to that assembly, in the smaller enterprises one could imagine more direct forms of workers' control being possible.

In addition, the fact that a feasible and desirable socialist economy would be primarily or predominantly a market economy does not mean that it would be *entirely* a market economy. On the contrary, such market-socialist economies would also have considerable state sectors in which were produced such goods and services as it was not deemed politically or ethically desirable to produce and distribute through a market. I am thinking here of such things as health care, education, and child care. State sectors could also produce some or all of such other basic goods and services as housing, mass transportation and other economic infrastructure, and perhaps (although this would be open to debate) a certain quantity of basic food and clothing to which every citizen would be entitled as a right. Alternatively, it could subsidize the market prices of such basic goods to ensure their easy availability to all citizens. The state would also have other important functions, including laying down and enforcing a politically agreed maximum and minimum income through a progressive tax system (as noted above), paying unemployment benefits (for there would be unemployment in this system), and creating and enforcing civil and criminal law. The state would *not*, however, own or control any mass media (which would be produced by competing collectives or cooperatives of writers, producers, technicians, journalists, etc.).

Since the state would therefore have a major role in this form of economy and society, the state bureaucracy would obviously be considerable and it would dispose of formidable powers. It would therefore be necessary that the activities of this bureaucracy be closely scrutinized and publicized to guard against abuse of power, and it would also be necessary for it to be both formally and actually responsible to a democratically elected government and popular assembly. The latter, therefore, would have to possess the constitutional powers to ensure that the openness and responsibility of the bureaucracy could be enforced.[50]

50. I do not include here the familiar Marxist/radical demand for state bureaucrats to be replaced by elected officials recallable "at will" by a popular assembly or subject to reelection at regular predetermined intervals. I am persuaded that arrangements like these would prejudice the possibility of such officials acting dispassionately in the general interest by introducing a

Obviously there would be considerable scope for political debate in this form of society—about the relative size and powers of the state and the market, about the most desirable maximum/minimum income differential (consistent with maintaining economic incentives for relatively scarce skills and abilities), about the desirable and feasible levels of unemployment payments and other welfare benefits—and about a myriad of other issues (see below). I therefore envisage that people holding different views about these matters would organize themselves into political parties or factions and would compete for governmental power in popular elections. To facilitate political organization and expression there would, of course, be complete (or as near complete as possible) freedom of speech and the media, of assembly, of protest, and so on. There would also be a wide variety of other organizations in "civil society"—including independent trade unions and organizations of enterprises (federations of collectives, cooperatives, etc.)—that would have political as well as economic or social roles.

This outline, being only an outline, leaves many questions unanswered and many issues unresolved. One important and difficult matter concerns the existence of a financial market as part of this socialist market economy. Would this be an economy, for instance, in which individual citizens and groups of citizens (organizations) could buy shares in enterprises and trade them on a stock market? If so, then even assuming the widest possible distribution of share ownership (consistent with a much more equal distribution of income than in all capitalist societies today) everybody's income would contain a "rentier" or "unearned" component. But more important, given such a market, more successful investors could rapidly become much richer than unsuccessful ones, thus upsetting the income-distribution norms. The only solution to this problem would be to tax away these capital gains entirely, and this would largely defeat the purpose of having a financial market in the first place. If, however, there was no financial market of this sort (which I think would be preferable from a social point of view), would

---

strong incentive among them to curry favor with influential individuals or interest groups that could ensure, or claim to ensure, their reelection. For an excellent discussion of this issue, making particular reference to the U.S. experience of an elected officialdom, see Polan, *Lenin and the End of Politics*, especially 67–74.

However, the omission of this conventional Marxist demand, and the acceptance of a need for career bureaucrats subject to professional appointment and promotion, is of course quite compatible with giving a popular assembly real powers of inquiry and, indeed, of demotion or even dismissal over state bureaucrats. It would also be necessary to give legally guaranteed rights of information and of redress of grievances to citizens in a socialist society, rights that they could enforce against the bureaucracy by a separate legal process *as well as* through a popular asssembly.

it be possible to devise a set of state or collective or cooperative financial institutions that would be genuinely flexible and responsive investment bodies providing for the capital needs of both state and market enterprises? This is the kind of issue in which "learning by doing" and trial and error seem the only rational way forward.

There are many other complex, unresolved questions in this outline. These include issues having to do with the known problems of collectively or socially owned enterprises in a market context (the postwar histories of Yugoslavia and Hungary are good learning grounds here);[51] issues having to do with the distortions in the use of resources that can arise from having both market and nonmarket enterprises and market and nonmarket (subsidized) prices in the same economy; as well, of course, as issues having to do with the kind of Keynesian "counter-cyclical" policies that would have to be pursued by a socialist market state (to prevent or iron out recessions, reduce unemployment, etc.).

As for the geographical extent of this kind of system, I envisage it as spreading gradually, from one nation-state to another, but eventually becoming a world-scale system with world-scale state and planning bodies overseeing a world market-socialist economy (subject to the same welfare and income differential rules, etc.). This itself is not, of course, without problems. Most notably, the larger the scale of the system the more attenuated its democratic controls can become and the more untrammeled may be the powers of world planners or world enterprise managers. But here one can only hope and suppose that as part of the "real movement which abolishes the present state of things" solutions to these problems, or at any rate partial solutions, could be devised as the system was growing. For example, it might be possible to devise novel combinations of world-level planning bodies with highly localized (sub-nation-state) decentralization of powers *if this was done with reference to different sectors and issues.* Thus one could, for example, treat the use of the world's natural resources as a centralized "world-level" planning issue and child care as a highly localized issue. One must also say, of course, that the growth of transnational corporations, as part of the internationalization of capital, and the growth of

---

51. See the discussion of some of these problems in Nove, *The Economics of Feasible Socialism,* part 3, 133–39 and 217. See also B. Horvat, *The Yugoslav Economic System* (New York: International Arts and Science, 1976); J. Meade, "The Theory of Labour-managed Firms and Profit-Sharing," *Economic Journal* (March 1972); L. Sirc, *The Yugoslav Economy under Self-Management* (London: Macmillan, 1979); and J. Vanek, *The General Theory of Labor-Managed Market Economies* (Ithaca: Cornell University Press, 1970).

genuinely transnational forms of capitalist economic organization (like the European Community), already provide frameworks transcending the nation-state in which the struggle for socialism can, and must, be carried on.[52] Indeed, I now believe that many present-day nation-states are already too small to be effective units of Keynesian economic management, let alone of socialist planning. So capitalism is forcing an internationalization of economic and political struggles, and both feasible and desirable visions of socialism and day-to-day socialist politics must accommodate and welcome this broadening of the struggle, not retreat from it.

It may be that when all is said, this vision of socialism will not be nearly so inspiring to the reader as Marx's (Godwin's) cryptic "From each according to his abilities, to each according to his needs," and that despite everything that has been said above. Perhaps this alternative vision seems little more than a program for the universalization and marginal radicalization of actually existing social democracy. Perhaps it is. But as I have already said several times in this book, what is rational and reasonable to desire and to struggle for is deeply a matter of specific social and historical context. And whereas in the Britain of 1964 such a vision, however rational, might not have seemed terribly inspirational or desirable, surely in the Britain of post-Thatcherite conservatism, or in contemporary America, or even, yes, in postcommunist Russia, it may now seem a consummation, as they say, devoutly to be wished.

And there is more. For if a society of "absolute equality" is neither feasible nor desirable; if a society in which "everybody" takes part "democratically" in planning is equally neither feasible nor desirable; if indeed the only feasible forms of a totally planned economy place awesome powers in the hands of a bureaucracy that, at the same time, cannot use those powers even remotely efficiently for the genuine benefit of the mass of the people; if, in short, all these things are chimeras or delusions—then when we have solved the economic problems of socialist construction in the (yes, rather mundane) way that I have outlined above, the real criteria by which, in the future, socialism is judged superior, or inferior, to capitalism may turn out to have nothing directly to do with these economic issues at all. On the contrary, in the late twentieth century it seems reasonable, rational to believe that in the future this choice may turn on such issues as:

52. For important discussions of transnationals and their political implications for socialists, see Rhys Jenkins, *Transnational Corporations and Uneven Development* (London: Methuen, 1987); Arghiri Emmanuel, *Appropriate or Underdeveloped Technology?* (New York: John Wiley, 1982); and Jim Tomlinson, *The Unequal Struggle?* (London: Methuen, 1982).

1. What women can achieve for themselves, and what can be achieved for them, in this form of market socialism, as against capitalism
2. How far the world's natural and environmental resources can be used, and not abused, in this form of market socialism, as against capitalism.
3. How far the potentialities of every individual—whether physical, intellectual, or cultural—are realized in this form of market socialism, as against capitalism.

The three criteria above are placed in the order in which they came to me, not necessarily in an order of importance. (The reader should in any case supply his or her own order of importance.) But clearly the third criterion in particular was at the heart of Marx's own original vision of socialism, and to a degree it subsumes the other two. For logically, women are a subclass of the class "all individuals," and without careful attention to the world's natural resources the third criterion cannot be applied anyway, so the second criterion may be regarded as a necessary condition of maintaining a world in which the third criterion can be applied.[53] To that extent, therefore, I believe that it is with reference to the third criterion above all that the desirability of the form of market socialism that I have outlined will have to be assessed. This criterion also constitutes a major point of continuity between the original Marxist point of view (which has taken such a pounding in this chapter) and the reformulated point of view by which I think it should be replaced. It is, of course, a criterion difficult or impossible to apply in general or in the abstract, but its application is usually tolerably clear with respect to particular issues in particular social and historical contexts.

The task, therefore, for Marxists is to continue the struggle for a world in which this third criterion is increasingly satisfied and to be victorious in that struggle. However, there is no hope of their doing this as long as the Marxist point of view is one with which reasonable and rational people living now, in the late twentieth century, cannot identify (and therefore one to which they cannot move or be moved). This chapter has suggested that if this is to happen—if Marxists are to succeed in moving people now— much in their original point of view will have to be abandoned, and without fear or regret. Indeed, Marxists must and should welcome the abandonment

---

53. This I take to be the central point of Bahro's work. See Rudolf Bahro, *The Alternative in Eastern Europe* (London: New Left Books, 1977), especially chapter 10.

of any redundant intellectual baggage if it will make them better convincers and persuaders and better able to advance, in however small a way, the struggle for a better world. In the next chapter, therefore, I will have a few more things to say about "rationally convincing" or "rationally persuading," and then my task will almost be done.

7

Marxism as a Point of View: Implications for Contemporary Practice

In chapter 5 I reached the surprising conclusion that the essence of the Marxist point of view on capitalism, that which in effect *makes* it Marxist, is a "rationally motivated willingness to act to transform capitalism." This conclusion was surprising because it is not what one might infer from the contemplative analogy of a "point of view." But it was also surprising because it suggests that what distinguishes Marxist analyses from other analyses of capitalist societies is *not* the empirical observations that Marxists made about such societies, nor even their theoretical explanations of these observations, but the use to which the observations and explanations are put. That use is, broadly, to rationally convince people who live in capitalist societies that such societies ought to be changed, and that they can be changed to a better form or forms of society through political action.

I went on to suggest, however, that in its original form the Marxist point of view on capitalism would not now produce a rationally motivated willingness to act to change capitalism. In chapter 6 I argued why this is, in detail, and reformulated the Marxist point of view with reference not only to the history of capitalism (especially since Marx's death) but with reference to the history of actually existing socialist societies since the Bolshevik Revolution of 1917.

In attempting this reformulation, I have endeavored to maintain the Marxist point of view as an immanent critique. That is to say, I have remained faithful to that tradition in Marxism that is suspicious of utopianism, of all attempts to judge or assess actually existing societies by reference to some imagined "perfect" state of affairs. For I think there is still great merit in Marx's well-known assertion that "communism is not for us a state of affairs which is to be established, an ideal to which reality will have to adjust itself. We call communism the real movement which abolishes the present state of things. The conditions of this movement result from the now existing premise."[1] My aim, in earlier chapters, was to challenge the way in which the concept of an immanent critique is understood, to show that it does not have the philosophical problems associated with it which Habermas and many others have identified. In this chapter I wish to challenge the conventional way in which Marxists have understood the phrase "the real movement which abolishes the present state of things." For, far too often, this phrase is trotted out as a prelude to a philistine discussion of the need (for example) to support trade-union activity, to engage in strike action, to join a sect and sell newspapers—in general, to do "real," "practical" things that will contribute to "the real movement"—rather than (for example) sitting around having abstruse discussions about the feasibility or desirability of socialism. Ultimately, this philistine understanding of Marx's famous phrase is based upon an utterly naïve philosophical dichotomy between "material reality" and "thought," the origins and philosophical supports of which I extensively analyzed in *Karl Marx and the Philosophy of Praxis* and which I shall not, therefore, repeat here.[2]

Rather, what we should note is that, in my conception, the *activities* that we call "learning" that (1) absolute material equality is neither feasible nor desirable, or that (2) abolishing classes is not tantamount to abolishing material inequality between persons, or that (3) a totally planned, complex industrial economy is neither feasible nor desirable, or that (4) a society based on the abilities/needs principle would be a miserable absurdity for those who lived in it *is part of "the real movement which abolishes the present state of things."* Or to put it another way, the activities that make up the learning of these things are part of what Marx's phrase *means*.

For there are, of course, a whole variety of practices or activities that can make up this "learning." Reading Alec Nove's book *The Economics of Feasible Socialism* is one such practice or activity, if one happens to be a reader of English. But equally, standing in a long queue on a bitterly cold January day in Irkutsk is part of that learning, as is losing one's job because one crossed a senior party official, as is going on holiday to the USSR and being unimpressed by the material standard of living, as is listening to a Soviet dissident on the BBC, as is reading *The First Circle*, by Aleksandr

1. Marx and Engels, *The German Ideology*, 56–57.
2. Kitching, *Karl Marx*, chapters 1 and 7.

Solzhenitsyn. All these activities, and many others, constitute ways of learning the truth of the four propositions in the preceding paragraph, and they also constitute rational reasons for believing them to be true. There are also, of course, irrational reasons for believing them to be true (for example, skimming *Reader's Digest* or listening to Ronald Reagan discourse on "the evil empire"). But propositions that are true (= that human beings have rational grounds for believing are true) can, of course, logically also be believed to be true, by other human beings, for quite irrational reasons. This latter fact, however, does not affect their truth (which is one of the reasons why ideology should always be distinguished from falsehood).

So, an important part of the history of the twentieth century has been the mass of people in actually existing socialist and capitalist societies learning that our four propositions above are true. However, the ways in which they have learned that (or the kinds of activities in which they have engaged so to do) have been rather different in the two cases. Since, as I have argued, these four propositions are true, it must be regarded as singularly fortunate that the mass of the people in both capitalist and socialist societies has learned that they are. And if we want to stick to some favored Marxist terminology, we can say that it is "material realities," especially in actually existing socialist societies, that have revealed that they are true.

Thus if Marxists wish to be part of "the real movement which abolishes the present state of things" *now*, then it is high time that they, too, learned, and publicly acknowledged, that these four propositions are true. For in doing so they would only be catching up with what the mass of the people in both capitalist and socialist societies have already learned, already know. I have argued in this book that, mainly for ideological and political reasons, Marxists in the twentieth century have conspicuously *lagged behind* "the real movement which abolishes the present state of things." And they are hardly likely to be able to play a leading role in helping to form the future state of affairs in the world until they do, at least, catch up with the real movement of historical activity and learning that is abolishing the present state of things in both East and West.

Much earlier in this book I also noted that one of the merits of seeing Marxism as a point of view—as a rational or reasonable point of view— rather than as a science, was that, in its metaphorical use, an evaluative "point of view" is something of which others have to be "persuaded" or "convinced." Whereas, semantically, a "science" is something that is to be "applied," and the notion of application implies an automaticity of result to which persuading or convincing are, semantically, an irrelevance. In the second part of this chapter, therefore, I wish to examine the practices of persuading and convincing more closely, with the aim of drawing out the implications of these practices for my reformulated Marxist point of view.

Persuading and Convincing: Science, Rhetoric, and the Limits of Reason

In a most interesting discussion of the practice of convincing, Stanley Cavell has pointed out that a close examination of this practice in interpersonal relations reveals that convincing somebody to believe something and/or to do something usually involves something more than simply giving him or her *good reasons* for believing it or doing it.

Cavell noted that convincers *do*, of course, give reasons, but they also do a number of other things, especially in interpersonal convincing. One typical activity, he notes, is to "make appeal to the existing commitments of the other." These commitments may be overtly acknowledged ("You say you love your mother, so how can you not visit her when she is sick, no matter how much it costs?") or may be implied in a situation ("Jenny is your daughter. You want the best for her, don't you? Then I am afraid you really must . . ."). Cavell also notes that convincers frequently "stand warranty" for the views that they express. Thus, "Look, I was in exactly your position a year ago, and I can tell you that it is far better to . . ." or "Look, if you decide to go, I will go with you and I'll tell them that . . . ." In other words, convincers, especially successful ones, often make statements about themselves, or pledge undertakings that they, as well as the other, will have to carry out, as part of the process of rationally convincing another to believe or to act.[3]

If Cavell is right here, and convincing, even rationally convincing, is not simply a process of "giving reasons" (however "good"), then this has some interesting implications for Marxism as "a rationally motivated willingness to act to change capitalism," especially if Marxism is conceived as a "science." For while scientists may analyze the world, predicting future events or trends, they do not—or at least natural scientists do not—*prescribe* actions or beliefs to that which they study. They do not "make appeal to the

3. Cavell, *The Claim of Reason*, chapters 9 and 12.

existing commitments" of atoms or rock strata, nor do they "stand warranty" personally for their views. For scientific views need no warranty save that provided by "science" or "the scientific method."

And thus it is that Marxists who think of themselves as scientists (even as social or human scientists rather than as some species of natural scientist) use modes of expression and undertake a type of intellectual activity that is deeply marked by the taboos of professional science, taboos that indeed derive from natural science. Thus, even when Marxist social scientists do "go so far" as to offer overt political or moral prescriptions, those prescriptions will be supported only by "good reasons"—something like "the weight of the (empirical) evidence" or "the strength of the argument," the latter involving logical coherence as well as empirical evidence. Such Marxists do not "make appeal to existing commitments" for the very good reason that as writers (and indeed as speakers) they often have no idea what the existing commitments of their audience are. Or they make the (usually sensible) assumption that these commitments are likely to be too diverse for any single appeal to work. More significantly, however, Marxists, as writers, seldom if ever stand personal warranty for the views that they are expressing. On the contrary, they usually adopt an *impersonal* mode of expression, involving the abolition of the self as subject or the elimination of the self from the text (often in the name of scientific objectivity). This practice in itself makes standing personal warranty linguistically or discursively impossible or forbidden.

Now, as Wittgenstein points out, there are very good reasons for adopting the "impersonal mode" of speech and writing, a mode that is distinguished by the elimination or minimization of first person singular forms of the verb and the personal pronoun and by the adoption of first-person plural forms (the ubiquitous academic "we") and the impersonal pronoun ("one"). Another common characteristic of this mode of language is the frequent use of passive forms of the verb and the minimization of active and transitive forms (which more frequently require reference to a subject).[4]

One of the most common and valid reasons for using the impersonal mode is to strengthen factual claims, or, more exactly, to stress the facticity or factuality of assertions. Thus, part of what makes "London is the capital city of the United Kingdom" a fact, a factual proposition, is that it is true *whoever asserts it* (and would be false, if it were false, whoever asserted it).

4. On the "impersonal mode" of expression and its role, see Pitkin, *Wittgenstein and Justice*, 231–40, and Cavell, *Must We Mean What We Say?* chapter 3, 36–96.

And we signal this facticity, this claim to factuality, precisely by using modes of speech and writing which make the identity of the asserter an irrelevance, which, in fact, linguistically *remove* the asserter as subject. Similarly, when we are making what we take to be valid arguments involving both factual statements and a process of reasoning from those statements, we also adopt the impersonal mode to signal that the claim to validity here transcends the individual who happens to be making it. Readers or hearers of the claim are then expected to understand that a judgment of the validity of the argument is not any kind of judgment of the arguer *as a person*. As Wittgenstein notes, there is nothing wrong with these impersonal modes of expression in their place, for in such places they serve their intended "objectifying" purposes well. One of the places where this impersonal mode of speech and writing clearly belongs is in science and, indeed, in scholarship. In fact, the use of these forms of speech and writing is one of the criteria by which we identify science and scholarship as such. It is one of the hallmarks of these activities as the activities that they are.[5]

However, if Cavell is right about convincing as a practice, then though providing evidence and giving good reasons is part of convincing, it is by no means the whole of this practice. Therefore, while the use of impersonal modes of speech and writing (which give force to factual claims and validity claims) may have some part to play in the practice of rational convincing and persuading, it is unlikely to be enough in and of itself for successful convincing. For here something more is needed. And that "something more" includes the use of forms of language that are much more self-revelatory, much more consciously reflexive, than are allowed by the conventional science-derived, academic canons of language use.

I am thinking here of statements about why a piece of writing or research was undertaken, statements that are much more personal and/or political than those usually found in the methodology sections of academic treatises. I am thinking about relevant, and occasionally irrelevant, autobiographical anecdote or detail. I am thinking of humor. I am also thinking of linguistic techniques—familiar enough to novelists, playwrights, and journalists—by which appeal is made to a reader's capacity for imaginative empathy. For example, "placing" her or him in the mind of an imagined character or characters, or "placing" her or him in situations (the queue in Irkutsk in January) in which appeal is made to the senses as well as to the intelligence.

5. Pitkin, *Wittgenstein and Justice*, 235–40.

In short, I have in mind a whole bundle of linguistic techniques that the ancient Greeks taught us to call *rhetoric*, in its original sense.[6]

In the original understanding of the term, and in the sense in which I am using it, the use of rhetoric is not incompatible with the careful selection and presentation of evidence, with care and exactness of argument, with a scrupulous treatment of opposing views, or with any of the other practices that are (rightly) emphasized and honored as the hallmarks of scholarly activity. The use of rhetorical techniques that can assist in the process of successful convincing is not incompatible with the highest standards of academic scholarship and objectivity, nor does employing such techniques amount to the substitution of "emotive appeals" for "appeals to reason." Rhetorical techniques can, of course, be abused or used badly or tastelessly (but then so can all the more conventional scholarly techniques and uses of language). But the possibility or even the actuality of such abuse does not provide any valid reason for excluding them from Marxist writing, and indeed there is every rational reason to include rhetorical techniques if that writing is meant to contribute, in however small a way, to the process of making people rationally or reasonably willing to change capitalism. If, that is to say, it is to help to move them to the Marxist point of view.

There is every reason to reject such uses of language, however, if Marxism is a hard science. For then, as I have already said, "convincing" a person or people to adopt the Marxist point of view is utterly beside the point. For if Marxism is a science, then once its "results" have been obtained and those results "applied" to the task of bringing about a socialist revolution, the question of persuading or convincing anyone does not enter into the matter. Equipped with this science, the scientific socialist possesses an understanding of the "true" or "real" material interests of the international proletariat. So equipped, she or he can utilize the inevitable crises of capitalism to build a political movement that will bring about the revolution.

I have said more than enough throughout this book about why I reject all these conceptions and propositions, and there is no need to repeat those arguments again. What is important to note, however, is the marked homology, the tight "fit," between this conception of Marxism and the uses of language in which it is embodied. For if one does not have to convince or persuade, *then it does not matter who one is,* and as a scientist one can simply disappear from the text and let the science "speak for itself." If one

---

6. For ancient Greek conceptions of rhetoric, see Ronald Beiner, *Political Judgement* (London: Methuen, 1983), especially chapter 5.

is appealing to material interests, *then one does not have to appeal to any-thing else* (imagination, empathy, morality, humor). And since one pos-sesses a scientifically guaranteed insight into what those interests are, such appeals are in turn guaranteed to be successful ("in the long run," of course!).

There are, however, many Marxists today, perhaps even the majority, who would reject the idea of Marxism as science in this full-blown determi-nistic sense. Yet, even as they reject it, they still make use of forms of language, of forms of expression, which originally embodied that full-blown conception and still get their residual power and force from it.[7] But if the view of Marxism as natural science (whether full-blown or attenuated in some way) is wrong, totally, hopelessly wrong and misconceived, then these linguistic forms may now be an empty shell and (to mix metaphors) a straitjacket. They may now be—indeed, they are in my view—a linguistic straitjacket that prevents Marxist writers from adopting other forms of lan-guage that could be rather more effective in persuading others to move to the Marxist point of view. For this straitjacket prevents Marxists from writing *movingly,* where "movingly" means not that one appeals to the emotions instead of to the reason, but that one appeals to the emotions as well as to the reason.

So it will be seen, I hope, that there is a deep and intimate connection between two central concerns of this book: between the analysis and cri-tique of Marxist uses of language that took up so much of its fourth and fifth chapters and the reformulation of the Marxist point of view that took place in its sixth. For the two are brought together in the linguistic exigen-cies or imperatives of "rationally convincing" or "rationally persuading" as

---

7. No one reference would capture what I am referring to here, but again the reader is directed to the language of *Economy and Society, Theoretical Practice, New Left Review* (especially in the 1970s), and to any of the works of Althusser, Poulantzas, Bettelheim, Laclau, and the "structural Marxist" tradition in general in the 1970s and early 1980s. Unfortunately, this tradition and practice (of a rigidly "objectified" form of writing) is also found in much positivistic Anglo-Saxon social science (not accidentally, as we can now see); indeed, the two traditions often mesh in a singularly ugly and dispiriting prose that has become quasi-hegemonic in social science—the journal *Critical Social Policy* is one example selected arbi-trarily from among many. E. P. Thompson's *Poverty of Theory* often scored palpable rhetorical hits against this form of writing, and he sensed, very rightly, that there was some deep organic connection between what was said and how it was said in Marxist structuralism. But in my view he never succeeded in grasping what the connection was (i.e., the reification of both language and the world) exactly enough. Indeed, he too often focused on the use of "concepts" in historical writing when a focus on propositions would have proved much more radically destructive of the Althusserian problematic.

practices. They are linked through a consideration of what people do when they rationally convince others to believe something or to do something and (therefore) by a consideration of what Marxists will need to do if they are to rationally convince others to move to the Marxist point of view. For Marxists will never speak movingly to others or write movingly for them so long as they are in thrall to a particular picture of science and to the uses of language which reproduce that picture constantly (even perhaps among those who do not subscribe to its full-blown version). And those uses of language are so effective in insinuating a picture of science because, of course, they originated with that picture and are still part of it.

However, when all this has been said, there remains one lasting merit of the traditional picture of Marxism as science, a merit to which, to this point, I have hardly made any reference at all, despite its being absolutely central to the leading themes of this book, especially to the theme of rationally convincing and persuading. This is the traditional Marxist concern with *material interests* and with basing the struggle for socialism on appeal to such interests and not on an abstract or naïve rationalism. If this book were simply to finish here, the reader would have every reason to convict me of just such a rationalism. For I might appear to think that my feasible and desirable socialism could be brought about simply by some cozy fireside chats in which people in general would be convinced of the need to bring about socialism by careful rational argument combined with some moving rhetoric. But I do not think that. Indeed, I think that the traditional Marxist opposition to abstract rationalism has some real merit to it. However, it also has grave weaknesses, based upon some overly simple conceptions of both "rationalism" and "material interests." So my task in the final section of this chapter will be to examine the strengths and weaknesses of the Marxist conception of material interests and to consider how far the critique of rationalism to which it gives rise affects or weakens the thesis that has been developed in this book.

Reason and Material Interests: The Limits of Antirationalism

To put the matter simply, it seems to me that in the Marxist tradition as a whole there has been a persistent tendency to slip from the (perfectly correct) observation that socialism cannot be brought about by rational conviction or rational argumentation *alone* to the (extremely errant and dangerous) proposition that it can be brought about without any need of rational conviction or argumentation *at all*.

However, this latter position can only be sustained if one holds to some version of the thesis that the working class (or women, youth, blacks, or whatever other revolutionary social category has been identified) has some *essential* material interest in the creation of socialism. And by "essential" I mean nothing less than the view that a revolutionary consciousness is somehow inscribed in the very *being* or *social situation* of the social group involved. As I have already said, I do not believe that Marx himself thought this about the working class (although there is some evidence in his writings to the contrary). In fact, the only serious and sustained attempt in the Marxist tradition to argue for this conception is Georg Lukács's *History and Class Consciousness*. It seems to me, however, that the argument which Lukács advances in that book is either metaphysical (since class consciousness is defined in such a way that no empirical evidence about the consciousness of any actual workers could refute it) or pernicious (in lending a spurious philosophical rationale to the substitution of the Leninist party for the working class on the grounds that the party is the embodiment of "true" proletarian class consciousness). It has never surprised me, therefore, that in his later years Lukács treated this work of his youth with some embarrassment.[8]

Leaving Lukács aside, however, and assuming that one does not believe that workers (or women, blacks, et al.) are essentially socialists in their very identity, then it follows that workers *become* socialists, women *become* socialists, blacks *become* socialists through processes that involve more than simply being a worker, a woman, and so on. Indeed the whole Marxist-Leninist tradition both implicitly and explicitly admits this as soon as it talks of the Leninist party as composing a "vanguard" of the working class, a vanguard of its most "advanced" or most "class-conscious" elements (elements that have gone beyond "trade union consciousness," etc.).

However, where the Leninist tradition departs from the position outlined in this book is in its conception of the additional processes that turn workers into class-conscious workers. For at this point it nearly always has resort to such examples as being a trade-union militant, taking part in strikes, experiencing class and political oppression "on the picket line," and so

8. See Lukács's own Preface to the 1967 edition of *History and Class Consciousness*, 9–39, and Kolakowski, *Main Currents of Marxism*, vol. 3, chapter 7.

forth. But this seems to be a perfect case of constructing unsafe generalizations from accurate, but specific, observations. For while it may be accurate to observe that, in some specific cases, people who become self-conscious socialists have led strikes or picketed (just as some women who become feminists have experienced domestic violence), it is most certainly inaccurate to say, as a general observation, that *all* people who lead strikes become socialists or that *all* women who experience domestic violence become feminists. It is even less plausible therefore to offer the general prescription that "becoming a socialist requires one to lead strikes" or that "becoming a feminist requires one to experience domestic violence."

In other words—and to state what is surely the obvious—while the experience of leading a strike, or confronting police on a picket line, or being arrested and beaten up after a demonstration may be part of the process of becoming a socialist for some people, these things are neither sufficient in themselves to make socialists (otherwise everybody who had ever been on strike would be a socialist) nor are they even necessary experiences in the making of all socialists. The reason for this is the one that we might expect—namely, that becoming a socialist involves an extra element over and above class or material self-interest or class political practices. And this element can even in some cases (many cases?) substitute for such interests. This element is—surprise, surprise—rational conviction about both the desirability and feasibility of socialism. This, in turn, is brought by critical thought, reflection, and study. Indeed, the actual practice of many Marxist and Leninist political sects (with their almost invariant emphasis on the "political education" of militants) implicitly admits this, even when their explicit ideology does not.[9]

But the most important thing here is to understand why this is, why this extra element of rational conviction is required. The reason is that what people, any people, take their material self-interest to be is *deeply affected by what they know*, both about their own situation and about the society in which they live. Thus if we take the vision of a feasible and desirable socialism outlined in this book, and we ask which groups or classes in contemporary capitalist and socialist societies would have a material interest in opposing the realization of such a vision, and which groups would have a material interest in supporting its realization, the answer turns out to be far more complex than one might suppose.

---

9. See Ellen Meiskins Wood, *The Retreat from Class: A New "True" Socialism* (London: Verso, 1986), chapter 8, and my "Reply," *New Left Review*, no. 163 (May–June 1987): 121–28.

For example, since my vision of a market socialism involves the abolition of the private ownership of the means of production, distribution, and exchange, then *all* the groups in contemporary capitalist society who currently own such assets would be deeply threatened materially by it, and these groups turn out to be those making up the "bourgeoisie" or "capitalist class" as conventionally understood. Even then, however, the struggle for such a market socialism might win the support of individuals from this rentier class who had become "renegades" out of rational conviction. It should also be noted, however, that all enterprise managers and workers who currently own equity or other financial assets would also be directly threatened by the realization of market socialism (since my variant of it involves the abolition of financial markets).[10] However, managers in their role as managers, and workers in their role as workers, would not be threatened by market socialism since they could continue to occupy such roles, although under somewhat different institutional conditions. And clearly many poor people and many women with children would benefit greatly from market socialism because of the more comprehensive and generous child-care resources and other welfare benefits made available by the state in such a system.

When we turn to the major social groups in currently existing socialist societies the situation is similarly complex. Clearly, many state bureaucrats in the currently existing socialist societies would be threatened by market socialism since their role and function would be abolished.[11] But equally many would still be required. Industrial and agricultural workers would, however, be in a very ambiguous position, since the stable and guaranteed employment that they enjoy in the current situation would be taken away. Yet most of the vast majority of workers who remained in employment would almost certainly experience a much faster growth of their real incomes than they enjoyed in, for example, the USSR from the 1930s or in China from the 1950s. In addition, the state in a market-socialist system would pay a much higher level of unemployment benefit (as a proportion of average earnings) than that currently available in most capitalist societies. Female workers would be in the same ambiguous position as male workers in the above respects, but, as women, they would undoubtedly benefit in other ways from market socialism, both through the provision of child care

---

10. For some data on the expansion of share ownership in Britain, see Charlie Leadbetter, "The Sid in Us All," *Marxism Today* (January 1987), and R. Fraser, *Privatization: The UK Experience and International Trends* (London: Longman, 1988), chapter 3.

11. Nove, *The Economics of Feasible Socialism*, 116–35.

by the state and, more important (for Russian and Chinese women), from the fact that commodities would become reliably available, eliminating the need for time-consuming queueing.

So what this all shows is the well-known philosophical fact that "material self-interest" and "class self-interest" are not at all the clear, unambiguous, or self-evident concepts that they are often taken to be, especially by more vulgar Marxists. Instead, they are deeply affected by the knowledge and other beliefs of the person in that class (or gender or ethnic) position. And to say this is only to say again that the making of socialists and of a conscious commitment to socialism is about more than "material self-interest" conceived in this vulgar way. In particular, while powerful minority groups or classes in both contemporary capitalist and socialist societies may have a fairly clear material interest in opposing market socialism, the majority of the populations in both types of society have no very strong material interest in opposing it. This does not mean, however, that such majorities will therefore support it. For whether they choose to support it depends upon what they *know* and *understand* about it as an alternative, and that in turn depends upon a host of other factors, most notably the political effectiveness of those who advocate such a change and those who oppose it. Here, indeed, is where politics becomes central, determining the types of understanding that come to predominate about market socialism as an alternative to current realities in East and West.

So I hope it will be clear that I do not suppose that the process of winning people to the modern Marxist point of view will simply be one of "civilized" persuasion and conviction. Indeed, there is every reason to suppose that it will involve, for example, strikes, demonstrations, and violent confrontations, with the processes of rational persuading and convincing woven into the warp and weft of these and other activities.

In fact, because I conceive things in this way I am increasingly dissatisfied with Habermas's ever more single-minded concentration on "rational communication" in his work. It seems to me to be absolutely right to see a genuinely democratic and free society as one in which "rational communication" can go on as uncontaminated as possible by the highly unequal power and knowledge relations that so compromise free speech and free debate in present-day capitalist democracies. To this extent I find Habermas's project illuminating and important. But it also seems to me dangerous to confuse this highly significant and helpful formal specification of what a genuinely free and democratic society would be with the actual social and political processes by which such a society or societies may be brought about.[12] For the latter, surely, will unavoidably be a complex and shifting combination of rational persuading and convincing with much less rational and highly conflictual processes. And there is no way (I am traditionally Marxist enough to believe) that this can be avoided. I also think that while a desirable and feasible socialist society of the type I have outlined would allow more social space for more genuinely equal and open discussion of a whole variety of personal, social, and political issues, it would certainly *not* be a society in which all decisions of all persons on all matters would be made rationally. No society composed of human beings will ever, in my judgment, be like that. And indeed I am enough of a nonrationalist to think that is a good thing and is in itself a bulwark of a kind of freedom.

This brings me to my final point. It is one of the strengths—not weaknesses—of Marx's own work that he simply took the existence of unequal abilities among human beings for granted. But it has, I think, been a weakness of the Marxist tradition in general that it has not given sufficient consideration or weight to the implications of both unequal abilities and differing interests among human beings in its conceptions of a desirable and feasible socialism.

Certainly, I see no point in hiding my view that the number of people in *any* society who will be deeply and passionately committed to creating socialism will always be a minority, probably even a tiny minority, of the whole. Similarly, if and when a world of market socialism is created, the number of people who will be deeply interested in playing an active role in its public institutions (whether in enterprise management, political parties, media and cultural collectives, or whatever) will also, I think, be a tiny minority of the whole. This does not mean that the struggle for socialism cannot be won, or that such a market socialism will somehow be flawed because it is not "perfectly democratic." (I trust that we have had enough of "perfect" anything by now.) It just means that *leadership matters*, both in the struggle for socialism in contemporary capitalism and, no doubt, in the socialist future (assuming, for a moment, that there will be one). It also means that leading people to socialism and leading them in a socialist society will almost certainly mean concentrating, most of the time, on immediate issues of pressing concern to the majority of people rather than on those grand themes that have dominated this book.

12. Richard J. Bernstein has made much the same point in *Beyond Objectivism and Relativism*, 193–205, and in *The Reconstructing of Social and Political Theory* (Oxford: Basil Blackwell, 1976), 223–26.

It was, and is, one of the strengths of the Leninist tradition in Marxism that it grasps very clearly the need for leadership in the struggle for socialism and in the socialist society. But where the Leninists erred (or where at any rate they turned an agonized historical necessity into a miserable ideological virtue) was in the scant attention they paid to the *forms* of leadership and to the need—the absolutely essential need in any socialist society worth the name—for the leadership to be responsible, genuinely and meaningfully *responsible*, to those whom they lead.

It is vital to say what this means "in a crunch," for it is in the crunch that it matters. It means that though "we" may, and must, endeavor to rationally persuade or convince people of the desirability and feasibility of socialism, in a democratic society one of their human rights is the right *not to listen to us*. Similarly, in the democratic market-socialist society of the future (?), though a leadership must try to convince of the desirability of a certain policy or course of action, it must be able to be deposed and replaced by another leadership if the citizens are not convinced or (again) if they just won't listen, for whatever reason.

All that one can say about such situations is that if people do refuse to do what is rational or reasonable to do in a given circumstance, this does usually rebound on them in some way, a way from which they will (hopefully) learn. In fact, that human beings *do* generally learn in this way ("the hard way," as we say) is part of what it means to say that they do usually, or at least fairly frequently, "act rationally." This being so, we Marxists can, like everybody else, have some hope for the future, but only if we too learn, albeit the hard way. This book has meant to be a small contribution to that learning. I hope that it has not been too hard.

PART FOUR

8

Darkness and Light:
Some Concluding Reflections

While thinking about this book and while writing it, I have been continually visited by two images. Both are rather commonplace, especially in philosophy, and there is little doubt that they derive, at any rate in part, from the reading that has most deeply influenced both this book and my earlier *Karl Marx and the Philosophy of Praxis*. But whether derivative or not, they were nonetheless important to me as I wrote this book—indeed, they more or less continually accompanied its writing—and both now seem to me of some significance. In fact, I now think that between them they distill the essence of Wittgenstein's later philosophy, or at any rate the aspects of it that have been most important to me and to this book as a project. I also came to feel that the very act of sharing them could be a help in elucidating that philosophy for others. So for both these reasons this chapter will be personal and introspective in tone, although the aim and issue of that introspection is not simply personal.

My first image was one of darkness. I am in a cave, but without Plato's fire, a mine gallery like that in which my father worked, a darkened and shuttered room. This, therefore, is not the darkness of night. It is an enclosed darkness. It is also silent. I think that it is a place like this, a silent and dark place (I am always alone in this image), which Marxists most fear. They fear that without science, without the certainties that science provides, without its guarantees, there is no way forward and one must stumble in the dark without any light to guide one's way. In fact, this is just the Marxist version of what Richard Bernstein has called the "Cartesian anxiety,"[1]

1. R. J. Bernstein, *Beyond Objectivism and Relativism*.

which has haunted Western philosophy from the eighteenth century until today and has continually fueled its neurotic epistemological obsessions. It is the anxious conviction that if there are no indubitable grounds, no securely establishable foundations for knowledge, then there is nothing but the darkness of skepticism, relativism, and doubt. And needless to say, I myself was one of the Marxists referred to above. For a long time, I shared both the fear of "subjectivism," "relativism," and so on and the conviction that science was the only possible light in this otherwise treacherous darkness.

The reason that Marxists have always been plagued by a particularly severe form of Cartesian anxiety is that for them—for us—a lot more hangs on the possibility of certainty, and a lot more is lost to skepticism and relativism, even than in mainstream Western philosophy. For, famously, we do not merely wish to interpret the world, we wish to change it. Hence it is vital, not merely that we have the guaranteedly right interpretation of the world, but that we have, as it were, the interpretation that is *so* guaranteedly right ("correct" is the favorite word) that it *will* change the world— and change it in the precise way that it is scientifically expected to change it.

I have endeavored to show, both in this book and in *Karl Marx and the Philosophy of Praxis,* that this heightened Cartesian anxiety too is misplaced. I have tried to show that one can analyze capitalism and socialism rationally, that one can aspire to and attain scholarly objectivity, and that one can politically persuade and convince in rational ways, all without any need either of the picture of science by which Marxists have been obsessed or of the foundations for knowledge that science supposedly provides. This is possible because the Cartesian anxiety, whether in its general form or in its heightened Marxist form, is generated by the same profoundly misleading picture of what it is for human beings to "doubt," "be certain," "know," "reason," and the like.[2] Hence the therapy for this anxiety pioneered by Wittgenstein, but followed by Sellers, Davidson, Quine, Rorty, and Cavell (among others), is to show, in very detailed ways, both how and why this picture is both enormously compelling and profoundly misleading.

I have also tried to demonstrate that a persuasive and convincing Marxist politics for the modern world can be formulated without the need for scientific foundations by actually doing it, by outlining such a politics in this book (and thus performatively realizing its possibility). And hopefully by

---

2. Wittgenstein, *On Certainty;* Morawetz, *Wittgenstein and Knowledge;* especially chapters 4 and 5; and Rorty, *Philosophy and the Mirror of Nature,* chapters 3 and 4.

doing this I will have helped to exorcise not only my own dark demons of skepticism, relativism, and subjectivism but those of others as well.

But the effectiveness of philosophical therapy, like the effectiveness of the psychotherapy with which Wittgenstein occasionally compared it, has ultimately to be judged by the patient. So it is up to the readers of this book, and especially those readers who think of themselves as Marxists, to attest whether the therapy has worked or not. Because, of course, if they do not so attest *it has not worked*, for there is no other criterion of its "working."[3]

Unfortunately, however, I think that the single greatest impediment to the therapy working is capitalism itself. For as I have remarked more than once in this book, Marxists must confront the massive, indubitable, hegemonic *actuality* of capitalism all the time. And the battle against that actuality is—or certainly seems—unequal enough without having to give up the one weapon ("science") that can confront that actuality with something as certain, as indubitable, as it itself appears to be. But, of course, Marxists and socialists do not need science to change capitalism, any more than lords and merchants and peasants needed science to change feudalism, or than the leaders and people of the former Soviet Union needed science to change actually existing socialism. They needed, and we need, only to *act* in the world on the basis of reason and interest. Of course, without science Marxists cannot know that capitalism will be changed into socialism and communism, but have they really *known* that? And if not, are they one whit worse off for admitting that they cannot know it but that they can rationally desire it and treat it as a possibility, a potentiality to be realized (by their actions, of course, but also by the actions of others)?

In my first image this is like my eyes adjusting to the darkness so that I find that it is not total darkness at all. It is to realize that it is possible to find one's way forward without the artificial light of science, even if it is a rather bumpy business, with many wrong turns, much falling over, and a continual fear that a pair of unassisted eyes will not be equal to the task. And of course there is no guarantee that they will be.

My second image is the total opposite of the first. It is an image of light. I am in a room made entirely of full-length mirrors, but they are peculiar in one respect. The mirrors do not reflect me, although I am the only person in the room. Instead, all I can see in them is a small, densely bearded,

3. See Wittgenstein, *Lectures and Conversations;* McGuiness, "Freud and Wittgenstein," in *Wittgenstein and His Times;* and the Preface to Pitkin, *Wittgenstein and Justice,* especially xi–xii.

red-haired little man with bright blue eyes and highly colored clothing. He calls himself Language.

I say to him, "If I'm not to become confused, it is of the utmost importance that you be absolutely precise."

He looks grave and implacably serious and says, "Precisely!"

And as he says this he comes suddenly into much clearer focus. His outline becomes very sharp, his colorful clothing is almost garishly defined, and, most strangely of all, he becomes rather *square*. His head and body are suddenly square-shaped and his legs are straight and dumpy. He stands foursquare and heavily in one spot.

But then I turn to another mirror and see him from a rather different angle. Inspired by this I say, "But of course, it is very difficult to say precisely what precision is. I mean what is precise in one context isn't precise in another, and anyway, do we always need to be precise? Don't we sometimes need to be vague?"

He smiles wryly at this and seems to stretch himself. His hard, square outline disappears, and the colors of his clothing become much less garish, more nuanced. He raises one arm above his head and jestingly assumes a ballet dancer's pose.

He says, "How true!"

Now I walk up to a mirror and peer at him closely. For suddenly he is much more difficult to see. In fact, he seems about to disappear. I say, "However, one must be careful here. Too much concentration on context, on the pragmatics of language, could simply become a means by which all exactitude, all rigor, is lost. There clearly is an important place for the tight definition of terms in any scientific use of language."

He frowns. He keeps his ballet dancer's pose and his outline becomes rather clearer again. Moreover, his square, dumpy legs reappear, but now combined with a lithe, sensuous torso. He looks totally out of proportion.

Now I say irritatedly, "You look ridiculous!"

He looks hurt. He says, "Do I? Well, if I do, 'tis you that have made me so."

Now I am frustrated and angry. I circle the room agitatedly peering in each of the mirrors in turn, examining him feverishly from every angle. But this does nothing for my exasperation.

Suddenly, he says, "Can I make a suggestion?"

He is smiling now. He has assumed his original rather nondescript shape, but his blue eyes are bright with amusement and he is standing in a relaxed pose with one hand on his hip. I say sullenly, "I suppose so."

He says, "Close your eyes and tell me a joke."

I say, "Don't be ridiculous. This is a serious business, a very serious business."

He says, "Oh, go on. Close your eyes, keep them tight shut, and tell me a joke."

I say, "What on earth good is that going to do?!"

He smiles mischievously again and says, "You'll see. Or rather you *won't* see. Go on!"

So rather reluctantly and ill-temperedly I begin.

"Well . . . er . . . There was this man who went to a psychiatrist. Asked what the problem was, he said, 'It's not me, doctor, it's my brother. He thinks he's a hen.' 'If that's true,' said the psychiatrist, 'it's pretty serious. How long has he been like this?' 'Oh, years,' said the young man, 'ever since he was a kid. But recently it's got much worse. He goes around the place almost bent double and clucking, and yesterday he tried to fly out of his bedroom window.' 'Good God!' said the psychiatrist, 'why haven't you done something about this long before now? He could really hurt himself.' 'We would have,' said the young man, 'but you see, doctor, the family needed the eggs.'"

Suddenly there is a peal of laughter and all around is the sound of breaking and exploding glass. When I open my eyes the mirror room has gone and I am alone in the open air on a bright, warm summer's day. I'm in a narrow country lane only a few yards from a pub. A friend is sitting in the pub garden with an empty beer glass on the table in front of him. He is reading a book by Althusser.

I stroll up to him and say, "Fancy a drink?"

He looks up in surprise, smiles, and says, "Oh yes, please. I'd have bought another one myself, but I came without my wallet and I'm six pence short. I suppose that's what he means by 'determination in the last instance by the economic.'"

I laugh. I know precisely what he means.

This makes a pleasing and amusing image, or series of images, and certainly it came to me again and again as I was struggling to get down the most explicitly Wittgensteinian pages of this book and to get their meaning and importance clear for myself and for others. Yet as a metaphor for Wittgenstein's later philosophy it has its limitations (of course). One serious limitation is that it suggests that Wittgenstein thought that the ordinary use of language was itself unproblematic, indeed that it was the embodiment of all wisdom. This is something of which he has often been accused, and along with this accusation has gone a more general one—that his later philosophy is utterly conservative. It is conservative, it is suggested, in that it deifies the ordinary use of language that happens to predominate in any society at any point in time as the standard by which all other uses should be judged. Thus, it is said, it endorses the ideological status quo in the most profound possible way.[4]

However, what such accusations miss is that Wittgenstein is not concerned, in his later philosophy, with any of the uses of language that are what one might call politically or ideologically problematic. He is not concerned with analyzing those forms or patterns of the use of language that are importantly varied and conflictual because they embody or reflect differences of interest or belief among different groups in society. In fact, he is only concerned with those uses of language that are almost entirely unproblematic—with that massive number of very mundane uses of language of which it can be universally agreed that "this is what we all say" or "those are the ways in which we all talk about these things." He is concerned with the close, even obsessive, analysis of these mundane cases *because he thinks that nobody, except philosophers or those treating philosophical questions, ever transgresses the rules of language use that they reveal.* He also thinks that philosophers themselves only transgress these rules unwittingly, in the course of trying to think profoundly, especially about epistemological issues.

In fact, this is one of the central paradoxes of language and of philosophy for Wittgenstein. For in his view it is *only* those people who are trying to think in a deep, philosophical way with language who will abuse it in the profound and subtle ways with which he is concerned. It is almost impossible to sum up all these ways in one brief formulation (which is why Wittgenstein has to be followed through the labyrinth of specific and varied examples of language use that he analyzes in his writings). But perhaps the nearest one can get to a general formulation is the following:

> People doing philosophy are, in general, inclined to take one
> use of a word or phrase, which is available in ordinary lan-

4. This is the central argument of Ernest Gellner's *Words and Things* (Harmondsworth: Penguin, 1963). For the case restated, see Robert John Ackermann, *Wittgenstein's City* (Amherst: University of Massachusetts Press, 1988), especially chapter 10; see also Cornforth,

guage, and then turn this into the "paradigm" use, often through fixing it in a definition. Thus, for example, they will fix on those uses of the words "know," "knowing," "knowledge," and so on that treat knowing as a form of perceiving or observing. In doing so, they either fail to notice other uses of these words (for example, "Boy, he really knows how to bat!" said while watching a cricket match), or they simply ignore them. However, they invariably do this at a cost. Because those other uses are "there" in language for a very good reason, usually the reason that the human *practice* involved (knowing, believing, thinking, imagining, expecting, etc.) is a lot more complex than can be grasped by one use alone. The net result, then, is that in making one employ the paradigm use, philosophers find themselves enmeshed in puzzles and paradoxes that disappear or are dissolved the moment that they are reminded of the other uses that they have neglected or ignored. In fact, assembling such reminders is the central technique of philosophy as therapy, and the technique employed over and over again in Wittgenstein's later philosophy. Often those reminders begin in ways that can seem almost embarrassingly banal and obvious, which is why this form of therapy requires patience from the patient. But if persevered with they can produce conclusions that are neither obvious nor banal, but both illuminating and therapeutic. Although, as noted before, whether they *are* illuminating or therapeutic is a matter to be finally determined by the patient him- or herself.[5]

In short, then, Wittgenstein's analytical techniques are designed to provide a sociological and anthropological dissolution of *epistemology*. But they do not, as he employs them, constitute a total sociology of knowledge or sociology of language. For he simply was not interested in the linguistic

---

Marxism and the Linguistic Philosophy, and David Pole, *The Later Philosophy of Wittgenstein* (London: Athlone Press, 1958), to which the excellent discussion in Fann, *Wittgenstein's Conception of Philosophy,* 98–105, is a reply.

5. The best general discussion of this issue (and of the merits and limitations of Wittgenstein's claim to have found a method to "dissolve" philosophical problems) known to me is in Cavell, *The Claim of Reason,* chapters 6 and 8. See also Richard Rorty's Introduction to *"The Linguistic Turn": Recent Essays in Philosophical Method* (Chicago: University of Chicago Press, 1967), especially 35–39.

forms or expressions of social conflict or in the historical processes of language change (although he does have one or two important, but isolated, insights into these latter processes).[6] It follows, therefore, that to be of most benefit to social scientists Wittgenstein's techniques will have to be developed by being applied to the socially problematic or conflictual areas of language use and by being used in the context of an explicit concern with language change as part of historical change. But I certainly believe that it is perfectly possible to do both these things, and indeed they are beginning to be done, with both Marxist and other social-scientific purposes in view.[7]

And if my second imagining risks doing injustice to Wittgenstein, it would probably also be frowned upon by Richard Rorty. Because, of course, it itself reproduces the equation of knowing with visual perception, the equation that is so profoundly and brilliantly criticized by Rorty in a book that is as full of mirrors as my imagined room. But I can perhaps be forgiven for that, so long as readers have *Philosophy and the Mirror of Nature* to which to repair for therapy.

What my second image *does* do, however, or at least what it did for me, is to remind me of one of the most extraordinary wonders of language. For it is our obedient and almost infinitely flexible servant, so long as we use it unself-consciously in the context of all the other practices that make up our lives. But it can become—indeed, almost always does become—the most tyrannical and quixotic of masters the moment that we reflect upon it. In fact, it took a genius like Wittgenstein to enter this hall of mirrors and to find his own way out. For real language is not the mischievous puck, the kindly leprechaun, of my imagining. "It" offers—"it" can offer—no advice, no formula for escape from its hall of mirrors. On the contrary, it just agrees with everything that is said in and of it and disagrees with everything that is said in and of it, and for those of us who are not geniuses *that* is only a formula for madness.

---

6. See in particular Bloor, *Wittgenstein*, especially chapter 7.

7. Most particularly in Pitkin's pioneering *Wittgenstein and Justice*, but also in Rubinstein, *Marx and Wittgenstein*, and in Bloor, *Wittgenstein*. However, by far the most significant recent neo-Wittgensteinian text in social/political theory is William E. Connolly, *The Terms of Political Discourse* (Oxford: Martin Robertson, 1983), which expands upon W. B. Gallie's notion of "essentially contested concepts" and applies it to a range of political ideas. For the original notion see W. B. Gallie, "Essentially Contested Concepts," in *The Importance of Language*, ed. Max Black (Ithaca: Cornell University Press, 1962), 121–46.

Bibliography

Abrams, P. *Historical Sociology.* Ithaca: Cornell University Press, 1982.

Ackermann, R. J. *Wittgenstein's City.* Amherst: University of Massachusetts Press, 1988.

Adler, R. P. *Understanding Television: Essays on Television as a Social and Cultural Force.* New York: Praeger, 1981.

Adorno, T. *Minima Moralia.* London: New Left Books, 1973.

———. *Negative Dialectics.* London: Routledge and Kegan Paul, 1973.

Adorno, T., and M. Horkheimer. *Dialectic of Enlightenment.* New York: Herder and Herder, 1972.

Aganbegyan, A. *The Challenge: Economics of Perestroika.* London: Hutchinson, 1988.

Aglietta, M. *A Theory of Capitalist Regulation.* London: New Left Books, 1979.

Althusser, L. *For Marx.* London: Allen Lane, 1969.

———. "Ideology and Ideological State Apparatuses." In *Lenin and Philosophy and Other Essays.* London: New Left Books, 1971.

———. "On the 22nd Congress of the French Communist Party." *New Left Review,* no. 104 (July–August 1977).

———. "What Must Change in the Party." *New Left Review,* no. 109 (May–June 1978).

Althusser, L., and E. Balibar. *Reading Capital.* London: New Left Books, 1970.

Amnesty International. *Prisoners of Conscience in the USSR: Their Treatment and Conditions.* Sydney: Amnesty International, 1980.

Anderson, M., ed. *Sociology of the Family.* Harmondsworth: Penguin, 1971.

Appel, M. W. *Ideology and Curriculum.* London: Routledge and Kegan Paul, 1979.

Armstrong, P., A. Glyn, and J. Harrison. *Capitalism since World War II.* London: Fontana, 1984.

Austin, J. L. *How to Do Things with Words.* Oxford: Oxford University Press, 1965.

———. *Philosophical Papers.* Oxford: Clarendon, 1961.

Ayer, A. J. *Language, Truth, and Logic.* 1936; Harmondsworth: Penguin, 1971.

Bachelard, G. *La formation de l'esprit scientifique*. Paris: Librairie Philosophique, Vrin, 1960.

Bahro, R. *The Alternative in Eastern Europe*. London: New Left Books, 1977.

Baker, G. P., and P.M.S. Hacker. *Essays on the "Philosophical Investigations."* Vol. 1, *Wittgenstein: Meaning and Understanding*. Vol. 2, *An Analytical Commentary on Wittgenstein's "Philosophical Investigations."* Oxford: Basil Blackwell, 1980.

Baran, P., and P. Sweezy. *Monopoly Capitalism*. Harmondsworth: Penguin, 1968.

Barone, E. "The Ministry of Production in the Collectivist State." In *Socialist Economics*, edited by A. Nove and D. M. Nuti, 52–74. Harmondsworth: Penguin, 1972.

Barrett, M. *The Politics of Truth: From Marx to Foucault*. Cambridge: Polity Press, 1991.

Bartley, S. H. *Principles of Perception*. New York: Harper and Row, 1969.

Beiner, R. *Political Judgement*. London: Methuen, 1983.

Bell, N. W., and E. F. Vogel. *A Modern Introduction to the Family*. New York: Free Press, 1968.

Benton, T. *The Rise and Fall of Structural Marxism: Althusser and His Influence*. London: Macmillan, 1984.

Bergson, A. *Planning and Productivity under Soviet Socialism*. Pittsburgh: Carnegie-Mellon University Press, 1968.

Bernstein, E. *Evolutionary Socialism: A Criticism and Affirmation*. Translated by Edith C. Harvey. London: Independent Labour Party, 1909.

Bernstein, R. J. *Beyond Objectivism and Relativism: Science, Hermeneutics, and Praxis*. Philadelphia: University of Pennsylvania Press, 1983.

———. *John Dewey*. New York: Washington Square Press, 1966.

———. *Praxis and Action*. London: Duckworth, 1972.

———. *The Reconstructing of Social and Political Theory*. Oxford: Basil Blackwell, 1976.

———, ed. *Habermas and Modernity*. Cambridge: Polity Press, 1985.

Bettelheim, C. *The Transition to Socialist Economy*. Hassocks: Harvester, 1975.

Beynon, H. *Working for Ford*. Wakefield: E. P. Publishing, 1975.

Bhaskar, R. "Realism." In *A Dictionary of Marxist Thought*, edited by L. Harris, V. G. Kiernan, and R. Miliband, 407–9. Oxford: Basil Blackwell, 1983.

———. *A Realist Theory of Science*. Sussex: Harvester, 1978.

Bloch, S. *Diagnosis: Political Dissent; An Abridged Version of "Russia's Political Hospitals: The Abuse of Psychiatry in the USSR."* London: Overseas Publishers, 1981.

Bloor, D. *Wittgenstein: A Social Theory of Knowledge*. London: Macmillan, 1983.

Bowles, S., and H. Gintis. *Schooling in Capitalist America*. London: Routledge and Kegan Paul, 1976.

Braverman, H. *Labor and Monopoly Capital: The Degradation of Work in the Twentieth Century*. New York: Monthly Review Press, 1974.

Brewster, B. "Fetishism in Capital and Reading Capital." *Economy and Society* 5, no. 3 (August 1976).

Brus, W. *The Market in a Socialist Economy*. London: Routledge and Kegan Paul, 1972.

Buck, T., and J. Cole. *Modern Soviet Economic Performance*. Oxford: Basil Blackwell, 1987.

Bukharin, N., and E. Preobrazhensky. *The ABC of Communism*. Harmondsworth: Penguin, 1969.

Callinicos, A. *Marxism and Philosophy*. Oxford: Oxford University Press, 1983.

Cardwell, D.S.L. *The Organisation of Science in England*. London: Heinemann, 1980.

Carr, E. H., and R. W. Davies. *Foundations of a Planned Economy*. Harmondsworth: Penguin, 1974.

Castells, M., and E. de Ipola. "Epistemological Practices and the Social Sciences." *Economy and Society* 5, no. 2 (1976).

Cavell, S. *The Claim of Reason: Wittgenstein, Skepticism, Morality, and Tragedy*. Oxford: Oxford University Press, 1979.

———. *Must We Mean What We Say?* Cambridge: Cambridge University Press, 1969.

Chenery, H., M. S. Ahluwalia, C.L.G. Bell, J. H. Duloy, and R. Jolly. *Redistribution with Growth*. Oxford: Oxford University Press, for the World Bank, 1974.

Churchland, P. M., and C. A. Hooker, eds. *Images of Science: Essays on Realism and Empiricism*. Chicago: University of Chicago Press, 1985.

Cliff, T. *State Capitalism in Russia*. London: Pluto, 1974.

Cohen, G. A. *History, Labour, and Freedom: Themes from Marx*. Oxford: Clarendon, 1988.

Connolly, W. E. *The Terms of Political Discourse*. Oxford: Martin Robertson, 1983.

Cornforth, M. *Dialectical Materialism: An Introductory Course*. 3 vols. London: Lawrence and Wishart, 1953.

———. *Marxism and the Linguistic Philosophy*. London: Lawrence and Wishart, 1965.

Corrigan, P. *Schooling the Smash Street Kids*. London: Macmillan, 1979.

Cowling, K. *Monopoly Capitalism*. London: Macmillan, 1982.

Cutler, A., B. Hindess, P. Q. Hirst, and A. Hussain. *Marx's "Capital" and Capitalism Today*. 2 vols. London: Routledge and Kegan Paul, 1977.

Dallmayr, F. R. "Critical Theory Criticised: Habermas's *Knowledge and Human Interests* and Its Aftermath." *Philosophy of the Social Sciences* 2 (1972): 211–29.

Desai, M. *Marxian Economic Theory*. London: Grey-Mills, 1974.

Deutscher, I. *The Prophet Outcast: Trotsky, 1929–1940*. Oxford: Oxford University Press, 1970.

Dobb, M. *Soviet Economic Development since 1917*. London: Routledge and Kegan Paul, 1966.

"Dr Althusser." *Radical Philosophy*, no. 12 (Winter 1975).

Dunning, J. H. *Economic Analysis and the Multinational Enterprise*. London: Allen and Unwin, 1973.

Durkheim, E. *The Rules of Sociological Method*. Translated by Sarah A. Solovay and John H. Mueller. Edited by George E. F. Catlin. New York: Free Press, 1938.

Eagleton, T. "Wittgenstein's Friends." *New Left Review*, no. 135 (September 1982).

Echevarria, R. "Critique of Marx's 1857 Introduction." *Economy and Society* 7, no. 4 (November 1978): 340–60.

Eckstein, A. *China's Economic Revolution*. Cambridge: Cambridge University Press, 1977.

Elger, T. "Valorization and Deskilling: A Critique of Braverman." *Capital and Class*, no. 7 (1979).

Ellman, M. *Socialist Planning*. Cambridge: Cambridge University Press, 1979.

Elson, D., ed. *Value: The Representation of Labour in Capitalism*. London: CSE Books, 1979.

Elster, J. *An Introduction to Karl Marx*. Cambridge: Cambridge University Press, 1986.

———. *Making Sense of Marx*. Cambridge: Cambridge University Press, 1985.

Emmanuel, A. *Appropriate or Underdeveloped Technology?* New York: John Wiley, 1982.

Engels, F. "Speech at the Graveside of Karl Marx." In K. Marx and F. Engels, *Selected Works*. London: Lawrence and Wishart, 1968.

Fann, K. T. "Wittgenstein and Bourgeois Philosophy." *Radical Philosophy*, no. 8 (Summer 1974).

———. *Wittgenstein's Conception of Philosophy*. Oxford: Basil Blackwell, 1969.

Feuer, L. S. "Karl Marx and the Promethean Complex." *Encounter* 21, no. 6 (December 1968).

———. "Lenin's Fantasy." *Encounter* 25, no. 6 (December 1970).

Feyerabend, P. *Against Method*. London: Verso, 1975.

Fransman, M. *Technology and Economic Development*. Brighton: Wheatsheaf, 1986.

Fraser, R. *Privatization: The UK Experience and International Trends*. London: Longman, 1988.

Fromm, E. *Marx's Concept of Man*. New York: Frederick Ungar, 1961.

Gadamer, H. G. *Truth and Method*. London: Sheed and Ward, 1981.

Galbraith, J. K. *The New Industrial State*. London: Hamish Hamilton, 1967.

Gallie, W. B. "Essentially Contested Concepts." In *The Importance of Language*, edited by Max Black. Ithaca: Cornell University Press, 1962.

Gamble, A., and P. Walton. *Capitalism in Crisis*. London: Macmillan, 1976.

Gellner, E. *Words and Things*. Harmondsworth: Penguin, 1963.

Geoghegan, V. *Utopianism and Marxism*. London: Methuen, 1987.

Geras, N. *Marx and Human Nature: Refutation of a Legend*. London: Verso, 1983.

Gerratana, V. "Althusser and Stalinism." *New Left Review*, nos. 101–2 (June 1981).

Geuss, R. *The Idea of a Critical Theory: Habermas and the Frankfurt School*. Cambridge: Cambridge University Press, 1981.

Gey, P., J. Kosta, and W. Qualsser. *Crisis and Reform in Socialist Economies*. London: Westview Press, 1987.

Gildea, R. *Barricades and Borders: Europe, 1800–1914*. Oxford: Oxford University Press, 1987.

Gill, J. H. *Wittgenstein and Metaphor*. Lanham, Md.: University Press of America, 1981.

Gillman, J. *The Falling Rate of Profit: Marx's Law and Its Significance to Twentieth-Century Capitalism*. London: Dobson, 1957.

Glasgow University Media Group. *Bad News* and *More Bad News*. London: Routledge and Kegan Paul, 1976 and 1980.

Glucksmann, M. *Structuralist Analysis in Contemporary Social Thought: A Comparison of the Theories of Claude Lévi-Strauss and Louis Althusser*. London: Routledge and Kegan Paul, 1974.

Glyn, A., and J. Harrison. *The British Economic Disaster*. London: Pluto, 1980.

Godwin, W. *Enquiry concerning Political Justice*. Harmondsworth: Penguin Classics, 1976.

Gold, D., C. Lo, and E. Wright. "Recent Developments in Marxist Theories of the State." *Monthly Review* 27, nos. 5–6 (1975).

Golschmid, H. J., H. M. Mann, and J. F. Weston, eds. *Industrial Concentration: The New Learning*. Boston: Little, Brown, 1974.

Goode, P., ed. *Karl Kautsky: Selected Political Writings*. London: Macmillan, 1983.

Gouldner, A. *The Two Marxisms*. London: Macmillan, 1980.

Grayling, A. C. *Wittgenstein*. Oxford: Oxford University Press, 1988.

Grossman, H. *Das Akkumulations und Zusammenbruchgesetz des Kapitalistischen Systems*. Frankfurt: Neue Kritik, 1967.

Habermas, J. *Knowledge and Human Interests*. Boston: Beacon Press, 1971.

———. *Theory and Practice*. Boston: Beacon Press, 1963.

———. *The Theory of Communicative Action: Reason and the Rationalization of Society*. 2 vols. Boston: Beacon Press, 1984, 1987.

———. "Towards a Theory of Comunicative Competence" and "On Systematically Distorted Communication." *Inquiry* 13 (1970).

———. "What Is Universal Pragmatics?" In *Communication and the Evolution of Society*, 1–68. Boston: Beacon Press, 1979.

Hacker, P.M.S. *Insight and Illusion: Wittgenstein on Philosophy and the Metaphysics of Experience*. Oxford: Oxford University Press, 1972.

Hacking, I. *Representing and Intervening: Introductory Topics in the Philosophy of Natural Science*. Cambridge: Cambridge University Press, 1983.

Hall, C., and L. Davidoff. *Family Fortunes: Men and Women of the English Middle Class, 1780–1850*. London: Hutchinson, 1987.

Hallett, G. *Wittgenstein's Definition of Meaning as Use*. New York: Fordham University Press, 1967.

Hannah, L. *The Rise of the Corporate Economy*. London: Methuen, 1977.

Harris, L. "The Science of the Economy." *Economy and Society* 7, no. 3 (August 1978).

Harris, R. *Reading Saussure: A Critical Commentary on the "Cours de linguistique générale."* London: Duckworth, 1987.

Harvey, D. *The Condition of Postmodernity: An Enquiry into the Origins of Cultural Change*. Oxford: Basil Blackwell, 1989.

Heer, F. *Europe: Mother of Revolutions*. London: Weidenfeld and Nicolson, 1964.

Hegel, G.W.F. *Science of Logic*. Translated by A. V. Miller. Foreword by Professor J. N. Findlay. London: Allen and Unwin, 1969.

Held, D. *Introduction to Critical Theory: Horkheimer to Habermas*. London: Hutchinson, 1980.

Hesse, M. *Revolutions and Reconstructions in the Philosophy of Science*. Brighton: Harvester, 1980.

———. *The Structure of Scientific Inference*. London: Macmillan, 1974.

Hilferding, R. *Finance Capital*. 1910; London: Routledge and Kegan Paul, 1981.

Hill, C. *The World Turned Upside Down: Radical Ideas during the English Revolution*. Harmondsworth: Penguin, 1975.

Hindess, B., and P. Q. Hirst. *Mode of Production and Social Formation*. London: Routledge and Kegan Paul, 1977.

———. *Pre-Capitalist Modes of Production*. London: Routledge and Kegan Paul, 1975.

Hirst, P. Q. "Althusser and the Theory of Ideology." *Economy and Society* 5, no. 4 (1976).

———. *Marxism and Historical Writing*. London: Routledge and Kegan Paul, 1985.

Hobsbawm, E. J. *The Age of Revolution.* London: Weidenfeld and Nicolson, 1962.

Hodgson, G. "The Theory of the Falling Rate of Profit." *New Left Review,* no. 84 (1974).

Holbraad, C. *The Concert of Europe: A Study of German and British International Theory, 1815–1914.* London: Longman, 1970.

Holton, G. *The Scientific Imagination: Case Studies.* Cambridge University Press, 1978.

Hook, S. *From Hegel to Marx.* Ann Arbor: University of Michigan Press, 1962.

Horkheimer, M. "Traditional and Critical Theory." In *Critical Theory.* New York: Herder and Herder, 1968.

Horvat, B. *The Yugoslav Economic System.* New York: International Arts and Science, 1976.

Hussein, A. "Crises and Tendencies of Capitalism." *Economy and Society* 6, no. 4 (November 1977).

Jameson, F. "Postmodernism; or, The Cultural Critique of Late Capitalism." *New Left Review,* no. 146 (July–August 1984).

Jaurès, J. *Le socialisme et l'enseignement.* Paris: G. Bellais, 1899.

Jay, M. *The Dialectical Imagination: A History of the Frankfurt School and the Institute of Social Research, 1923–1950.* Boston: Little, Brown, 1973.

Jenkins, R. *Transnational Corporations and Uneven Development.* London: Methuen, 1987.

Jessop, R. *The Capitalist State.* London: Martin Robertson, 1982.

Karol, K. S. "The Tragedy of the Althussers." *New Left Review,* no. 124 (1980).

Kautsky, K. *Terrorismus und Kommunismus: Ein Beitrag zur Naturgeschichte der Revolution.* Berlin: E. Berger, 1919.

Keat, R., and J. Urry. *Social Theory as Science.* London: Routledge and Kegan Paul, 1975.

Kenny, A. *Wittgenstein.* Harmondsworth: Penguin, 1973.

Kingston, W. *The Political Economy of Innovation.* The Hague: Martinus Nijhoff, 1984.

Kitching, G. N. *Development and Underdevelopment in Historical Perspective.* London: Methuen, 1982.

———. *Karl Marx and the Philosophy of Praxis.* London: Routledge, 1988.

———. "Modes of Production: Suggestions for a Fresh Start on an Exhausted Debate." *Canadian Journal of African Studies* 19, no. 1 (1985).

———. "Politics, Method, and Evidence in the 'Kenya Debate.'" In *Contradictions of Accumulation in Africa,* edited by H. Bernstein and B. K. Campbell. Beverly Hills: Russell Sage, 1985.

———. "Reply to Meiskins Wood." *New Left Review,* no. 163 (May–June 1987).

———. *Rethinking Socialism.* London: Methuen, 1983.

Klemke, E. D.; R. Hollinger, and A. D. Kline, eds. *Introductory Readings in the Philosophy of Science.* Buffalo: Prometheus Books, for Iowa State University, 1969.

Kline, M. *Mathematics in Western Culture.* London: Allen and Unwin, 1954.

Koestler, A. *The Sleepwalkers.* Harmondsworth: Penguin, 1964.

Kolakowski, L. *Main Currents of Marxism.* 3 vols. Oxford: Oxford University Press, 1981.

Kornai, J. *Economics of Shortage.* Amsterdam: North-Holland, 1980.

Kripke, S. A. *Wittgenstein on Rules and Private Language.* Oxford: Basil Blackwell, 1982.

Kuhn, T. *The Structure of Scientific Revolutions.* Chicago: University of Chicago, Press, 1970.

Laclau, E., and C. Mouffe. *Hegemony and Socialist Strategy: Towards a Radical Democratic Politics.* London: Verso, 1985.

Lakatos, I., and A. Musgrave, eds. *Criticism and the Growth of Knowledge.* Cambridge: Cambridge University Press, 1970.

Lane, D. *The Socialist Industrial State.* London: Allen and Unwin, 1976.

Lange, O. "On the Economic Theory of Socialism." In *Socialist Economics,* edited by A. Nove and D. M. Nuti, 92–110. Harmondsworth: Penguin, 1972.

Laslett, P., ed. *A Critical Edition of John Locke's "Two Treatises of Government."* Cambridge: Cambridge University Press, 1960.

Lauden, L. *Progress and Its Problems.* Berkeley and Los Angeles: University of California Press, 1977.

Leadbetter, C. "The Sid in Us All." *Marxism Today* (January 1987).

Little, D. *The Scientific Marx.* Minneapolis: University of Minnesota Press, 1986.

Lukács, G. *History and Class Consciousness.* London: Merlin Press, 1971.

Lukes, S. *Marxism and Morality.* Oxford: Oxford University Press, 1987.

Lyotard, J.-F. *The Postmodern Condition: A Report on Knowledge.* Manchester: Manchester University Press, 1984.

Macintyre, S. *A Proletarian Science: Marxism in Britain, 1917–33.* Oxford: Oxford University Press, 1980.

Maier, C. S. *Recasting Bourgeois Europe: Stabilization in France, Germany, and Italy in the Decade after World War I.* Princeton: Princeton University Press, 1975.

Malcolm, N. *Wittgenstein: A Memoir.* Oxford: Oxford University Press, 1958.

Mandel, E. *Late Capitalism.* London: New Left Books, 1975.

———. *Marxist Economic Theory.* London: Merlin Press, 1971.

Marcuse, H. *Eros and Civilization.* London: Sphere, 1969.

———. *One-Dimensional Man.* London: Routledge and Kegan Paul, 1963.

———. *Soviet Marxism.* Boston: Beacon Press, 1958.

Markus, G. "Planning the Crisis: Some Remarks on the Economic System of Soviet-type Societies." *Praxis International,* no. 3 (1981).

Marx, K. *Capital.* Vol. 1, *A Critical Analysis of Capitalist Production.* Translated (from the third German edition) by Samuel Moore and Edward Aveling. Edited by Friedrich Engels. Moscow: Progress, 1965.

———. *Capital.* Vol. 3, *Capitalist Production as a Whole.* Moscow, Progress Publishers, 1972.

———. "The Civil War in France." In *K. Marx and F. Engels: Selected Works.* London: Lawrence and Wishart, 1970.

———. "Critique of the Gotha Programme." In *K. Marx and F. Engels: Selected Works.* London: Lawrence and Wishart, 1970.

———. "Introduction to a 'Contribution to the Critique of Hegel's Philosophy of Right.'" In K. Marx and F. Engels, *Collected Works,* vol. 3. London: Lawrence and Wishart, 1975.

———. "On the Jewish Question." In K. Marx and F. Engels, *Collected Works,* vol. 3. London: Lawrence and Wishart, 1975.

———. *The Poverty of Philosophy.* New York: International Publishers, 1963.

———. *Theories of Surplus Value,* part 2. London: Lawrence and Wishart, 1969.

Marx, K., and F. Engels. *The German Ideology.* Part 1, with selections from parts 2 and 3. Edited by C. J. Arthur. London: Lawrence and Wishart, 1970.

————. *Selected Correspondence*. Moscow: Progress Publishers, 1955.

Matthews, K. *Privilege in the Soviet Union*. London: Allen and Unwin, 1987.

McCarthy, T. *The Critical Theory of Jürgen Habermas*. Cambridge, Mass.: Harvard University Press, 1978.

McGinn, C. *Wittgenstein on Meaning*. Oxford: Basil Blackwell, 1984.

McGuiness, B. *Wittgenstein and His Times*. Oxford: Basil Blackwell, 1982.

McLellan, D. *Karl Marx: His Life and Thought*. London: Macmillan, 1973.

Meade, J. "The Theory of Labour-managed Firms and Profit-Sharing." *Economic Journal* (March 1972).

Meisel, J. H., ed. *Pareto and Mosca*. Englewood Cliffs, N.J.: Prentice-Hall, 1965.

Meiskins Wood, E. *The Retreat from Class: A New "True" Socialism*. London: Verso, 1986.

Meisner, M. *Mao's China: A History of the People's Republic*. New York: Free Press, 1977.

Mepham, J., and D. H. Ruben, eds. *Issues in Marxist Philosophy*. 3 vols. Brighton: Harvester, 1979.

Middlemas, K. *Politics in Industrial Society*. London: André Deutsch, 1979.

Mill, J. S. *On Liberty*. 1859; London: Dent, Everyman, 1962.

Miliband, R. *Marxism and Politics*. Oxford: Oxford University Press, 1977.

————. *The State in Capitalist Society*. London: Weidenfeld and Nicolson, 1969.

Mises, L. von. "Economic Calculation in the Socialist Commonwealth." In *Socialist Economics*, edited by A. Nove and D. M. Nuti. Harmondsworth: Penguin, 1972.

Moore, B., Jr. *The Social Origins of Dictatorship and Democracy*. Harmondsworth: Penguin, 1966.

Morawetz, T. *Wittgenstein and Knowledge: The Importance of "On Certainty."* Brighton: Harvester, 1980.

Morris, C. "Foundations of the Theory of Signs." In *Foundations of the Unity of Science: Towards an International Encyclopedia of Unified Science*, vol. 1. Edited by O. Neurath, R. Carnap, and C. Morris. Chicago: University of Chicago Press, 1955.

Mount, F. *The Subversive Family: An Alternative History of Love and Marriage*. London: Allen and Unwin, 1983.

Munting, R. *The Economic Development of the USSR*. London: Croom Helm, 1982.

Nabseth, L., and G. F. Ray, *The Diffusion of New Industrial Process: An International Study*. Cambridge: Cambridge University Press, 1974.

Nagel, E. *The Structure of Science*. New York: Harcourt, Brace and World, 1961.

Neurath, O. *Empiricism and Sociology*. Translated by P. Foukes and M. Neurath. Edited by M. Neurath and R. S. Cohen. Dordrecht: D. Reidel, 1973.

Nichols, T. *Capital and Labour: Studies in the Capitalist Labour Process*. London: Fontana, 1980.

Nicolaus, M. Foreword to K. Marx, *Grundrisse: Foundations of the Critique of Political Economy*. Harmondsworth: Penguin, 1973.

Nove, A. *The Economics of Feasible Socialism*. London: Allen and Unwin, 1983.

————. *Glasnost in Action: Cultural Renaissance in Russia*. London: Unwin Hyman, 1989.

————. *The Soviet Economic System*. London: Allen and Unwin, 1977.

Page, L. R. *Karl Marx and the Critical Examination of His Works*. London: Freedom Association, 1987.

Pareto, V. *A Treatise of General Sociology*, vol. 4. New York: Dover, 1935.

Penrose, E. T. *The Growth of the Firm*. Oxford: Basil Blackwell, 1968.

Phillips, D. L. *Wittgenstein and Scientific Knowledge*. London: Macmillan, 1977.

Pitkin, H. F. *Wittgenstein and Justice*. Berkeley and Los Angeles: University of California Press, 1973.

Polan, A. J. *Lenin and the End of Politics*. London: Methuen, 1984.

Pole, D. *The Later Philosophy of Wittgenstein*. London: Athlone Press, 1958.

Pollock, F. *Die planwirtschaftlichen Versuche in der Sowjetunion, 1917–27*. Leipzig: C. L. Hirschfeld, 1929.

———. "State Capitalism: Its Possibilities and Limitations." In *The Essential Frankfurt School Reader*, edited by A. Arato and E. Gephardt. Oxford: Basil Blackwell, 1978.

Poulantzas, N. *Political Power and Social Classes*. London: New Left Books, 1973.

Radice, H., ed. *International Firms and Modern Imperialism*. Harmondsworth: Penguin, 1975.

Ranciere, J. "On the Theory of Ideology." *Radical Philosophy*, no. 7 (Spring 1974).

Rhees, R., ed. *Recollections of Wittgenstein*. Oxford: Oxford University Press, 1984.

Rizzi, B. *Le bureaucratisation du monde*. Paris, 1939.

Robertson Elliot, F. *The Family: Change or Continuity?* London: Macmillan, 1986.

Robinson, J. *The Economics of Imperfect Competition*. London: Macmillan, 1933.

———. *An Essay on Marxian Economics*. London: Macmillan, 1942.

Roderick, R. *Habermas and the Foundations of Critical Theory*. London: Macmillan, 1986.

Roemer, J. F. *Analytical Foundations of Marxian Economic Theory*. Cambridge: Cambridge University Press, 1981.

Rorty, R. *Philosophy and the Mirror of Nature*. Oxford: Basil Blackwell, 1980.

———, ed. *"The Linguistic Turn": Recent Essays in Philosophical Method*. Chicago: University of Chicago Press, 1967.

Rowbotham, S. "The Women's Movement and Organising for Socialism." In *Beyond the Fragments*, edited by S. Rowbotham, L. Segal, and H. Wainwright. London: Islington Community Press, 1979.

Ruben, D. H. *Marxism and Materialism*. Brighton: Harvester, 1977.

Rubinstein, D. *Marx and Wittgenstein: Social Praxis and Social Explanation*. London: Routledge and Kegan Paul, 1981.

Runciman, W. G. *Relative Deprivation and Social Justice*. London: Routledge and Kegan Paul, 1966.

Saich, T. *China: Politics and Government*. London: Macmillan, 1981.

Salvadori, M. *Karl Kautsky and the Socialist Revolution, 1880–1938*. Translated by Jon Rothschild. London: New Left Books, 1979.

Saussure, F. de. *Course in General Linguistics*. Translated by Wade Baskin. Edited by Charles Bally and Albert Sechehaye, with Albert Reidlinger. London: Peter Owen, 1960.

Sayer, A. "Abstraction: A Realist Interpretation." *Radical Philosophy*, no. 28 (1981).

———. *Method in Social Science: A Realist Approach*. London: Hutchinson, 1984.

Sayer, D. *Marx's Method*. Brighton: Harvester, 1979.

Schlick, M. *Philosophy of Nature*. New York: Philosophical Library, 1949.

Schumpeter, J. A. *Capitalism, Socialism, and Democracy*. London: Allen and Unwin, 1976.

Searle, J. R. "Minds, Brains, and Programs." *Behavioural and Brain Sciences* 3 (1980).
———. *Speech Acts*. Cambridge: Cambridge University Press, 1969.
Sen, A. "On the Labour Theory of Value: Some Methodological Issues." *Cambridge Journal of Economics*, 2, no. 2 (1978).
Shonfield, A. *Modern Capitalism*. Oxford: Oxford University Press, 1965.
Sik, O. *The Third Way*. London: Wildwood House, 1976.
Silverstone, R. *The Message of Television: Myth and Narrative in Contemporary Culture*. London: Heinemann Education, 1981.
Simon, B. *Education and the Labour Movement, 1870–1920*. London: Lawrence and Wishart, 1965.
———. *Two Nations and the Educational Structure*. London: Lawrence and Wishart, 1974.
Sirc, L. *The Yugoslav Economy under Self-Management*. London: Macmillan, 1979.
Smith, A. *On the Nature and Causes of the Wealth of Nations*. 2 vols. Edited by Edwin Cannan. 1776; London: Methuen, 1961.
Steenson, G. P. *Karl Kautsky, 1854–1938: Marxism in the Classical Years*. Pittsburgh: University of Pittsburgh Press, 1978.
Stretton, H. *The Political Sciences*. London: Routledge and Kegan Paul, 1969.
Suchting, W. A. *Marxism and Philosophy: Three Studies*. New York: New York University Press, 1986.
Theobald, D. W. *An Introduction to the Philosophy of Science*. London: Methuen, 1968.
Thomas, K. *Religion and the Decline of Magic*. London: Weidenfeld and Nicolson, 1971.
Thompson, E. P. *The Poverty of Theory and Other Essays*. London: Merlin Press, 1978.
Thompson, N. *The Market and Its Critics*. London: Routledge, 1988.
Tomlinson, J. *The Unequal Struggle?* London: Methuen, 1982.
Toulmin, S. *The Philosophy of Science*. New York: Harper Bros., 1953.
Trotsky, L. *The Revolution Betrayed: What Is the Soviet Union and Where Is It Going?* London: New Park Publications, 1973.
van Fraasen, Bas C. *The Scientific Image*. Oxford: Clarendon, 1980.
van Parijs, P. "The Falling Rate of Profit Theory of Crisis: A Rational Reconstruction by Way of an Obituary." *Review of Radical Political Economics* (Spring 1980).
Vanek, J. *The General Theory of Labor-Managed Market Economies*. Ithaca: Cornell University Press, 1970.
Venable, V. *Human Nature: The Marxian View*. London: Denis Dobson, 1946.
Volosinov, V. N. *Marxism and the Philosophy of Language*. Cambridge, Mass.: Harvard University Press, 1973.
Waissmann, F. *Wittgenstein and the Vienna Circle*. Edited by B. F. McGuiness. London: Basil Blackwell, 1967.
Waldrop, M. Mitchell. *Man-Made Minds*. New York: Walker, 1987.
Weber, M. *Economy and Society: An Outline of Interpretive Sociology*. Edited by Guenther Roth and Claus Wittich. New York: Bedminster Press, 1968.
Widgery, D. *The Left in Britain, 1965–68*. Harmondsworth: Penguin, 1976.
Williams, K. "Facing Reality: A Critique of Karl Popper's Empiricism." *Economy and Society* 4, no. 3 (August 1975).
———. "Problematic History." *Economy and Society* 1, no. 4 (November 1972).

Williams, R. "Marxism, Structuralism, and Literary Analysis." *New Left Review*, no. 129 (September–October 1981).

———. *Television: Technology and Cultural Form*. London: Fontana, 1974.

Wittgenstein, L. *The Blue and Brown Books: Preliminary Studies for the "Philosophical Investigations."* Oxford: Basil Blackwell, 1958.

———. *Lectures and Conversations on Aesthetics, Psychology, and Religious Belief.* Edited by C. Barrett. Oxford: Basil Blackwell, 1967.

———. *On Certainty.* Oxford: Basil Blackwell, 1979.

———. *Philosophical Investigations.* Oxford: Basil Blackwell, 1953.

———. *Tractatus Logico-Philosophicus.* Translated by D. F. Pears and B. F. McGuiness. Introduction by Bertrand Russell. London: Routledge and Kegan Paul, 1961.

———. *Zettel.* Oxford: Basil Blackwell, 1967.

Wright, E. Olin, ed. *The Debate on Classes.* London: Verso, 1989.

Wright, E. Olin, A. Levine, and E. Sober, eds. *Reconstructing Marxism: Essays on Explanation and the Theory of History.* London: Verso, 1992.

Wyndam Goldie, G. *Facing the Nation: Television and Politics, 1936–76.* London: Bodley Head, 1977.

Index